D0934343

Politics and Planning

625678

Institute for Research in Social Science Monograph Series

Published by The University of North Carolina Press
in association with the Institute for Research in Social Science
at The University of North Carolina at Chapel Hill

Harriet Irving Library

MAY 13 1980

University of New Brunswick

Politics and Planning
A National Study of American Planners

by
Michael Lee Vasu

The University of North Carolina Press
Chapel Hill

© 1979 The University of North Carolina Press
All rights reserved
Manufactured in the United States of America
ISBN 0-8078-1342-7
Library of Congress Catalog Card Number 78-10440

Library of Congress Cataloging in Publication Data

Vasu, Michael Lee.
   Politics and planning.

   Bibliography: p.
   Includes index.
   1. Land use, Urban—United States—Planning.
2. City planning—United States.   3. United States
—Social policy.   4. Planning.   I. Title.
HD205 1979.V37   309.2′12′0973   78-10440
ISBN 0-8078-1342-7

for my sister Colleen Vasu Fike
. . . in loving memory.

Contents

Tables

Foreword

A glance at any community newspaper is likely to show stories with such headlines as: "City Planning Commission to Meet," "Planners Schedule Hearing to Consider Highway Relocation," or "Citizens Group Protest Plan for Rezoning." At the state level increasing attention is given to planning, whether for industrial growth, growth management, or for a better "quality of life." Even in the national government, where "planning" was long an unpopular word following the demise of the National Resources Planning Board in the 1940s, the new Department of Energy is charged with preparing a "National Energy Plan"; the highway plans for the Department of Transportation have had enormous impact, intended and unintended, on life in America; and the first steps at least have been taken within the Department of Housing and Urban Development toward comprehensive national urban planning.

Who are these planners? Where do they come from? By what values do they live and work? These are some of the questions that Michael Lee Vasu addresses in *Politics and Planning: A National Study of American Planners*. The core of the study is a unique data base: the results of a national mail survey of a cross section of the membership of the principal association of planning professionals, The American Institute of Planners. This survey was conducted by Vasu while he was a research associate of the Institute for Research in Social Science and the data are available for further, secondary analysis by others through the Institute's Social Science Data Library. By themselves these data permit a description and interpretation of the profession, and an identification of points of agreement and disagreement among planners. In comparison with data for national samples of the whole population, comparisons that Vasu supplies, the data locate a planning "elite" by reference to the population that elite serves.

As a study of an important American professional group, this volume should be of interest to multiple audiences. Most obviously, it will be of interest to those seeking to understand the nature of the contribution that the people we call "planners" make to those important policy decisions we call "planning." In this sense the study contributes both to our understanding of what now is, and also of what will be, as professional planning continues to grow in importance. On these subjects Vasu has conclusions to draw and an argument to present; one of the attractive features of the book, however, is the author's ability to separate his personal evaluations from the conclusions that follow directly from the data analysis, thus permitting others with other value premises to incorporate his findings into their own conceptions of correct policy.

Secondly, the study will be of interest to those engaged in the professional training of planners. "Planning" is one of those professions in which some planners receive formal training as such, while others slip into service by circuitous routes. By comparing the differences in values and behaviors of those formally trained as planners with those without such indoctrination, Vasu points to some conclusions as to the current status of planning as a defined academic subject.

Finally, as a study of a major American professional group the volume should be of value to all those concerned with professionalization and the comparative study of professions. Many comparisons suggest themselves, whether to lawyers, educators, journalists, public policy analysts, or whatever; to me one of the most interesting parallels is found in the self-study of the profession of landscape architecture conducted but a few years ago.[1] As the parent profession—of Frederick Law Olmsted and many others—from which "planning" schismatically withdrew, landscape architecture defines a professionalization with many similar interests but subject to quite different economic influences. Fortunately, the American Society of Landscape Architects self-study made use of similar survey techniques and facilitates comparative examination.

With this book the Institute for Research in Social Science launches a new series of studies in social science to be published by The University of North Carolina Press under the joint sponsorship of the Institute and the Press. As director of the Institute I am delighted thus to resume a relationship with The University of North Carolina

---

1. Albert Fein, *A Study of the Profession of Landscape Architecture* (American Society of Landscape Architects, McLean, Va., 1972).

Press that has been so often productive of quality publication and
sound scholarship through the fifty-five years since the foundation of
the Institute for Research in Social Science by Howard W. Odum in
1924.

Frank J. Munger

Acknowledgments

In the course of this undertaking, I have incurred numerous debts to individuals who contributed their time, expertise, and encouragement to this research. Most of these debts cannot be adequately repaid. Nonetheless, I want to express my sincere thanks to those people who have made this research both a pleasure and a reality. I hasten to add, of course, that while these individuals share whatever merit the book contains, its inadequacies are my responsibility alone.

I am particularly indebted to Professor Frank Munger, Director of the Institute for Research in Social Science (IRSS) at the University of North Carolina at Chapel Hill, for the institutional support that made this research possible. Angell Beza, Associate Director for Research Design for the Institute, was extremely giving of both his time and expertise in the sampling and design phases of this study. The staff of the Statistical Laboratory at IRSS, in particular Bill Reynolds, is owed a special thanks for their assistance in a variety of computer-programming and methodologically related concerns. David Kovenock, Director of the Comparative State Elections Project at the University of North Carolina at Chapel Hill, availed me of his considerable experience in conducting large-scale-survey research, as well as his expertise on matters of both analysis and style. I thank Elizabeth Martin, Associate Director of the Louis Harris Political Data Center at UNC Chapel Hill, for her assistance in the use of various data sources, as well as her methodological advice during the context of the study. Needless to say, neither Dr. Martin nor any of the organizations whose data I utilized are responsible for my analysis or interpretations. Susan Clarke, Director of Research Programs for the Institute, provided me with her professional assistance, scholarly encouragement, and her friendship throughout the entire course of the project. All of her contributions are highly valued. Various individuals read the manuscript at specific stages. Frank Munger, John S. Jackson, and Charles Goodsell in particular provided me with valuable comments. The scholarly assistance of my colleagues G. David Garson, Oliver Williams, and J. A. Clapp is both recognized and appreciated. Bonita Samuels and Vonda Hogan typed the manuscript with extreme efficiency. My research assistant, Abigail Wilson, performed numerous tasks associated with the final preparation of the manuscript.

I also owe a special thanks to my parents, Lee and Eileen Vasu, for their continued encouragement in all my pursuits. And I wish to express my sincere thanks to my wife, Ellen, whose emotional support and statistical and computer-programming competence were essential at every juncture of this endeavor.

Chapel Hill, N.C.
May 1978

Politics and Planning

Chapter 1

Planning and Politics: The Interface

Introduction

The onset of a variety of problems, oil and natural gas shortages, inflation, eroding center cities, which appear to defy solutions by the traditional institutional arrangements of American federalism, is currently engendering a cry for more and better "social planning." Moreover, this plea is emanating from unusual quarters and among strange political bedfellows. Among its proponents are individual and collective representatives of corporate America, as well as the traditional proponents of centralized planning of the political left. For example, in a speech 7 January 1970 to the Bond Club of New York, IBM's chairman of the board, Thomas J. Watson, Jr., called for national planning: "In most businesses," he said, "and certainly in highly technological industries, the United States has learned how to set fairly precise goals. We've learned that we have to implement them, step-by-step, in a disciplined way over a long period of time. I believe that the complexity of our modern economy demands national goal setting and planning closely paralleling that which is commonplace in industry." He concluded, "It's a sad thing, a very sad thing when a nation like this has to creep into a new decade with its tail between its legs. I don't want to do that again. I want to sail into the 1980s—and I want to see flags flying and hear bands playing. We can do that, I'm convinced, if we're willing to take a hard, cold and constant look at how we're running the biggest enterprise in the world."[1]

In addition, proposals for social planning have also been forthcoming from those elements of the political spectrum whose ideological legacy emanates from the New Deal. Among the expressions of this vision of social planning are the Humphrey-Hawkins Bill and the National Goals and Priorities Act, which called for a Council of Social Advisers modeled on the Council of Economic Advisers, and would employ a variety of behavioral-science methodologies in a comprehensive endeavor to chart a planned course for the American body politic.[2]

3

A more far-reaching vision of American social planning is that of "a pluralist commonwealth" projected by Gar Alperovitz, director of the Cambridge Policy Studies Institute. This vision of a radically decentralized form of American social planning rejects mere changes in the institutional structures or the management practices of federalism, advocating in their place a fundamental reordering of the American economic and political system.[3]

Clearly, social planning in all its forms enjoys an expanding legitimacy and has acquired political support that ranges from the board room of IBM to the tabloids of American Socialism. At the basis of this bizzare political consensus among otherwise incompatible political philosophies is the firm belief that all important human endeavors can and should be planned. Indeed, to individuals inculcated within the highly rationalized culture of a modern industrial society to suggest otherwise seems almost primitive.

One can be assured, however, that while a strong political consensus on the need for some form of planning exists, there are a variety of different perspectives on just what planning is or what is the best method to achieve it. Indeed, much of the consensus on the need for planning thoroughly collapses at that juncture at which one moves from some abstract and amorphous notion about planning's necessity to any concrete expression of its reality. Part of this, of course, is a function of the different interests of the actors involved, and part of it is because "planning" can mean all things to all men. However, planning has at least two dominant faces, one economic, the other decidedly political.

Economists are prone to discuss problems of planning in terms of control over the allocation of goods and services. The political theory of planning, however, revolves around the corresponding problems of accountability for the coordination of people and the public and private associations to which they adhere. While the techniques of economic planning have been developed and improved to an extent unimagined by even the proponents of planning in earlier generations, in the United States it is the concern over predictions of what planning will be like in the *political* sphere that constitutes the greatest anxiety about the spread of this orientation toward public policy.

These concerns are both valid and familiar: 1984, Brave New World, Communism, Bureaucracy, Red Tape. These symbols represent ideas that run deep in the popular mind, and in the thought of politicians, academicians, and planners for that matter. In the common rejection of what these symbols are presumed to represent, conservatives and radicals find a common meeting ground. At the center is the fear of Bureaucracy, the image of a society out of control in the name of control. Or, as it is sometimes put, behind the symbols is the quite valid and probing question, Who is to control the planners? Much of this concern results from the fact that planning's essence is to centralize power in order to control allocation for ends that would not otherwise be achieved, and in centralizing power it thereby creates in itself a value which many would want to call their own. Moreover, the decentralization of planning to the regional, state, or local level does not solve the problem of the power of planners, but merely enables it to be replicated on a smaller scale where false logic suggests it will do less harm.[4] In other words, regardless of any lofty goals conceived and formulated by any planning structure or law that might be enacted, one essential theoretical perspective that endures is the role orientations of the planners themselves. It is difficult to underestimate the capacity of planning professionals to implement preexisting ideas regardless of the legal-structural framework established by government. More fundamentally, the question of role orientations raises the question of what, substantively (as opposed to structurally), planning is! It raises the differences between New Deal conceptions of planning to reorder priorities and mobilize resources toward national goals on the one hand, and the value-free municipal-reform orientation toward planning as rationality within given parameters. It raises questions that are essentially political, questions to which this study shall speak.

It is an explicit assumption of this book that the social and environmental complexity of the next two decades will generate an even greater demand for planning in the United States, and that there will be an exponential increase in the ideological distance that separates the Herbert Hoover administration from the Humphrey-Hawkins Bill. Moreover, the growth of planning in the public sector in this country will result in a concomitant growth in the influence of the planner on public policy. A society socialized to revere credentials will instinctively turn for guidance to those possessing formal education and membership in professional planning organizations. American society, in other words, will look more and more to the planners to employ their expertise, to do what they are trained to do; namely, plan. The American Institute of Planners is the national organization of public, private, federal, state, local, health, land-use, transportation, and economic planners. Its membership is the subject of this book.

This research is, in essence, a national study of the conceptions of planners themselves toward a variety of factors inherent in the planning process. The essential purpose of this book is to provide a profile of planners with respect to their perception of both the planning function and their role in it. In so doing, we will hopefully expand our understanding of the planner's influence on the conditions of American life. The choice of the planner as the subject of this research was motivated by the highly political nature of both the planning process itself, and the recommendations made by planners as participants in that process.

In a very fundamental sense, then, the focus of this book is on the standards and ideologies of the American planning profession. And, while much of the discussion in subsequent sections is about the urban planner, this is simply to underscore that most formal planning in the United States up to now has taken place and continues to take place at the subnational level. It is at this level, therefore, that we must evaluate the past accomplishments of planning, as well as assess the political factors inherent in the planning process. Nonetheless, the political issues that are raised and addressed throughout this book are inherent in any planning endeavor at any level of government. In fact, many of the issues addressed—the existence of a solitary public interest, the possibility of comprehensive rational planning in a pluralistic society, the role of the planners as expert in a democratic framework—become more important as one moves up formal lines of authority and jurisdiction. They become, in fact, imperative for a body politic even considering engaging in the tenuous balance between national planning and democratic government.

In order to address these important issues, however, it is essential to provide a framework for discussion that includes both a definition of planning and some perspective on its form and function in the American governmental context.

Planning: Definitions and Perspectives

Planning can be conceptualized as both a generic process and a function of government. In the generic sense, planning has been described by Marshall Dimock as "thinking before acting, establishing objectives before setting out aimlessly to attain fuzzy goals."[5] Planning in the generic sense is virtually a synonym for rational activity, or as Alan A. Altshuler states, "simply the effort to infuse activity with consistent and conscious purpose."[6] Planning as a function of government, however, has a variety of dimensions that need clarification if a common understanding of the process is to be achieved. One definition of planning is a process for the "rational" and "equitable" distribution of societal resources in a socialistic state. In this context planning is the antithesis of laissez faire market capitalism, and the embodiment of Marxist economics. It is also by implication national planning. The first limitation of the general use of the term is to define planning as one function of government in the United States.

The concept of planning as a function of government, however, needs further delineation. First of all, while planning in the generic sense occurs at all levels of government, very little (if any) formal national planning currently occurs in the United States.[7] In addition professional planners fill a variety of positions in agencies that span multiple levels of government. For these reasons it is necessary to operationalize *planning* along additional criteria. In the United States, *planning* commonly refers to the function of local government concerned primarily with the use of physical space.[8] The two important elements in this operational definition, planning as a function of local government and planning as a process concerned with the use of physical space, merit additional elaboration. Donald T. Allensworth summarizes succinctly the place of planning in the context of American federalism. "In the United States, no one government or level of government has the complete responsibility for planning. The most important public planning powers are decentralized in our federal system; they are lodged in numerous local governmental units across the nation. All levels of government have at least some planning function, and all levels carry on activities that affect community development and comprehensive planning."[9] Allensworth's comments underscore the essentially decentralized nature of the planning function in the United States and its primarily local character. Moreover, while all levels of government influence the character of American planning, the implementation of planning is, in effect, a local governmental responsibility. A clearer understanding of the planning process in the American governmental structure necessitates some discussion of the powers of the federal, state, and local governments with respect to the planning function.

The federal government's interest in planning emerged late in the history of the nation, and specifically in the arena of the federal courts, when in *Euclid* v. *Ambler Realty Co.* (1926) the court legitimized zoning to separate nonconforming uses.[10] However, the first federal initiatives directed to a larger focus than the limited dimensions of zoning did not emerge in a real sense until the depression.

The collapse of the stock market and the subsequent economic upheaval created for a brief time in the United States a political climate favorable to national planning. The National Resources Committee and its successor, the National Resources Planning Board, reflected in their conception a reevaluation of the very fundamentals of laissez faire economics and rugged individualism. In addition, the election of Franklin D. Roosevelt brought to the presidency a man committed to the ideology of planning and to giving that ideology a concrete expression. In the early days of the Roosevelt administration a supportive Congress, under the watchful eye of a reluctant Supreme Court, produced the Agricultural Adjustment Act, the Tennessee Valley Authority Act, the National Industrial Recovery Act, as well as the legislation to produce the Civilian Conservation Corps. And, with the support of the president, Secretary of the Interior Harold L. Ickes, inaugurated the National Planning Board.[11]

These various legislative and executive acts represented more than a commitment to public works and economic stabilization, they reflected a new perspective on the role of government and planning. The resulting possibility for a change in the ideological balance of power was obvious to both the opponents and supporters of the administration's programs. Many of these new agencies, in particular the National Resources Planning Board, provided a potential infrastructure for American national planning. The board, which became an instrument of the executive office in 1940, was ostensibly restricted to reviewing public works, but became actively involved in a variety of endeavors ranging from economic trends and transportation, to promoting state and local planning. The board's mere existence posed a severe threat to its opponents, who seized upon the temporary economic prosperity brought on by the war, as well as shifting coalitions in Congress, to abolish it in August 1943, and to add a provision to the legislation which precluded transfer of the board's functions to any other agency.[12]

However, much of the New Deal legislation produced enduring effects on the character of American planning. The National Housing Act of 1934, for example, established the Federal Housing Administration to insure loans for housing improvements and mortgages.[13] Another federal involvement from the perspective of planning emerged in the form of the United States Housing Act of 1937, which made available financial assistance for state and local governments to provide housing at the local level. This legislation, however, was more symbolic than real, since it produced only 26,000 housing units in the next four years.[14]

The next significant stage in the federal government's involvement in basic planning, which assumed a somewhat more comprehensive perspective, was the Housing Act of 1949. Established in an era of postwar center-city deterioration, the legislation provided for various programs of urban renewal. It especially called for federal money to subsidize the purchase, aggregation, and subsequent land clearance by local governments for the purpose of eventual resale to private developers.[15] The first federal legislation directed "specifically and exclusively" at urban planning was The Housing Act of 1954.[16] The act provided federal money to state and local governments to establish and fund comprehensive planning. Planning received continued support in the housing measures of 1956 and 1959 and subsequently in the model-cities legislation in 1966. In the Demonstration Cities and Metropolitan Act of 1966 the federal government provided funding for eliminating both physical and social blight in America's inner cities. While the housing legislation of 1968, 1969, and 1970 has only modified provisions of earlier acts, the Housing and Community Development Act of 1974 included a variety of federally assisted housing programs of a different focus. Among the provisions of the legislation was a new rental leasing program for moderate- and low-income families, and the provision of expanding the public-housing concept to include rehabilitated or existing private housing, acquired by enabling the Department of Housing and Urban Development to engage in contractual arrangements with private developers and local housing authorities. The federal government has additional and continued impact on state and local planning in the form of grant-in-aid programs in areas such as highways, sewer and water facilities, and mass transit, all of which directly affect planning at the local level.[17] However, the overall impact of federal programs has been to provide direction by stimulating the planning process through the incentive of financial aid.

The states, as actors in the decentralized American federal system, also have had an impact on planning. The influence of the American states has been most pronounced in two general areas. "The state government has two important roles in urban planning and development: (1) authorizing localities to engage in certain planning and related activities; and (2) directly operating substantive programs in planning and urban development and directly regulating some kinds of land use."[18] In the first regard, states have been exercising their traditional role of granting legitimacy to local governmental powers in the area of planning by passing enabling legislation. In the second regard, state governments have been directly involved in planning on a statewide basis. However, the direct impact of state planning has been limited primarily because many important planning and land-use powers have been delegated to local governments.[19]

The delegation of these powers to local governments has created an environment for planning in the United States that makes the activity highly decentralized and local in character. David C. Ranney states, "The fact remains that most local planning is done by the individual municipal governments within the metropolitan areas."[20] The activities of local planning include the development of plans and subsequent implementation of those plans by utilizing the legal tools of zoning, subdivision regulations, and building codes. Planning-agency organization varies from state to state with the three most common organizations being the semiindependent planning commission, the executive staff agency, and the legislative staff agency.[21]

In addition to the local character of planning in the United States, it was stated that planning as an activity is concerned with the use of physical space. This qualification at the present time distinguishes American planning from the ideological implications of a more comprehensive type of social planning practiced in many socialistic countries. Yet, this distinction, while clear in practice, is not always clear in the ideology of the planning profession. For example, consider Charles Abrams's definition of city or urban planning as "the guidance and shaping of the development, growth, arrangement, and change of urban environments with the aim of harmonizing them with the social, aesthetic, cultural, political, and economic requirements of life."[22] Despite Abrams's eloquent and encompassing definition, planning as a function of government in the United States has as its primary objective the regulation of the use of physical space. As Ranney notes, "The physical planning activities of government may be based upon broad social science research or upon narrower design considerations. In either case the focus of planning is on land use."[23] In addition, it should be stated that the formal role of planning in the United States is currently advisory.

Any analysis of the planning function must also include the acknowledgment that both the nature of the planning process, and the recommendations made by planners as participants in that process, are inescapably political. This fact is central to any past analysis of planning impact, as well as any future assessments of its probable effects. In addition, it is a characteristic that pervades the planning function at any level of government; it emanates in effect from the very essence of the endeavor. Moreover, the inherently political nature of the planning process is exacerbated, because planning as function of government is characterized by a great deal of administrative discretion.

With respect to this consideration, Alan Altshuler in his classic work, *The City Planning Process*, contends that local political officials seldom give planners any clear objectives to guide the value-choice aspects of their work and that there is some evidence that local politicians avoid making policy commitments "during the early life of any idea." He concludes that to the extent that these two factors are operating, "city planning is one of the extreme examples of administrative discretion to be found in American government."[24] Altshuler's contention is supported empirically by a study of the planner's function from a focus which, from the perspective of organization theory, can be typologized as programmed versus nonprogrammed behavior. Utilizing self-reports to evaluate the frequency with which planners found it necessary to deviate from routine in order to work effectively, Deil S. Wright states that "planner behavior, as perceived and reported by the planner himself, tends to include substantial nonprogrammed activity."[25]

The discretionary character of the planning process is extremely relevant to students of political behavior, because the planning process serves many of the same functions as, and in many ways is isomorphic with, politics. As a consequence of the political nature of the planning process, the criteria upon which recommendations by planners are based are never exclusively rational or technical, but are highly political in content. In addition, the political factors inherent in planning are crucial for evaluating planning's past impact on public policy and for assessing the political dilemmas and obstacles that will emerge under any potential scheme to enlarge the planning function at the national level. The remainder of this chapter will seek to establish the conceptual framework for this research by demonstrating the commonality between politics and planning.

Planning: The Nature of the Process

The nature of any planning process is highly political. In addition, planning has a significant effect on public policy decisions relating to the physical-land-use aspects of American cities. In order to explicate the interrelationship between planning and politics, and to substantiate the foregoing contentions, it is necessary to define the concept *politics* and then to demonstrate the similarity between politics and planning. For the purpose of this study, the following definitions will be employed:

1. Politics is the exercise of power leading to the determination of who gets what, when, how.[26]
2. Politics is the authoritative allocation of values.[27]

The former definition emerges from the classic work of Harold D. Lasswell. The perspective taken in the definition underscores the distribution of income and opportunity functions implicit in politics as a cross-cultural activity. The latter definition, from the work of

David Easton, reflects the systems approach to political science within the discipline with particular emphasis on the synonymous nature of politics, the political system, and the government as an instrument for the authoritative allocation of values. It will be demonstrated that by both these definitions of politics the nature of the planning process in the United States and the individual planner's input into that process are highly political in character.[28]

Norman Beckman asserts that planning is political in the direct sense that Lasswell uses the term when he says, "Planning helps to determine 'who gets what, when, and how,' and to do that is to function politically."[29] The process of planning, and by implication the individual planner's input into that process, has marked policy consequences for the distribution of income and opportunity in our nation's urban areas. David C. Ranney asks:

How much land should be devoted to housing for low-income families in a community and what priority should low-income housing have relative to other aspects of a city's physical development? Those low-income people who feel that their present living facilities are inadequate would favor a plan which places a very high priority on the development of housing units that meet their needs. The downtown merchants who feel that they need to have more affluent customers living nearby, would favor a plan which places a high priority on replacing "slums" with middle and upper-income housing or with parking garages. Whose values come first in this case, the low-income slum dweller or the downtown merchant?[30]

Clearly, the answers to the preceding questions fall into the domain of "who gets what, when, and how." Precisely how planning is involved in determining "who gets what, when and how" must be explicated, since the formal power of the planner is supposed to be advisory. The two ways that have been postulated are: through routine decision with high policy content and through the structuring of the agenda of policy making.

Francine F. Rabinovitz contends that frequently the planner has the opportunity to administer projects in which the administrative and policy character overlap. After asserting the long-recognized argument that the separation between policy making and administration is in many ways mythical, she states, "In locating a new park to separate cheaper developments from expensive residential areas or marking areas of the community as dilapidated, the planner is exercising power no less important than that of the traditional wielders of authority."[31] Much of the capacity of the planner to exercise this power is a result of his or her expert status. There is evidence to indicate that the planner's expertise is utilized in conjunction with that of the city manager to provide a nonpolitical or technical motif for what is really policy innovation.[32] In addition, the very nature of planning as a function of government does much to affect the economic vitality of an area. Planners' recommendations can have profound influence on a variety of policy-related matters that involve real economic stakes. "The planner is called upon to make recommendations on sites for highways, hospitals, schools and other community facilities. In some cities the planner is responsible for scheduling capital expenditures to be made by the government."[33]

In addition to controlling routine decisions with high policy content, planners do much to establish and structure the agenda of policy making. "Whether he likes it or not the planner is a key participant in the politics of planning. His initial decisions will often generate actual or potential conflict."[34] Thomas Dye contends that in many cities the planning staff can project an "image of the city of the future and thereby establish the agenda of community decision making."[35] Altshuler argues that planners in America have adapted to their political environment and increased their power by seeking harmonious personal relations with politicians.[36] Planners have assumed this strategy, because "most politicians are cautious men who make no more decisions than they have to, and who try to make these appear beyond the realm of reasonable controversy. They tend to have a high regard for expertness as a mechanism of consensus: that is, as one which minimizes the number of seriously controversial decisions which politicians have to make."[37]

The capacity of the planner to limit the scope of the agenda of political decision making in order to assure successful planning has, of course, important implications for the content and character of public policy in any real or envisioned political arena. It is also directly relevant to Peter Bachrach and Morton S. Baratz's critique of community power studies.[38] In an article that addresses the continued debate between sociologists and political scientists as to the locus of community power, Bachrach and Baratz provide a perspective on power directly relevant to the present discussion of planning. They assert that there are two faces of power, neither of which sociologists see, and only one of which political scientists take into account. In their analysis they reject the traditional sociological approach to the study of community power, reemphasizing the criticisms of this approach that have emerged. That is, they assume an elite power structure exists which is stable over time, and that the "reputational approach" of sociologists employed to identify political influentials incorrectly equates reputed with actual power.

Yet, as Bachrach and Baratz have noted, while political scientists in their criticisms have isolated the particular deficiencies inherent in the sociological approach to the study of community power, they have overlooked one face of power themselves. In their methodological and conceptual commitment to the pluralistic approach to power, which focuses not on the sources of power but on its exercise, political scientists have implicitly defined power as participation in decision making through an examination of concrete decisions. Bachrach and Baratz focus on the deficiency of the pluralist approach by contending that it does not take into account the possibility that power may be exercised by limiting the scope of decision making to relatively safe issues—ones which do not constitute a threat to particular power groups. In addition, they indicate that the pluralistic model provides no objective criteria for distinguishing important and unimportant decisions. They also indicate that, with respect to the exercise of power, one must recognize that power over concrete decisions is only one exercise of power, and that while factors such as the capacity to limit the agenda of decision making may produce complex measurement problems for researchers, any complete concept of power must include both its faces.

Of course power is exercised when A participates in the making of decisions that affect B. But power is also exercised when A devotes his energies to creating or reinforcing social and political values and institutional practices that limit the scope of the political process to public consideration of only those issues which are comparatively innocuous to A. To the extent that A succeeds in doing this, B is prevented, for all practical purposes, from bringing to the fore any issues that might in their resolution be seriously detrimental to A's set of preferences.[39]

The analysis of nondecisions, that is the exercise of power in the form of limiting the forum of public decision making by eliminating from consideration certain alternatives, is directly related to any analysis of the planning process in the United States. It is related because non-decisions themselves are the result of an exercise of power—the power to limit the scope of the agenda.

The specific relevance of the foregoing is twofold. In the first regard planners, as experts, can exert a significant impact on how policy alternatives are chosen by determining how problems are structured.

For many experts the only relevant actor is the Prince, who happens to pay wages, supply office space, provide status, and offer access to the substance of the research; these evident attributes make the Prince an attractive target for experts' attention.

This means that in many instances experts and planners tend to emerge as the equivalent of selective filters for communication and decision in the social system. They use their available time to consult in selected circles. Since they limit participation in planning they permit information and influence to flow only within a selective portion of the body politic.[40]

The planner's professional vernacular and array of ostensible esoteric techniques can be employed in the service of a variety of different values to give rational veneer to what is, in essence, simply a given set of opinions. In this sense the planner's expertise can be employed to limit the range of policy choices considered. Moreover, many scholars in the area of planning suggest that American planners possess a history and heritage which is transmitted through formal training and expressed in specific professional standards and values, and that this professional world view is an important element in any planning recommendation. Since the nature of these professional values limits the range of alternatives the planner is willing to consider, he or she becomes a political actor, exercising one of the two faces of power which leads to the determination of "who gets what, when, how."

The second definition of politics is Easton's concept of politics as the authoritative allocation of values. It will be demonstrated that planning shares a common core with politics in that the subject matter of both is inherently normative or value-laden in content. Altshuler indicates a central feature of the planning process when he states: "Significant planning problems are never simply technical; they always involve the determination of priorities among values."[41] The essential normative character of the process is, perhaps, best expressed in the ideal object of that process; namely, the matter or general plan. T. J. Kent describes it as essentially a community's statement about the major policies concerning its physical development.[42] Planner Charles Abrams describes the general plan as "a comprehensive, long-range plan intended to guide the growth and development of a city, town, or region, expressing official contemplations on the course its transportation, housing, and community facilities should take, and making proposals for industrial settlement, commerce, population, distribution, and other aspects of growth and development."[43]

Two factors emerge from either of these definitions. First of all, transportation, housing, community facilities, etc., require choices from among a variety of alternative policies, and secondly those choices must be made in reference to some statement of community goals; for example, in the first context, what type of transportation should the community pursue—rubber or rail—and in what (if any) mix; what type of housing—some public or exclusively private; what type of community facilities—additional police stations or an opera house? When such questions are answered, they clearly discriminate among the variety of real and potential interests in the community, rewarding some interests and depriving others. Also, the answers to such questions imply some statement of community goals to provide the criteria on which to evaluate and order the various alternatives.[44]

It can be demonstrated, however, that the nature of those community goals in the planning process are such that they implicitly overlap with (and cannot be separated from) the values they represent. Herbert Simon in his classic *Administrative Behavior* provides a definition of values, and a distinction between facts and values that illustrates this point. Factual or empirical propositions, according to Simon, are statements about the observable world and the manner in which it functions. In theory they can be tested to ascertain whether they are true or false. Normative or value propositions on the other hand are of an ethical nature, statements about the good or the preferable, and are not susceptible to empirical testing to ascertain whether they are true or false.[45] Simon utilizes the fact-value dichotomy to discuss decision making in the organizational context. He describes organizational behavior as purposive; that is, oriented toward goals.[46] He contends that each decision in an organizational context involves the selection of a goal and a behavior relevant to it. Decisions that lead to the selection of final goals are factual judgments.[47] In other words, the goals themselves are not completely reducible to (and cannot be defined exclusively on the basis of) empirical criteria alone. Simon presents an illustration of the inherent fact-value overlap in an applied decision-making context that is worth quoting at length:

> *An Illustration of the Process of Decision.* In order to understand more clearly the intimate relationships that exist in any practical administrative problem between judgments of value and fact, it will be helpful to study an example from the field of municipal government.
>
> What questions of value and fact arise in the opening and improvement of a new street? It is necessary to determine: (1) the design of the street, (2) the proper relationship of the street to the master plan, (3) means of financing the project, (4) whether the project should be let on contract or done by force account, (5) the relation of this project to construction that may be required subsequent to the improvement (e.g., utility cuts in this particular street), and (6) numerous other questions of like nature. These are questions for which answers must be found—each one combining value and factual elements. A partial separation of the two elements can be achieved by distinguishing the purpose of the project from its procedures.
>
> On the one hand, decisions regarding these questions must be based upon the purposes for which the street is intended, and the social values affected by its construction—among them, (1) speed and convenience in transportation, (2) traffic safety, (3) effect of street layout on property values, (4) construction costs, and (5) distribution of cost among taxpayers.
>
> On the other hand, the decisions must be made in the light of scientific and practical knowledge as to the effect particular measures will have in realizing these values. Included here are (1) the relative smoothness, permanence, and costs of each type of pavement, (2) relative advantages of alternate routes from the standpoint of cost and convenience to traffic, and (3) the total cost and distribution of cost for alternative methods of financing.
>
> The final decision, then, will depend both on the relative weight that is given to the different objectives and on judgment as to the extent to which any given plan will attain each objective.[48]

In the preceding example, Simon's separation of the administrative decision-making process into the purpose and the procedure inherent in each decision is synonymous with his identification of decisions that lead to goals as value judgments, while those leading to their implementation are classified as factual judgments. The decisions that lead to planning priorities and the priorities themselves are, also, in the domain of value judgments. Implicitly, therefore, the "rational" (in the sense that the term is utilized synonymously with factual or empirical) rank ordering of ultimate planning goals is a contradiction in terms.

The foregoing analysis is directly relevant to any consideration of the planning process, because planning as a function of government has the ascribed objective of taking a comprehensive perspective toward making recommendations about the urban growth and developmental process. Planning in the United States drew its inspiration from the conviction that it "should encompass all important social, economic, and political factors that impinge on urban growth."[49] Altshuler contends that planners aspire to a degree of comprehensiveness which attempts to determine the overall framework in which urban development takes place, and that planners "generally feel that they must recommend public regulation of the uses to which every bit of urban area land may be put."[50] Any process that seeks such objectives is implicitly political. Dennis R. Judd and Robert E. Mendelson maintain that planning is political in the direct sense that David Easton uses the term because of its "involvement in allocating socially valued resources."[51] If the planning process is involved in the allocation of socially valued resources, then decisions are correct only to the extent that they can be compared to some criteria which we have stated are essentially value-laden in content. The correct decision about a community's posture toward public housing, for example, may be presented by a planning agency accompanied by a strong rational technical motif: elaborate land-use charts, a cost-benefit analysis, and a myriad of graphs and computer output. However, the decision itself, to recommend or reject public housing, is predicated on some conception of community goals and is, therefore, political.

In summary, then, we may conclude that the nature of the planning process and the planner's input into that process are highly political in the sense that planning does much to determine "who gets what, when, how" in urban America. It does so through the control planners have over routine decisions with high policy content, and through their capacity to influence the agenda of community decision making. Planning is political also because of its involvement in the allocation of values. Indeed, like politics, the subject matter of planning is essentially normative or value-laden.

Planning: The Basis of the Recommendations

One particular question that emerges from the previous discussion is, Upon what criteria do planners base their recommendations? The answer is of considerable importance, given the planner's real and potential affect on public-policy output. One alternative would be to contend that decisions are predicated on an empirical theory of planning. However, planning possesses very little theory that can be utilized as a basis for land-use-related decisions. In the absence of a cohesive empirical theory, and given the value-laden nature of the process, one could conclude that "there are no planning policy decisions which do not involve value judgments."[52] Even when making recommendations based on ostensibly technical criteria, planners are required to choose among values, and are acting in some sense to establish priorities among those values. Norton Long contends that the question is not whether planning will reflect values, but which values planners will reflect.[53]

If planning recommendations are based upon values, the nature of those values needs to be discussed. Do the recommendations have any relationship to a core set of values unique to the profession, or are those values random in the sense that they are idiosyncratic to the individual planner? How, in practice, does the planner approach the value-laden aspects of his work? Altshuler provides one example of how decisions are made in practice by outlining the essentially intuitive character of the planning director's recommendations:

> The director focusing on innovation is bound to face several major political handicaps. Like any goal-generalist evaluator, he will rarely be able to base his ultimate defense of any proposal on reasoning as tight as one would expect from an engineer defending recommendations within his specialty. His efforts at persuasiveness will be further hampered, moreover, by his obligation regularly to throw out provocative (and thus potentially controversial) ideas and his need to resist routinization of his concerns (and thus his patterns of argument). By the time consensus envelops any idea, he will no longer have any reason to be interested in it. At best, nonetheless, his reasoning may be akin to that of a judge who in a difficult case makes his central decision intuitively, after examining the available evidence, but who then

writes his defense of that decision for all the world to see. The defense is society's safeguard against the uninformed and careless use of intuition.[54]

If, as he contends, the director's reasoning is based on intuition similar to that utilized in the judicial system, one should note that judicial decisions throughout the course of American constitutional history have led to a variety of diverse, if not mutually exclusive, conclusions. In addition, Altshuler's discussion does not deal with the questions previously raised; that is, the basis of this institution. Does it stem from values unique to the planning profession and socialized into the planner by his professional training, or does it stem from the idiosyncratic values of the individual?

In reality, the basis of any recommendation made by a planner or any professional is probably the result of an interaction of his own values with the values of his profession, his expertise, and the situation in which he finds himself. Nonetheless, the influence of professional socialization cannot be discounted. The professional socialization of the doctor toward the ultimate value of preserving life cannot be disassociated from his or her attitudes toward euthanasia. Similarly, the legal profession's strong value commitment to due process as a primary value legitimizes a young attorney's defense of a known criminal.

There is considerable support for the contention that the planning profession itself possesses a unique history and heritage that has been identified as exerting an independent influence on the attitudes of planners toward their professional standards and their attitudes toward the government.[55] In a recent work dealing with the status of planning ideology, political scientists Judd and Mendelson argue that planners "constitute an identifiable elite not only because they see themselves as such—note their noblesse oblige sentiments—but also because they share a core set of values."[56] These values, expressed in the form of professional standards and ideologies, affect the nature of planning recommendations. "In practice, planners tend to base their decisions on professional standards and ideologies which are acquired through training and experience. At the same time, however, the criteria for planning the use of urban space are not totally objective, but are based on a series of value premises. Some of these premises underlie the professional standards on which planning decisions are based."[57]

The origin and specific content of these standards and ideologies are related to the history and heritage of planning and will be more clearly explicated in the next chapter. However, it seems apparent that understanding the attitudes planners hold toward factors inherent in the planning process is important in ascertaining the planner's past or future impact on public policy. Understanding these attitudes is also important for the following reasons. The determinants of any planning outcome in any real or envisioned context will be the result of an interaction between the governmental structure by which the planning function is bound (its objective context), and the standards and ideologies of the planners themselves (the subjective context).[58] If these standards and ideologies have clear and explicit direction, and the literature suggests they do, then an understanding of these attitudes becomes an important element in understanding public policy. In addition, while the analysis of planners' attitudes is certainly important under current planning conditions, it becomes far more crucial given the expanded role of the planner implicit in the previously mentioned proposals for American social planning. Guy Benveniste's prophetic analysis is well worth noting.

Rapid and accelerating technological changes with their economic, social, and psychological consequences are an important factor in creating excessive bureaucratic uncertainty, which in turn results in bureaucratic fear. As the future becomes more uncertain, the bureaucracy becomes more rigid and rule-ridden. It therefore performs less well, and this accelerates the spread of the malaise. At that point, planning and systems expertise appear to be palliatives, and the call for systematic, comprehensive planning becomes generalized.

Therefore, just as a traditional society evolves the roles of warriors and shelter builders to deal with constant, if uncertain, elements in its environment, we are now evolving the role of expert or planner in response to the threat posed to individual decision-makers confronted by choices in situations where the outcomes are too uncertain and the penalties for error too heavy.[59]

Yet, despite these considerations a review of the literature indicates a dearth of information about the attitudes of planners. As Francine F. Rabinovitz states, "Studies of the background and perceptions of planners are unfortunately few and contradictory."[60] Much of the discussion about planners that emerges from the literature is in the form of case studies by various authors focused on specific arenas;

consequently, many of the generalizations made about the planners' attitudes toward their work are predicated on these isolated cases. Very few of the hypotheses about the kinds of attitudes they hold toward factors inherent in the planning process have been subjected to empirical analysis.[61] David C. Ranney has written, "Unfortunately, the politics of planning has received very little attention from the students of political behavior."[62] This research has been undertaken to address this deficiency.

Conclusions

It seems appropriate at this point to summarize the foregoing analysis and to outline the general research objectives of this study. First, I have sought to establish the conceptual framework for this research by demonstrating the interface between politics and planning. The nature of the planning process was compared to two classic definitions of politics. In this regard, planning was defined as political in character because of its involvement in the determination of "who gets what, when, how." Also, the nature of the planning process, like politics, was shown to be essentially value-laden and as a result planning could not be regarded as an exclusively rational-technical enterprise. Consequently, the values, attitudes, and self-perceptions of planners themselves become an important object for empirical analysis.

In addition, the criteria on which planners tend to base their recommendations were explored. It was concluded that in practice planners base their recommendations to some extent on professional standards of city planning and related attitudes toward government, and that these standards have been identified as having their origin in the history and heritage of the planning profession. Finally, the growing popularity of planning as a panacea for the complexity of the future was underscored and the contention stipulated that the growth of the planning function would result in a concomitant growth in the influence of the planner on the formation and implementation of public policy.

The principal objective of this research is to test empirically certain hypotheses emerging from the literature about planners in an endeavor to provide a profile of the planners with respect to attitudes they hold toward factors inherent in the planning process. In this regard, the subsequent chapter will examine the history and heritage of the planning process in an attempt to isolate specific influences on the professional standards of planning. The expression of these professional standards in the form of the two major strains of planning doctrine—traditional planning doctrine and advocacy—will be outlined.

The substance of following chapters will explore concerns related to themes developed within the context of this framework. Specifically, chapter three will focus on the professional standards of planning by analyzing a national sample of the members themselves. The objective of this endeavor will be to discover the distribution and direction of planners' attitudes toward various features of the planning process. Among the concerns we will explore is the question of whether or not planning is indeed a profession. Moreover, the role of the planner, advocate, or technician, will be examined, as will the question of the status of planning theory. In addition, the possibility of comprehensive rational planning in a pluralistic society and the desirability of national planning for the United States will be investigated. These attitudes will be compared and contrasted from the perspective of traditional planning doctrine and advocacy to assess which, if either, has exerted the greatest influence on the attitudes of planners. Also, particular concern will be given to what extent cleavages exist within the planning profession among various subgroups of the membership; for example, between public versus private planners and those possessing exposure to formal planning education versus those that do not.

Chapter four will compare and contrast planners with themselves and with a representative sample of the U.S. public on the dimensions of political ideology, political-party identification, and various measures of political participation. One particular objective of this chapter will be to determine if the planners' presumed political liberalism is simply an artifact of the limiting scope of the case studies on which this hypothesis is based, or, if the planner is indeed more liberal than Americans of similar educational, economic, and social class backgrounds.

Chapter five will test a variety of hypotheses related to the presumed influence of the philosophy of municipal reform on the attitudes of the planner, as well as on the development of various planning standards and ideologies. The major tenets of reformism which have been emphasized as exerting an influence on planning doctrine will be empirically examined; for example, the central question of the existence of a public interest and whether or not planners, by virtue of their professional training, are in the best position to be neutral judges of the public interest. Moreover, this chapter will assess the impact of the municipal-reform movement's distinct antipolitical bias by measuring levels of political cynicism among planners, as well as attitudes toward the role of government in general. Again, the purpose of this endeavor is to assess the enduring impact of traditional planning ideology versus the emerging influence of advocacy planning on the perceptions of planners.

The final chapter will seek to integrate the findings of this study with that of existing research and to assess if the planning profession does indeed possess a coherent professional doctrine which because of its empirical or normative quality is capable of providing the practicing planner, as well as his client, with direction in the resolution of specific policy dilemmas. In so doing, this research will shed some light on the central political question in any form of planning, by any level of government, in any real or envisioned context, which is legitimacy, or, in its less eloquently phrased version, the question generic to the political theory of planning: "Who will control the planner?"

Chapter 2

Profiles in the Literature

Introduction

The literature provides a profile of the planner with respect to the attitudes he presumably has toward factors inherent in the planning process.[1] The basis of these attitudes is assumed to be found, in part, in the history and heritage of the planning profession and to have been transmitted through formal training and experience. These attitudes, which are expressions of professional standards and ideologies, have been identified as influencing the nature of planning recommendations. It will be the purpose of this chapter to explore the history and heritage of planning in the United States in an attempt to examine the origin and content of such attitudes. In addition, the chapter will explicate the relationship between certain historical factors and dominant strains of planning ideology or doctrine; namely, the traditional ideology of planning and advocacy. After this relationship is established, the theoretically distinct assumptions made by each of these ideologies will be presented. Thus, the framework can be established to assess which of these two professional doctrines, if either, is most clearly reflected in the perceptions of planners themselves.

Planners and Planning: A History and Heritage

It has been asserted that the planner enters the planning process with a "set of values and procedures" which constitutes the planner's heritage.[2] This heritage contains three closely related elements: an environmental deterministic view of urban problems, a utopian vision, and a political-reformer outlook.[3] The basis of this heritage is presumed to be found in the history of the planning profession. This heritage has been identified as exerting an influence on the way planners perceive and interpret their work and to be "an important part of the process by which planning decisions are made."[4]

The assertion that planners tend to concentrate on the physical land-use related elements of the community rather than stressing larger social concerns has its roots in the planning profession's strong association with the housing-reform movement and in the professional background of many of the early planners. The housing-reform movement began as a reaction to adverse consequences the Industrial Revolution had for American cities. The crowded conditions of the slums generated by the massive influx of European immigrants and the movement of indigenous rural inhabitants seeking jobs in cities engendered a concern for the deteriorating physical environment. One of the first expressions of this concern was in the New York Tenement House Law of 1867. New York was among the first American cities to focus on the conditions of tenement housing, which is not surprising, since New York was already the largest city in the nation with the highest proportion of ethnic population, urban poor, and crowded slums.[5] The focus of the 1867 law was on the physical features of the tenements, and it possessed a strong strain of environmental determinism: "Primarily, however, the law of 1867, like later laws, assumed that a slum was a physical entity, whatever else it was; control of physical abuses was *per se* a contribution to solving the evils of the slum."[6]

Planners were involved in this movement and accepted many of its assumptions. The housing-reform movement was essentially concerned with social consequences of physical conditions, the foremost of which was overcrowding. The New York Tenement House Committee of 1894 presented figures which indicated that the population density of Manhattan Island exceeded that of the most crowded European cities.[7] The housing-reform movement had a strong noblesse oblige bias and was predicated on the prevailing assumption that social conditions could be altered by simply manipulating housing design. Lawrence Friedman's comment on the provisions of the New York Tenement House Law of 1901 expresses this viewpoint. "Nonetheless, the physical emphasis was primary. The provision on overcrowding, for example, reflected strong views on the noxiousness of dark and uncirculated air, as much as anything else. Moreover, nonphysical reforms were pursued through physical means."[8]

The movement to reform housing in the United States was primarily under the leadership of two men, Jacob Riis initially, and subsequently Lawrence Veiller. Largely through their efforts, the

New York Tenement Housing Acts of 1867 and 1901 were enacted. Jacob Riis's *How the Other Half Lives*, an account of the squalor and dehumanization of New York slum life, was in the tradition of reformist literature of the time and very influential in motivating housing reformers. Lawrence Veiller was involved in establishing criteria for minimum standards in housing and is considered the father of modern housing codes.[9] Both men shared the conviction that the social values of the poor could be molded by changing their physical environment. Veiller asserted, "We all live up to our environment, more or less, like the beggar in the bed of the king."[10] The housing-reform movement's environmental-deterministic philosophy greatly influenced the planning profession and was largely adopted by it. The First National Conference on City Planning and the Problems of Congestion in 1909 was itself initiated by New York City housing reformers. In 1910 the American Institute of Architects and the American Society of Landscape Architects held another planning conference considered to be the origin of planning as a movement in the United States.[11] Among its members was a large proportion of planners instrumental in housing reform. Despite its noblesse oblige sentiments and environmental-deterministic philosophy, the housing-reform movement expressed a decided concern for social justice and equity. In addition, the housing reformers did not avoid the suggestion of public action as a means of addressing societal problems. The legacy of support for positive government, the concern for the underprivileged, and larger social welfare interests are emphasized by contemporary planners as a part of their professional heritage.[12]

The 1910 planning conference began a move toward a separate professional identity for the planning movement. The conference also took on an even stronger physical perspective, moving away from the somewhat larger goals of the housing-reform movement, and focusing on the aesthetic features of the city. This period in the history of planning became known as the City Beautiful Movement. The essence of this movement had its expression in the neoclassic form given to the City of Chicago in preparation for its world's fair in 1893. The City Beautiful Movement with its concern for the aesthetic features of the city engaged the support of civic-minded businessmen, politicians, and planners, and many American cities began the process of municipal beautification. The movement exemplified an even greater emphasis on physical determinism within the planning profession, which is understandable in retrospect, given the professional background of many of these early planners. "Most of those professionals who self-consciously labeled themselves planners were, by professional training, architects and engineers. Their proposals for changing city life—a concern that had led them to identify with the reformers in the first place—quite predictably reflected their training."[13]

Planners' concern with physical environment, exemplified in the city-beautiful movement, was the result of a shift of emphasis away from larger social concerns. Planners began to seek legal ways to control the chaotic and unplanned growth typical of most cities. The tool to achieve this purpose was zoning. Planners were instrumental in enacting the first zoning ordinance adopted by New York City in 1916. At the same time, however, enthusiasm for the City Beautiful Movement began to subside as American municipalities became concerned with the values of economy and efficiency. The impact of this movement on the planning profession has been described as follows:

The City Beautiful Movement had its greatest impact between 1900 and 1915, but by 1920 the movement had undergone a shift in emphasis, which has been referred to as "city efficient" or "city useful." . . . Many engineers who were concerned with the practical problems of public health and the efficient movement of the automobile entered the planning profession. Lack of beauty did not bother the new utilitarian planners as much as the other problems which the city faced. City efficient was not a departure from the emphasis on physical rearrangement as a solution to urban problems. The physical design bias was still there; only the emphasis of that design changed.[14]

The influence of the legacy of environmental determinism on planners has never been adequately assessed. However, one impact of environmental determinism on contemporary planners has been expressed by Melvin Weber in his analysis of the traditional view planners have taken of their role. "The city planners' responsibilities relate primarily to the physical and locational aspects of development."[15] This view, which implicitly accepts the separability of the whole city into physical versus social aspects, may merely reflect the propensity of any profession to structure the world in a fashion consistent with its body of knowledge and techniques. Nonetheless, the fact remains that the planners' methodology is heavily imbued with physical/design tools which can, indeed, seduce the planner into a purely physical focus on phenomena having enduring social consequences. Zoning, for example, has done much to establish both the physical and social mosaic of metropolitan America. Moreover, an assertion forthcoming from a variety of quarters is that all too often planners reduce the complexity of the city to physical design considerations (and that even these are chosen from a limited array of possible design standards), and in so doing they fail to recognize the profound social and political effects of their policy recommendations.[16]

There is, however, clear evidence that some planners have begun to expand their traditional role definition, as well as their conception of the planning process, in an explicit recognition of the complexities of urban life and the social consequences of their actions. Some planners have called for a reorientation of physical planning to include priorities that extend beyond physical development.[17] Others have asserted that planners have always been concerned with the social and economic factors inherent in their profession.[18] Herbert Gans, for example, calls for planners trained specifically in policy formation.[19]

Much of the recent literature suggests that planners may now consider social and economic planning as a legitimate goal for public planning to pursue. Various articles on "social planning" attempt systematically to define and defend planners' input into a type of planning that extends beyond the limited focus of the physical plan. There exists, nonetheless, a controversy within the planning profession on what public planning's legitimate scope of concern should be. It has been suggested that this controversy is a function of the interaction between the legacy of environmental determinism in the profession, the new demands on planning, and the divergent attitudes of certain socially oriented planners. The controversy extends to both the legitimate scope and the purpose of public planning and has been expressed by Frieden:

Another conflict concerns the purpose of planning. To some socially oriented people in the field, planning involves a process of redistributing resources through public action. They see planning as a way of redressing inequities that arise through the operation of the private market. . . .

To others, however, planning is neutral with respect to the distribution of resources to different groups. It is more concerned with the conservation of resources and with efficiency and economy in urban development.[20]

A specific purpose of the subsequent chapter will be to assess what impact the legacy of environmental determinism has had on the attitudes of the membership at large, particularly their perceptions about the nature of the planning function, as well as their convictions about the legitimate scope of authority of the public-planning process. More specifically, we will address the question, Do planners believe that the legitimate scope of the public planning function should be expanded to include factors other than the physical development of the community? Moreover, we will assess the prevailing conception among planners about their definition of planning; that is, do planners think it is a strictly technical activity involving application of the profession's engineering and design tools to a given problem, or an activity in which physical/design tools, as well as other techniques, provide a veneer for what is in reality policy innovation?

The second element of planners' heritage is a presumably utopian vision and is directly related to the environmental determinism that characterized the early history of planning. Ranney asserts that the planner's preoccupation with the physical environment as a means of addressing social problems has led to a reliance upon land-use standards derived from "ideal" communities. "Put another way, the ideal community is the planner's conception of utopia and is primarily a physical representation of the utopia." The tendency has resulted from the fact that planning has "very little theory that can be used as a basis for the development of land use standards."[21] In some sense, planning's traditional physical orientation led quite predictably to a search for a utopia that could be expressed in a physical form. In their search for this physical utopia, planners borrowed extensively from a variety of existing "ideal" communities both in the United States and in Europe.[22] It is Jane Jacobs's belief that foremost among the influences on professional planning standards were the conceptions of a young English court reporter, Ebenezer Howard, whose "Garden Cities," she asserts, exerted paramount influence. According to Jacobs, Howard did not understand the dynamics of large cities, and so his conception of planning was suburban (in terms of the physical qualities it emphasized), static, and paternalistic. "Both in his preoccupations and in his omissions, Howard made sense in his own terms but none in terms of city planning. Yet virtually all modern city planning has been adapted from, and embroidered on, this silly substance."[23]

While Jacobs may be accused of overstating her case, Howard's influence on the evolution of planning standards was nonetheless substantial. His conception of the ideal community was physically expressed in the city of Letchworth, England, and is described by Mel Scott:

The town included 3,800 acres owned by a corporation in which some of the most prominent English statesmen, intellectuals, and philanthropists were stockholders. Intended to embody the best features of both city and country and to be self-sustaining, it included residential, commercial, and industrial areas carefully planned by the architects Raymond Unwin and Barry Parker for a maximum population of some 30,000. Surrounding these areas was an agricultural and recreational greenbelt considered an integral part of the town and a permanent assurance against encroachment by other developments or the expansion of the town beyond its planned size.

Howard thought of Letchworth as an evangelical demonstration of the way to deter further sprawling growth of London and other large cities, and to initiate the development of whole clusters of garden cities which in the aggregate world offer all the economic, social, and cultural advantages of the vital but disorderly urban complexes of his day.[24]

Howard's ideas were given organizational form in the United States by the creation of the Garden City Association of America in 1906, and were an important part of the agenda for the National Conference on City Planning and the Problems of Congestion of 1909. In addition, at the conference the early fathers of American city planning also expressed clear admiration for the planning manifested in what were considered the far more orderly cities of Germany.[25] Finally, American planners were also influenced by indigenous endeavors at creating the ideal community based on both religious or economic values and expressed in such American examples as Oneida, New York, and Pullman, Illinois.[26]

From the work of Howard and others, planners presumably have inherited a series of professional standards, predicated on these ideal communities, which are at the basis of many planning recommendations.[27] Moreover, while the physical design assumptions inherent in these planning standards have been addressed elsewhere, the political assumptions have been less adequately explicated.[28] For example, one obvious political assumption in all these ideal communities is the very real requirement of a generous use of public authority to implement planned development of this type on a societal scale. At the very minimum is the requirement of extensive public control—if not ownership—of land, as well as a very directive series of public-policy regulations to harness the market mechanism. Also, it is obvious that this type of public control of development is not in accordance with the assumptions emerging from free-market economics; namely, that the market, and not the public sector, is the more preferable resource allocator. In addition, it is obvious that professional standards which support such an orientation toward an expanding public sector, as well as postulate the general conviction that planning of this scale is desirable, are decidedly at variance with dominant values of the American political system. An example of such values would include interest-group pluralism, and the decentralized structure of power that is inherent in American federalism. In other words, the political expression of the utopian vision of planners, if indeed it exists, would be reflected in a series of political attitudes among planners that could be characterized as very liberal by the conventions employed to distinguish ideological perspectives in American politics.

Subsequent chapters will focus on the impact of this utopian vision on the professional standards of planning by empirically analyzing the conceptions of the membership on a variety of political attitudes this vision clearly implies. First, we will explore the attitude of the planner toward the role of positive government in implementing planned change along a variety of related dimensions. The general question of the planner's position on the desirability, as well as the feasibility, of comprehensive national planning by the federal government will be investigated. In addition, we shall address in a later chapter the general question of whether the planner's utopian vision is anchored in the realization that planning of the type he desires is a specific expression of support for expanded government control. Also, we will compare and contrast planners with a national sample of Americans with respect to their political ideology and determine if, indeed, the planner is more politically liberal than Americans of similar socioeconomic status.

I have one final comment on the legacy of a utopian vision and its impact on planning standards; planning on a scale implied in the ideal communities outlined previously implies an arsenal of theory, both normative and empirical in content, capable of providing a necessary and sufficient justification for a planning function of this magnitude. It requires in essence a body of knowledge and techniques sufficient to constitute a theory of planning that is capable of providing the practicing planner with answers to questions about both the means and the ends of planning. The extent to which planners perceive that planning in fact possesses such a theory is a question we will investigate in the subsequent chapter.

Planners: The Machine and Municipal Reform

The last feature of the planners' heritage is to be found in the association of the planning movement with that of the municipal-reform movement.[29] The two movements flourished simultaneously and had overlapping membership. Also, it has been indicated that planners shared many of the underlying attitudes and assumptions of municipal reform, and presumably this early association is an important element of the contemporary planner's heritage.[30] Among the ideological tenets of reformism that have influenced planning doctrine, and which will be analyzed in the subsequent section, are the commitment to a solitary public interest and a concomitant antipolitical bias. Additionally, the reform movement's support for rationality, the political neutrality of expertise, and the tendency to centralize executive influence in order to make government more efficient, are identifiable influences of reformism on traditional planning doctrine.[31] One consistent contention emerging from the planning-related literature is that the planner has a political reformer's outlook; that is, the planner's attitudes toward the political process have been shaped by the philosophy of municipal reform. Moreover, a great deal of the debate between the proponents of the traditional ideology of planning and the proponents of advocacy centers around issues whose origin is to be found in the philosophy of municipal reform. For these reasons, the following section will discuss the history of municipal reform and its impact on planning theory in some detail.

The municipal-reform movement arose in reaction to a style of political-party organization known as the "machine," which dominated, at one time or another, the politics of most major American cities between the Civil War and the New Deal.[32] While the political machine took on a variety of forms, it has been generally defined as "a party organization that depends crucially upon inducements that are both specific and material."[33] The machine has been compared, allegorically, to a brokerage organization whose "business" consisted of trading votes for public services. Devoid of ideology, save that of self-sustainment, the machine prospered through a linkage mechanism that tied the party organization to the needs and aspirations of the successive waves of ethnic groups arriving in search of the American dream. For many of these immigrants, the American dream required an adjustment to the harsh realities of urban life. The immigrants frequently found themselves crowded into unsafe tenements, and they often lacked adequate education and the ability to speak English. In addition, they frequently were unfamiliar with the American culture and mores, and were the subject of religious and ethnic hostility from native Americans.[34]

The political machine, in some sense, provided the mechanism to address many of the economic and social problems faced by America's new urban masses. The machine, in effect, moved into the power vacuum created by the withdrawal of many native Yankee Americans, who were reacting to the growing power of "new" urban social groups and reflecting their distaste for the political culture of the immigrant. This political culture is perhaps best exemplified in George Washington Plunkitt's contention "that when a man works in politics, he should get something out of it."[35]

The machine existed by operating an informal exchange mechanism that traded various services for electoral support. At the apex of the machine's organizational pyramid loomed the boss,

who was at the top of the chain of command, was served by a number of ward leaders who were responsible for distributing the favors and collecting the votes. Each ward leader, in turn, had a staff of precinct captains who made most of the initial contacts with the voters. Precinct captains and ward leaders were generally chosen by some elected party official and given an appointed job by the party which would allow them to have a reasonable income while pursuing their major work for the party. The ultimate objective of this work was to deliver the votes on election day. This was a full time job, which required frequent visits to the neighbors, doing various tasks for the party and generally being available to the voters. For the most part, the precinct captains and ward leaders asked individuals to exchange their votes for tokens of friendship, although cash, coal, or turkeys at Christmas time were occasionally given to the loyal electorate.[36]

The machine, from a structural functional perspective has been characterized by Fred Greenstein as basically a highly disciplined party hierarchy that effectively exercised control over both nomination to public office and ultimately those offices themselves. The leadership of the party, frequently lower class or ethnic in origin, was tied organizationally to the voters through a cadre of party loyalists motivated by tangible, rather than ideological, rewards.[37] Working from a political structure that could "get things done," the machine politician avoided abstract ideologies and public issues and focused on the real and private desires and needs of his constituents. "If a family is burned out I don't ask whether they are Republicans or Democrats and I don't refer them to the Charity Organization Society, which would investigate their case in a month or two and decide they are worthy of help about the time they are dead from starvation. I just get quarters for them, buy clothes for them if their clothes were burned up, and fix them up till they get things runnin' again. It's philanthropy, but it's good politics, too—mighty good politics."[38] In order to generate the revenue to sustain its self-serving altruism, the machine freely extended political privilege to various interests.[39]

The political machine has been the subject of much pejorative analysis primarily because of its real and documented corruption and the "private regarding" ethos that gave sanction to this style of politics.[40] Robert Merton, however, in a seminal work dealing with the "latent functions" of the machine, outlines its importance in filling the vacuum created by the fragmentation of political power in urban government. According to Merton, the machine provided a centralization of authority that facilitated the growth of free enterprise. In the process of its questionable interactions with businessmen, the machine enabled American cities to acquire badly needed capital improvements in such areas as transportation and public utilities. The machine also personalized government and provided a mechanism of upward social mobility for ethnic groups and others denied access by the larger culture. Finally, the machine served as an employment agency that offered a public-service alternative to unemployment and provided social-welfare activities.[41] The political machine prospered during a time when the existing structures of local government were unwilling or unable to address the problems inherent in rapid urbanization and immigration and, in that sense, was clearly functional for the American city.

The decline of the political machine is associated with changes in the social and economic environment and the alteration of certain structural features of the political process which severed the linkages that tied the machine to its clientele.[42] In the first regard, the depression and evolution of positive government created a condition by which the federal government subsumed many of the machine's social-welfare functions. Also, the nativistic sentiments that resulted in a restrictive immigration policy served to curtail the flow of immigrants who constituted much of the social base of the political machine.[43] The second factor in the decline of the machine was the rise of the municipal-reform movement. This movement's success in implementing a variety of structural changes in local government (nonpartisan elections, at-large constituencies, council-manager government) in essence weakened the structural foundation of the machine as a party organization and, therefore, contributed to its demise.

The origins of a reform style of politics began in the United States shortly after the Civil War, and as stated previously, began primarily in response to the real and perceived abuses of machines and bosses.[44] This reformist impulse in politics culminated in what has been called the Progressive Era of American politics.[45] In a very real sense, the foundation of the Progressive movement was built on a style of reform-oriented, muckraking journalism. The impact of Progressive Era journalism was intensified because it flourished at a time of rapid urbanization and a concomitant expansion of newspaper and magazine circulation.[46] The focus of the muckrakers was frequently corruption in city politics and business. Lincoln Steffens's *The Shame of Cities*, a caustic diatribe on political machines in a variety of American municipalities, epitomized the righteous indignation that characterized much of the writings of the times.[47] The municipal-reform movement, which was a product of the Progressive Era, found its institutional expression in the creation of the National Municipal

League, founded in 1894. The effect of the movement was to intro-
duce profound and enduring changes in the political and structural
features of the contemporary American city.[48]

The machine and reform styles of politics have been compared and
contrasted both in terms of their social base and the conception of
politics with which each have become associated. To the extent that
the political machine was "ethnic," the social base of the reform
movement was indigenous Yankee American. From what Richard
Hofstadter calls "the clash between the needs of the immigrants and
the sentiments of the natives"[49] emerged two distinct political ethics,
which expressed divergent views on both the philosophy and function of government.

It has been argued that all governments perform two essential
functions, the service function and the political function.[50] The former
refers to the provision of goods and services that are not provided or
cannot be provided by the private sector. The latter refers to the management of conflict generated in the process of determining "who
gets what, when, how." In one sense the machine epitomized the
political function and the municipal reform movement epitomized
the service function of government. In a very real way, the political
machine with its party loyalties, its overt acceptance of political corruption, and its personal style, was a distinct conception of the
political world. It reflected a different ethos, which "took for granted
that the political life of the individual would arise out of family
needs," and which viewed "civic relations in terms of personal obli-
gations, and placed strong personal loyalties above allegiance to
abstract codes of law or morals."[51] This style of politics has been
appropriately called the "private-regarding" ethos.[52] The municipal-
reform movement, conversely, emphasized a style of politics presumably expressing a different ethic, which was both an Anglo-Saxon
Protestant style of politics, and a public-regarding ethos. This style
contained an "emphasis upon the obligation of the individual to
participate in public affairs and to seek the good of the community 'as
a whole.'"[53]

The reform movement also expressed a distinct ideology relating to
the conduct of public affairs. Primary in this ideology was a commitment to a public interest that should prevail over competing private
interests. This belief in the existence of a solitary public interest,

which could be identified and acted upon, was related to the anti-political bias expressed in the negation of the "evil theory" of politics that conceptualized the city as a political body.[54] The assumption of the reformers that "politics" denoted illicit demands in opposition to the interests of the community as a whole understandably led to their proposals for removing "politics" from government.

They attempted to effect this removal by advocating changes in the structure of local government and the manner of electing public officials.[55] The reform movement recommended a series of structural changes, which constituted the program of reform. Among the elements of the program were initiative, recall and referendum, the short ballot, opposition to immigration, home rule, nonpartisan and at-large elections held separately from national and state elections and, finally, the council-manager form of government and master planning.[56] While the styles and strategies of reform were varied, three elements of the program have been identified as most characteristic: the council-manager form of government, nonpartisanship, and master planning.[57] The subsequent analysis will focus on these three.

The council-manager form of government personified in one sense the "Anglo-Saxon Protestant middle-class ideal" in municipal politics; moreover, it expressed much of the philosophy of politics behind municipal reform.[58] It was first recommended by the National Short Ballot Organization in 1911 and later adopted by the National Municipal League.[59] Its principal protagonist, and some say father, was Richard Childs, an advertising man who devoted his life to municipal reform. Childs reflected a dominant feeling of the Progressive Era in his commitment to the belief that politics and administration should and could, in fact, be separated. It was upon this principle that he structured this form of government.[60]

John Porter East, biographer of Childs, underscores the influence of Frederick Taylor's classic *The Principles of Scientific Management* on Childs. Embracing the scientific management of Taylor, the council-manager concept emphasized the efficiency that would result from the proper application of expertise to local government. If efficiency was the goal, structure was the key in Childs's schema. He regarded the failures of government, exemplified in the political machine, not as failures in the capabilities of the body politic, but as the result of inadequate governmental structures; that is, structures which would separate the vagaries of politics from the "business" of government. According to East, "It is Childs' belief that from the properly constituted structural arrangements will flow the public interest."[61] In this sense the council-manager plan expressed the prevailing view of reformers that "the interests of the community as a whole should be determined in disinterested ways and then carried into effect expeditiously and efficiently by technicians."[62] In order to pursue these goals, the centralization of executive authority was required to combat the debilitating effects of checks and balances on municipal efficiency. "The principal symbols of the city manager plan were in harmony with the idea that government should be strengthened and made capable of rendering service, rather than weakened to prevent it from doing harm."[63]

The "business" of government was to be taken literally, since the manager form was an expression of the business model of corporate organization. The manager/expert, like his corporate-president prototype, was responsible for administration. The council, the board of directors for the corporation, represented the policy-making element.[64] The implicit assumption apparent in the council-manager plan was that efficiency was the principal goal of government, and that expertise was the foremost mechanism for its realization. This philosophy even today is commonly associated with "good-government" advocates.

Stemming from this philosophy, or perhaps giving birth to it, was the belief that there is no "Democratic or Republican way" to run local government. In Childs's cosmology, the vicissitudes of national politics had no relation to the problems of local government. At the local level, government was a matter for experts applying rational-technical efficiency in pursuit of the public interest.[65] The council-manager form was seen as a mechanism to address the lack of centralized influence that was characteristic of the weak-mayor/council form of government that prevailed in many machine-dominated cities. While municipal reformers at various times advocated the strong-mayor/council and commission forms of government, respectively, each subsequently fell into disfavor. East maintains that Childs's commitment to scientific management was manifested in his belief in the "one best form," the council-manager plan, and the "one best man," the manager.[66]

If Childs and other reformers were not unaware of politics, they placed political considerations secondary to the ideal of efficiency. In addition, to the extent that politics implied political-party machines and not electoral democracy, clearly the objective of the council-manager form was expressed in Childs's own evaluation of the principal accomplishment of the plan; namely, the destruction of the political machine.

The second major structural change proposed by reformers was nonpartisan elections. Philosophically, it was in keeping with the attitudes of reform. To the reformers the city was, in fact, a nonpolitical entity in pursuit of governmental efficiency. Therefore, the prospect of partisan or party-dominated politics, which tended to divide rather than pursue the public interest, had no place.[67] In fact, the entire concept of interest-group pluralism with its focus on separate demands was at variance with government by the community as a whole.[68] The intent of nonpartisanship was to remove local politics from the control of national politics, and to insulate the local community from the national political party framework. Since there was no Democratic or Republican way to run a city, the presence of the Democratic or Republican party was extraneous to good government. The proposed intent of nonpartisanship was to produce more qualified candidates, who were not motivated by political-party reward. In addition, it was conceived as a mechanism for insuring the accountability of the candidates to the interests of the community as a whole, and as a mechanism for destroying the influence of the political machine. In order to further insure the community's interests as a whole, the removal of party labels from ballots was advocated in conjunction with at-large, rather than ward, representation. The urban community prior to municipal reform was a decentralized political structure predicated on a system of ward-based politics. The wards represented not only a grass-roots political organization in the urban community, but also racial and ethnic pluralism. The reformers objected to this "structure of government which enabled local and particularistic interests to dominate."[69] The nature of those "particularistic interests" has caused some scholars to suggest that the stated objectives of the reform movement obscure its real intent; that is, to reestablish the dominance of the indigenous elite over the laboring class by instituting structural mechanisms guaranteed to disable the machine, and effectively disenfranchise the great unwashed. Whatever the merits of this contention, recent empirical studies have indicated variations in the public policy and voting turnout associated with council-manager government and nonpartisan elections.[70] The substance and implications of these findings will be addressed in a subsequent chapter.

The third major proposal associated with the municipal reform movement is the concept of master planning. The impact of reformist ideology and its preference for particular organizational structures have been dominant influences on the planning profession both in the actual form which the classic model of planning assumed and as the basis for a great deal of contemporary controversy over the nature of planning doctrine. Indeed, much of the doctrinaire debate within planning revolves around support for (or criticisms of) such pivotal questions as the existence of a solitary public interest, the role of politics in the planning process, the proper organizational locus of the public planning function, and questions of values and rationality, goals, and political power in the planning process. A review of the literature in planning reveals two dominant strains of planning doctrine: traditional ideology and advocacy.[71] The former expresses a conceptual legacy whose roots are clearly in the reform ideal, the latter is in essence a rejection of many of the assumptions of reformist thinking.

Master Planning and the Traditional Ideology of Planning

The first commonality between the traditional ideology of planning and various elements of reformism is the commitment to the concept of a solitary public interest. Indeed, the pursuit of the public interest is in some sense at the very foundation of the classical model of planning, and in many ways dictates its structure and content. Richard S. Bolan succinctly summarizes the relevant features of the classical model and the planner's perspective on the policy-making process:

1. The planning commission (with its professional staff) is an advisory body which assists government in formulating policy. Its view is comprehensive in

that no aspect of community development is assumed to be beyond its responsibility. It is also comprehensive in the sense that the planning commission is the guardian of the *whole* public interest rather than any particular special interest.

2. From this, it is assumed that the planning commission is both capable and responsible for establishing long-term development goals which provide a broad perspective and give substance to short-term particularistic community decisions. Planning is construed to be the antithesis of nihilism and is thus responsible for developing the broadest and highest aspirations to give meaning and purpose to the community's day-to-day activities.

3. These long-term goals are expressed by a long-range comprehensive or master plan whose salient features include a map of what the pattern of land-use development will be at some distant point in the future and some general policies as to how the community should be guided as it attempts to strive for that end-state.

4. With this, it is assumed that short-term, small-scale development decisions are to be measured against the yardstick of the master plan. The master plan would essentially eliminate debate on goals and on general means so that debate could focus on relatively narrow grounds of particular means.[72]

The linkage between various aspects of the model clearly explicates its implicit and explicit political assumptions.[73] For example, in order for the planning commission to exercise its function as guardian of the public interest, there must be by definition a public interest. In addition, the rhetoric associated with the master plan indicates that this public interest is superior to other particularistic or pluralistic interests. Accordingly, the master plan exemplifies a comprehensive perspective on community development. The master plan, as such, becomes the medium of expression for long-range goals and the criteria by which short-range development proposals are evaluated for their conformity to the physical expression of the "public interest." Putting the philosophical viability or political success of the model aside, it exemplifies a central precept of traditional planning doctrine, the existence of a solitary public interest and a de facto rejection of political pluralism as a precept. Judd and Mendelson contend that "even those planners who stress the complexity of the city—as most planners do—often speak of one public interest."[74]

In many ways the public-interest doctrine has been the edifice of the planning profession's source of legitimacy or, in other words, this doctrine has been its philosophical justification for the intervention of public authority in the private-market mechanism.[75] A very fundamental assumption of the government's role in planning is "that the natural processes of the private market cannot allocate land uses that benefit the public as a whole."[76] Consequently, planning is seen as a mechanism for addressing this dysfunction and the planner is empowered to invoke both his profession's commitment to a larger public interest, and his rational expertise in its pursuit to support the implementation of planning objectives. Planner Richard S. Bolan recognizes the role of philosophical justification in practical planning proposals when he states, "Of major importance in any proposal is the degree to which it can be argued on ideological grounds."[77] In effect, the technical aspects of many planning-policy questions (for example, public housing) are secondary to the ideological dimensions of the argument that they are related to some conception of the "public interest."

In some sense, as Altshuler notes, since planners in their comprehensive generalist role deal with many more aspects of public policy than do various subject specialists, "claims to comprehensiveness, if they are to be persuasive, must refer primarily to a special knowledge of the public interest."[78] The claim is one that in traditional planning ideology is pervasive. "Planners have always believed in some unified public interest or general welfare which was the special responsibility of the planning profession."[79] Moreover, in traditional planning ideology the centrality of the concept of a solitary public interest and the special knowledge in the planning profession of both its nature and dimensions is recognized by many planning theorists. "The implications of the challenge to the public interest doctrine are clear, direct and serious—and, if true, shattering. If there is no unifying public interest to be served, if the science and art of planning is to be placed in the service of each special interest group in a pluralist society, what happens to the concept of comprehensiveness?"[80]

The challenges to this doctrine, which have emerged from both within and without the planning profession, are exacerbated, because the assumption in traditional planning doctrine, that planners possess a unique perspective in their ability to judge the public interest, is said also of the politician. While both claim the ability, each rests his claim on different sources of legitimacy. "The politican's claim rests on his popular election, his knowledge of the community, his sensitivity to human needs, and his personal wisdom. The planner's claim is one of professionalism and research."[81] The juxtaposition of planner and politician, and the negative feelings of the former for the latter, are expressions of the shared variance between planning and elements of the municipal-reform movements. Deil Wright indicates that two complementary themes emerge in the findings of research on local planning: "First, a distinct anti-political bias exists among planners. Second, and closely related to the first, is the observation that as professional planning norms become more pervasive there is a consequent atrophy in the planner's capacity to affect public policy."[82] The planner's disdain for the political process is, presumably, a legacy of the ideology of municipal reform.[83] This contention is supported by some limited empirical evidence which suggests that the degree to which planners are effectively socialized into traditional professional norms is associated with their willingness to engage in overt political activities.[84]

The antipolitical bias of planners is in keeping with the traditional values of reform. To the reform movement, politics connoted the pursuit of private interests at the expense of the interests of the community as a whole. This belief, coupled with the assumption that politics and administration could be separated, did much to dictate the preference for certain structural features of local government discussed previously. The political cynicism that characterized the early planning movement was itself related to preferences for the one best public planning structure.[85] As Ranney contends, "Planners have traditionally distrusted local government, viewing it as a pawn of special interest groups."[86] In order to insulate planning from the vagaries of politics, planning as a governmental function evolved under the semiindependent planning agency.[87] The concept of the semiindependent planning commission was predicated on many of the prevailing assumptions of municipal reform. Planning was conceived of as a rational technical enterprise in pursuit of the whole community's interest. As a technical process with no Democratic or Republican parameters, the independent commission's salient features incorporated in the Standard Planning Enabling Act of 1928 were designed to remove politics from planning.[88] The independent planning commission, composed of appointed laymen, in effect divorced the planning function from the control of elected officials.[89] The justification, valid or not, was the presumed immunity from political pressure and a concomitant ability of the commission to take a comprehensive view of the community's interest.

The comprehensive focus of planning itself has generic similarities to the doctrine of the interest of the community as a whole, emerging from the ideology of municipal reform. The model of comprehensive planning, which was at first physical and later somewhat social in conception, expresses many of the assumptions of traditional planning ideology. For example, among the elements that would have to be included in any definition of comprehensive planning would be coordination, projection, rationality, and control.[90] The terms *coordination* and *projection* express what is implied by planners in the term *comprehensiveness*. As Melville Branch contends, two basic characteristics of comprehensive planning are the integration of parts, and the projection into the future.[91] The coordination aspect of the planning functions has been compared metaphorically by Branch to physical coordination in the human organism, which is a type of holistic integration or gestalt.[92] Not surprisingly, Branch sees comprehensive planning as a distinct process, an intellectual discipline, and the most important of human endeavors.[93] The implications of the ideal of comprehensive planning reflect, again, the commonality it shares with the ideology of municipal reform. As Altshuler notes, comprehensive planning assumes a special knowledge of the public interest by planners, because truly comprehensive planning seeks to "plan in detail the future evolution of all important economic and social patterns."[94] Implicit in this level of coordination or integration is the assumption that community goals can be measured and a value matrix, as it is called by planners, can be established.[95] Also, proponents of comprehensive planning assume coordination is possible because the "common interests of society's members are their most important interests and constitute a larger proportion of all their interests. They must assert that conflicts of interests in society are illusory, that they are about minor matters, or that they can be foreseen and resolved by just arbiters (planners) who can understand the total interests of all parties."[96] In effect, like the ideology of reform the assumptions of comprehensive planning repudiate, or at least place in a secondary position, many of the contentions of political pluralism.

The coordination element of comprehensive planning pertains primarily to its scope. The objective of comprehensive planning, however, is projection or the ability to predict and direct the community's development in line with the master plan and the public interest.[97] In the ideology of traditional planning doctrine, the method to achieve this goal is rationality, "not political horse trading but rational thought was to guide the cities' future."[98] Robert Goodman summarizes these sentiments: "The planning of cities was to be entrusted to professionals, who would supposedly consider all interests of the city in their objective, scientific, nonpolitical analyses and then arrive at a comprehensive plan."[99]

Traditional planning doctrine, like reformism, has been heavily imbued with elements of scientific management, particularly with respect to the role of the value-free technician expressed in the belief that planners were "politically neutral, that planners did not take sides in community conflicts, but rather worked for something we sometimes called 'the community as a whole.'"[100] In traditional planning doctrine, rationality, efficiency, and neutrality are core elements that bind together the components of the classical model.[101] According to the model, the planner as expert, freed from the constraints of values, imbued with comprehensive focus and a scientific method, works toward the achievement of everyone's common interest. "Planners typically defend the claim that their work can add to the sum of human welfare by referring to the 'comprehensiveness' of their point of view. Since they also speak frequently of the 'rationality' of their prescriptions, the implication often seems to be that their breadth of concern enables them to conceive clearly rational solutions to policy choice problems."[102] Some scholars contend that many of the assumptions of the classical model still dominate the planning profession's preference with respect to the role planners should assume; namely, that of technician.[103]

The last element of the comprehensive planning model and the traditional ideology with which it is associated is control or, more precisely, political control. In order to implement the comprehensive plan, some degree of control is implicit. As previously stated, the independent planning commission was created in an attempt to remove planning from politics and from the mainstream of the political system. One commonly noted feature of the municipal-reform movement was its attempt to centralize political power in an endeavor to "rationalize" the governmental process and thus make it more efficient.[104]

According to Altshuler, opponents of planning have contended that planners have a bias toward centralized political authority which is reflected in their support for an expanded governmental role.[105] Judd and Mendelson observe: "Taking on the tasks of saving mankind and ushering in and administering a new utopia, the planners have confidently asked for sufficient power to accomplish their mission. To counteract the unplanned 'effects of industrialization and urbanization' the planners' power must be increased, for planning must face the major domestic and international problems of the twentieth century. To undertake these tasks planners must not be hampered by 'too little authority and territorial limitations.'"[106] Indeed, some planning theorists suggest that of "all the functions of government, the one least conducive to decentralization is planning,"[107] and go on to note "the centralization of power is not inherently undemocratic, only the extent to which its use is accountable to the popular will."[108] Robert Goodman contends that the classic example of the philosophy of "nonpolitical" scientific planning is Rexford Tugwell's fourth-power status for planning, in which it was advocated that planning acquire the status of a fourth branch of government whose function would be to establish social policy.[109] According to Tugwell's conception, the planning branch of government would be concerned, in a fashion reminiscent of Progressive Era thinking, with pursuit of a factual or empirical basis for social policy, one "dictated by contemporary resources, techniques and circumstances, rather than by political expediency."[110] While a review of planning literature suggests many theorists prefer an expanded role for government, others predict it as the ultimate and logical consequence of the rationalization of society. Accordingly, society will be pushed by virtue of problems ecological and social in nature toward "the inexorable expansion of the federal government as the dominant device for social control."[111]

Advocacy: A Rejection of the Philosophy of Reform

The classical model of planning and the traditional planning ideology clearly no longer command consensus within the planning profession. In fact rather than consensus, an evaluation of planning doctrine reveals a heterogeneity of perspectives, a conceptually dynamic process, and an introspective search for a statement of values and a body of knowledge and techniques of sufficient quality to give planning some theoretical structure. However, some scholars suggest that the influence of the traditional ideology of master planning is still strong in spite of the fact that many of its fundamental assumptions have been called into question in varying degree by proposals for middle-range and advocacy planning. The intensity and scope of the criticism has varied from attacks which sought to reduce the scope of planning to middle-range objectives or to adjust planning to the realities of the political system by linking planning to the executive or the legislative branches, to the total rejection of the political and philosophical assumptions on which the classical model of comprehensive planning has been predicated.[112]

Early criticisms of the classic model emerged from within the profession as attempts to change the focus of planning while retaining the ideal of comprehensiveness. Robert Walker, among others, benefiting from his experience with planning's fleeting national prominence, recognized planning's ultimate dependency on the political process and advocated that planning be tied to the executive, if it was to be effective as well as comprehensive. T. J. Kent accepted similar assumptions, although he presented a different medium in suggesting that planning be tied to the city council or legislative branch.[113] Both in effect questioned the possibility that successful comprehensive planning would emerge from structures such as the independent planning commission, which sought to insulate planning from politics. Martin Meyerson called for planning to focus on middle-range objectives.[114] Altshuler has described the practice of middle-range planning as "planning for the achievement of goals that are general, but still operational."[115] Alan Kravitz argues that middle-range planning was and is an attempt to salvage the classic model of planning by attempting to adapt the ideals of comprehensiveness and rationality to the realities of the behavioral studies of political systems that questioned them.[116] From these studies by political scientists and sociologists, various issues were raised about the viability of the comprehensive-planning model given the characteristics of the local political systems themselves. Among the most pervasive have been Edward Banfield's critiques of comprehensive planning, in which he questions many of the essential assumptions of the comprehensive-planning ideal. Among his conclusions are the following: it is difficult to establish any but the most abstract goals in a pluralistic community, the decentralized nature of American community politics mitigates against the ideal of comprehensiveness, and there is enormous complexity in predicting change in the environment.[117] In addition, the contradictions between the decision-making styles and the time frames of politics versus planning have been richly elaborated by both Altshuler and Theodore J. Lowi.[118] However, among the most systematic critiques of the comprehensive rational decision-making model is Charles E. Lindblom's critique of the positivist approach to truly scientific-rational comprehensiveness, which focuses on the inability of the decision maker to truly consider all values in the goal-formation process because of the realities of the political system and the incomplete information available.[119]

The most significant assault on the traditional ideology of planning, however, has been advocacy planning. The advocacy movement in planning was a child of the sixties, and like so many ideas of that peculiar decade, the impact of advocacy has been more significant than its detractors would care to concede, yet far less profound than its proponents once envisioned. Advocacy planning in a sense fed upon the very real inequities and discrimination evident in the political system in such areas as housing, health, education, and welfare. To the theorists of the advocacy movement these failures of the political system to provide equity were partly the result of failures in the form and substance of the planning profession.

The critics of the Vietnam War and civil rights advocates ultimately turned to the very foundation of the American political system (capitalism and the existing institutions of representation) in search of a culprit for the particular malady manifested in the direction of American public policy. Likewise planners, or more precisely some theorists within the profession, looked to the very foundation of the planning profession and isolated their own culprit for America's badly planned cities, the traditional ideology of master planning. In retrospect it is apparent that advocacy seized upon and reflected the generally diminishing respect for expertise and rationality characteristic of the decade. Moreover, advocacy legitimized political solutions to planning problems at a time when "political solutions" were clearly the preferred medium of exchange in the marketplace of ideas.

In addition, since advocacy drew its inspiration from the legal model of advocacy, it placed great emphasis on the role of the planner as serving a particular client. And since many advocate planners became associated with clients who had traditionally been excluded from the political process, advocacy planning quickly acquired the legitimacy bestowed by the times on events or ideologies that attempted to address the concerns of the socially disenfranchised.

However, advocacy was (and is) more than a new planning style—it is predicated upon assumptions that are totally antithetical to the major assumptions of the traditional model of planning. For most important questions in planning theory (for example, the nature of the planning process, the role of the planner, the existence of a public interest, the importance of expertise, and the client served) advocacy posits a decidedly different set of professional standards for its adherents. The substantial challenge of advocacy to the very foundation of traditional planning ideology warrants analyzing specific points of divergence between it and the traditional ideology of planning. The following section will compare and contrast advocacy with the traditional ideology of planning.

In a seminal article, Paul Davidoff laid the foundation for advocacy planning. Advocacy planning rejects outright the fundamental assumption of traditional planning ideology; that is, the existence of a solitary public interest in which all social groups share equally. He states, "Determinations of what serves the public interest, in a society containing many diverse interest groups, are almost always of a highly contentious nature."[120] This rejection of the existence of a uniform public interest obviously casts doubt on the planner's unique professional capacity to integrate objectively the diverse elements of the general plan into a holistic plan expressing that public interest. The doctrine of advocacy in effect rejects a pivotal assumption in the classic model of comprehensive planning "that planners can resolve conflicts among goals in expert fashion."[121] In advocacy-planning doctrine the general plan is merely an expression of group interests. Advocate planners "deny both the notion of a single 'best solution' and the notion of the general welfare it might serve."[122] Rather than rejecting pluralism characteristic of traditional planning ideology, advocacy embraces pluralism as a reality of political existence. The acceptance of pluralism in advocacy planning is basic to its decidedly political posture. Unlike traditional ideology, which sought to remove politics as a part of planning, "advocacy planning here appears as a new kind of politics."[123] Moreover, in the advocacy doctrine there are Democratic and Republican, racial and ethnic, rich and poor, and self-interest parameters in all community goals, and therefore, in all elements of the planning process. In effect, planning is perceived as inherently partisan. The pluralistic and partisan assumptions of advocacy lead to an understandably divergent view of the role of rationality in the planning process. Quite predictably, a doctrine that invites open debate about social values is at odds with the rationality manifested in the apolitical scientific planning of the classic model, a rationality that implies the ability to assess objectively the public interest and to establish "logically or experimentally the relationship between proposed means and the ends they are intended to further."[124]

Advocacy planning contends that there are no neutral, value-free criteria for evaluating a plan. Therefore, it opposes the right of a group of professionals, i.e., planners, to devise in exclusively rational terms a unitary plan serving a unitary public interest. Because all important choices on the right course of action in planning are "always a matter of choice, never of fact,"[125] the doctrine of advocacy proposes plural plans and a plural planning process to reflect the diversity of interests inherent in a community. When the concept of a neutral basis for the creation or evaluation of plans is denied, the traditional role of the planner as a neutral expert or technician is also questioned. According to advocacy, as the term implies, the planner is seen as espousing particular values. Unlike the planner's role in traditional ideology the planner's client is no longer the public as a whole, but specific subgroups of that public. Rather than attempting to reduce planning considerations to questions of expertise by contending they are technical, the advocate planner accepts the strong normative content in all planning questions and represents his client accordingly. In addition, the client of the planner becomes both the private and public sector, creating in many cases the opportunity to engage in a different kind of planning—"a vigorous class and race oriented planning on behalf of the new urban constituency"[126]—a type of planning no longer confined solely to the physical forms of the city.

Also, with respect to the consideration of governmental control, advocacy espouses a tendency toward pluralized control rather than centralized control by the government. Advocacy, which recognizes the societal movement toward bureaucracy and expertise, stresses a plurality of expertise.[127] In effect, since there is no neutral value-free method to establish community goals, all groups require the technical competence of the planner in pursuit of their separate interests. In this sense planning policy, like all public policy, is the result of compromise and the product of group interaction rather than the one best solution of a rational, value-free algorithm. Finally, advocacy planning rejects a purely physical focus for the planning function and, in fact, embraces social planning, including supporting a new professional training for the planner that would incorporate the skills necessary for such a holistic endeavor.

Clearly the overall impact of advocacy planning has been to question much of the theoretical basis of the comprehensive model of planning and the traditional ideology of planning that gave substance to it. As such, advocacy provides its adherents with an alternative professional world view on most elements of the planning process, and therefore becomes an important vehicle for expressing, as well as understanding, the attitudes of the planning profession.

Conclusions

The objective of this chapter was to examine the literature in an attempt to suggest a profile of the planner with respect to the attitudes he presumably has towards factors inherent in the planning process. We indicated that the attitudes planners hold were assumed to be found in part in the history of the planning profession, and to be transmitted through formal training and experience. These attitudes, which are expressions of professional standards and ideologies, were identified as a significant influence on the character of planning recommendations and, therefore, worth explicating. The first influence outlined was the impact of the legacy of environmental determinism, which we indicated has influenced the planning profession to become more preoccupied with the use of physical space, rather than the search for larger social objectives for the planning function. Moreover, the impact of the planner's presumed utopian vision was

traced in the literature to the ideal community on which many contemporary standards for good planning are predicated. The political
orientation implied by these standards was outlined and the contention stipulated that the implications of implementing planning of this
scope and scale would predispose planners to political convictions
that would be very liberal by the conventions of American political
ideology.

Moreover, the history and heritage of the planning profession was
explored in an attempt to examine specific influences on the professional standards of planning. The association of the planning movement with that of the municipal-reform movement was examined. It
was noted that the two movements occurred simultaneously and had
overlapping memberships. In addition, it was indicated that the planning movement shared many of the underlying attitudes and assumptions of municipal reform and that the ideology of municipal
reform is an important element of the contemporary planner's heritage. Among the ideological tenets of reformism that we emphasized
as having influenced planning doctrine were the municipal-reform
movement's distinct antipolitical bias and its commitment to the
concept of a solitary public interest. Also, the reform movement's
support for rationality, neutral competence, and the tendency to centralize executive influence in the interest of efficiency were identified
as important influences on traditional planning doctrine.

Finally, the two distinct strains of planning doctrine were examined:
traditional planning ideology and advocacy. Traditional planning doctrine was underscored as expressing an ideological and conceptual
legacy whose roots are clearly in the philosophy of municipal reform.
Advocacy on the other hand was characterized as essentially a rejection of many of the assumptions of reformist thinking. We concluded
by observing that the bipolarity of these two ideologies made them
important conceptual anchor points by which to compare and contrast the attitudes of the profession.

It is very apparent that a planner committed to the merits of
advocacy planning would approach the planning function in a distinctly different manner (theoretically as well as practically) from his
counterpart who accepted the world view of planning postulated by
the traditional ideology. Moreover, one could clearly hypothesize a
very different set of planning-policy recommendations—for an iden-

tical substantive problem—emerging from planners of these diverse ideological persuasions. Yet, there is no clear and systematic evidence to suggest where the majority of planners would lie on a continuum bounded at one end by the traditional ideology of planning and on the other by advocacy. Indeed, it was the lack of adequate empirical data on how planners perceived the planning function and their role in it that initially served to motivate this research. Since there are no clear data that suggest otherwise, I will begin with the general working hypothesis that the professional standards of planning (in both education and in practice) express a clear preference for the traditional ideology of planning. However, we will look to the planners to resolve the question of which, if either, of these two rather diverse ideologies in fact most adequately reflects the majority opinion within the planning profession. In order to begin our analysis, the next chapter will outline the components of the methodology employed in the study with particular emphasis on the sampling design and procedures, as well as general statistical considerations. In so doing, we will provide the background necessary for interpreting the data as well as assessing the attitudes of planners themselves toward the issues we have raised in these first two chapters.

Chapter 3

The Professional Standards
of Planning

Introduction

In the first chapter of this work it was stated that the planning process serves many of the same functions as politics, and in many ways is isomorphic with it. In addition, it was noted that traditional planning doctrine, like the philosophy of municipal reform, has been heavily imbued with elements of scientific management, particularly with respect to the rationality, efficiency, and neutrality of the planner and the planning process.[1] Moreover, it was underscored that the objective of comprehensive planning is to guide and direct the community's development in line with the master plan and the public interest.[2] In the ideology of traditional planning doctrine, the method to achieve this goal is rationality; "Not political horse trading but rational thought was to guide the future."[3] Robert Goodman summarizes this perspective: "The planning of cities was to be entrusted to professionals who supposedly would consider all interests of the city in their objective, scientific, nonpolitical analyses and then arrive at a comprehensive plan."[4] Accordingly, the planning staff represented both "a comprehensive viewpoint and a scientific approach."[5] The general or master plan thus represented the expression of this comprehensive perspective and served the function of a criterion against which short-range development decisions could be measured.

Obviously, there exists an inherent contradiction between a conception of planning which posits that planning is political in substance, and one which underscores the scientific, value-neutral, and comprehensive core of the undertaking. Indeed, such a contradiction is not only apparent, it is real and exists in the literature focusing on "planning theory."[6] Moreover, the juxtaposition of the two perspectives on the nature of the planning process is in many ways a manifestation of the larger question relating to the two dominant strains of ideology within the planning profession; namely, traditional planning doctrine and advocacy.[7] The purpose of this chapter is to begin the empirical analysis of how planners themselves view their profession and their role in the planning function, as well as to assess the relative influence of the two previously outlined strains of planning ideology on the conceptions of the membership at large. In order to begin analyzing these important concerns it is necessary to outline the methodology employed in the development of this research.

Research Design

The research design was formulated in such a fashion as to facilitate addressing the principal research objectives of the study. It was decided initially that achieving our research objectives would require a comparison of planners at two levels: internally, (within themselves) and externally (with a representative sample of the U.S. public).

In regard to the first level of comparison (internal), subgroups of planners within the profession have been identified in the literature as possessing characteristics that could produce potential attitudinal cleavages within the profession; namely, planners formally educated within the discipline of planning versus those with other academic degrees, and public-agency versus private-sector practitioners. We therefore concluded that any assessment of professional standards or attitudes among planners would have to be analyzed within the context of the amount of formal planning education a planner possesses, since such exposure is obviously an important medium for the transmission of planning standards. Secondarily, the dichotomy formed by public-agency planners versus those employed in private enterprise has been identified in the case-study literature as exemplifying an important point of cleavage in the planning profession, and therefore represents a second basis of comparison among planners.[8]

In regard to the second level of comparison (external), the design includes both the data on planners collected as part of this research project, and data on the American public compiled in the National Data Program for the Social Sciences from the 1974 General Social Survey.[9] Our study collected data about planners' attitudes by means of an anonymous mail questionnaire for reasons I will discuss subsequently. The data on the attitudes of the American public were collected by means of interviews administered to populations sampled by both the National Opinion Research Corporation (NORC) and the Inter-University Consortium of Political Research (ICPR) of the Institute for Social Research at the University of Michigan in 1974.

The Construction of the Survey Instrument

The decision to utilize a self-administered questionnaire was reached because the geographical distribution of the population made it the only pragmatic means of obtaining the required number of respondents.[10] The major weaknesses of the mail questionnaire (the problem of nonreturns, the potential for misinterpretation of questions, the inability to follow up on misinterpreted questions) were assumed to be less significant than the advantages of geographical scope, the reduced costs, and the greater uniformity in the format in which the questions could be posed.[11] In addition, the particular character of the population (college-educated professionals) we believed would result in a higher return rate than the small return rate commonly associated with large-scale survey research utilizing mailed questionnaires.[12]

The instrument was pretested on a subsample of planners, which included practicing planners working in both the public and private domains, as well as faculty members in the field of planning, and graduate students in city planning. While the pretest included only sixty respondents, it proved valuable for several reasons. First, a few general problems relating to questionnaire construction were isolated and changed accordingly. Second, specific questions that were found to be ambiguous and, therefore, likely to cause problems in the general field test were located and eliminated. Finally, the time required to complete the questionnaire was evaluated by the respondents and determined to be reasonable.

The final questionnaire included a letter of endorsement by the Institute for Research in Social Science, University of North Carolina at Chapel Hill, which provided the funding for the American National Planners Study.[13] Considering that the population consisted of professional planners, it was determined initially that two mailings would be sufficient to generate an adequate response rate. The first mailing was followed three weeks later by a postcard in order to insure a maximum response rate.[14] The sampling was conducted in the fall of 1974 and all returns were received by January 1975. The methodology employed in the development of the survey instrument and its relationship to the research design is outlined in the following paragraphs.

The 1974 NORC data was utilized to measure the American public's attitudes toward national priorities with respect to spending on a variety of policy dimensions. Data on subjective identification of political ideology were employed as well. Since the universe sampled in the 1974 NORC survey includes the total noninstitutionalized population of the continental United States eighteen years of age or older, it provides a very representative criterion group against which to judge planners' responses.[15]

The questions utilized on the planners' questionnaire, which focused on a series of national priorities and subjective ideology, were identical or nearly identical to those in the 1974 NORC study so that comparisons of planners and the U.S. public on the same dimensions would be facilitated. Likewise, many questions employed were identical or similar to those used in previous studies of planners.[16] Also, additional items included on our questionnaire are from the CPS 1974 American National Election Study (ICPR). Consequently, whenever possible, the questions were designed so that the results of this research may be compared with those of other studies. In addition, standard measures of political attitudes were used (Domestic Social Welfare Scale; Political Cynicism Scale).[17] Finally, a variety of new questions were included to test certain hypotheses that have been generated from the literature but have not as yet been subjected to empirical testing.

In the creation of new questions an effort was made to focus on significant areas of controversy within the literature of planning. In order to avoid the inherent subjectivity of this type of endeavor, a subset of the pretest sample was selected as a panel to evaluate various items according to their importance as issues in contemporary planning doctrine, and from this a composite set of questions emerged. In addition, in order to minimize response-set bias, the items in the "Planners and the Planning Process" attitude scale were designed so that various questions were stated positively while others were worded negatively.[18]

Sampling Design

The total population for this research includes all Full, Associate, and Intern members of the American Institute of Planners. The sampling frame is the 1974 *Roster of Members of the American Institute of Planners*. Consequently, the term planner is operationally defined by membership in the AIP, one of the two major national organizations to which planners belong.

The theoretical justification for choosing the AIP can be best explicated by a comparison of the different natures of the two organizations and the relevance of that difference for purposes of this research. The American Society of Planning Officials is a self-defined "service" organization, whose purpose is to facilitate communication among all groups in planning. Membership in ASPO is open to all interested persons. The American Institute of Planners, on the other hand, is a self-defined "professional" organization of urban and regional planners in America. Unlike that of ASPO, membership in the AIP is not open, but rather is restricted to professional planners and is controlled by formal examinations. The AIP also publishes a professional journal that provides a medium for the discussion of critical issues in the field of planning. Because of the unique character of the AIP as a professional organization, we believed that any research which addresses itself to the attitudes of planners is justified in using the membership of the AIP as a valid basis for generalization. The reason for this is clear. The AIP serves as a forum for the important theoretical debates about issues that are critical in any planning process. The AIP does not include all planners as members; however, it is also clear that the American Bar Association or the American Medical Association would by definition exclude those lawyers and doctors who are not members. Yet any research which addressed itself to professional standards or changing convictions in the fields of medicine or law would clearly be on solid empirical grounds, if those organizations (ABA, AMA) were chosen as a basis for generalizations. We are convinced that the same logic applies to the AIP. We do not suggest that the AIP incorporates all those who would refer to themselves as "planners," although we suggest no realistic sampling frame could achieve that objective. However, as a simple empirical finding, our research discovered a substantial overlap (67.8%) between the AIP and ASPO membership rolls (see Appendix C). Nonetheless, apart from the foregoing we are convinced that the AIP is the appropriate sampling frame on which to base conclusions about the professional standards and convictions of the American planning profession.

Sampling Procedures

A random sampling procedure was employed in which every member of the population had an equal chance of inclusion.[19] Specifically, a unique number was assigned to the name of each Full, Associate, and Intern member included in the 1974 *Roster* of the AIP. A simple random sampling procedure, rather than a systematic, multistage or stratified sampling procedure, was utilized because: (1) a simple random sample requires minimum advance knowledge of population characteristics; and (2) it renders high precision relative to sample size, and it is the basic assumption underlying many statistical techniques.[20] Finally, there were no theoretical reasons for employing a stratified sample.

It was predetermined that a large sample size would be needed in anticipation of a general tendency toward a rather low response rate to the mail questionnaires. The sample itself was generated utilizing the random-number generator program RANDU (*Scientific Subroutine Package Version III, Programmer's Manual, Program Number 360A-CM-03A*, IBM, August 1968). The final total response rate to the initial and follow-up mailings of 1,145 questionnaires is 67.6% (N = 775). This response rate is considered high for a mailed questionnaire and allows for a high degree of precision. Questions of precision of course necessitate the discussion of sample size. The targeted sample size was 1,067, allowing for a tolerated error of plus or minus 3% at the .95 confidence level. The final return rate allows for a tolerated error of plus or minus 4% at the .95 confidence level.[21]

Sample Representativeness

To assess the representativeness of the sample, all known or approximated parameters were compared to sample statistics. In addition, various sample characteristics are presented to provide a profile of the American Institute of Planners with respect to additional relevant characteristics. The following comparisons using our Survey of Planners sample are made on the basis of the most complete enumeration of population characteristics available that are found in the AIP *Roster* data compiled by the American Institute of Planners and published in the June 1974 *AIP Newsletter*.[22] Table 3.1 indicates that the sample is highly representative with respect to both sex and age. However, there is a noticeable overrepresentation of Full members and, conversely, an underrepresentation of Associate members.

The following section attempts to provide some perspective on the breakdown of the sample with respect to educational background and place of employment. As Table 3.2 demonstrates, planners repre-

Table 3.1

Age, Sex, and Membership Grade: Representativeness of Survey of Planners

Characteristic	Survey of Planners Sample* (%)	AIP *Roster/ Newsletter* (%)
Sex		
Male	92.3	92.5
Female	7.7	7.5
Membership grade		
Full	46.0	35.8
Associate	47.6	56.0
Intern	6.4	8.2
Age		
Median	35.9	35.0

*The N size for the survey of planners for this table is 765. The N size for the AIP *Roster/Newsletter* varies. In the case of membership grade and age, the entire population of the AIP is enumerated (N = 9818). In the other case, sex, the response is reported in the *Newsletter* as reflecting 48% of the membership (those who returned their roster form). See: *AIP Newsletter*, June 1974. Appendices B and C contain additional material relevant to both the sample and the methodology employed in the study. Appendix C, for example, has additional sample demographics. Appendix B has material related to scale construction and validation. Membership grade percentages were computed exclusive of Intern and Honorary categories.

sent a wide range of educational backgrounds at the undergraduate level.

With respect to graduate school education, only 18.9% of the planner's sample had no graduate training whatsoever, and 15.6% were working toward the completion of a master's degree in planning. Moreover, 15.8% of the planners were pursuing graduate work in a field other than planning, while 48.0% had a master's degree and 1.7% a Ph.D. in planning. It is relevant to note that in the largest professional organization of planners in the United States, a significant proportion of the planners do not have a formal degree in planning. This is not surprising since Deil Wright found an even larger proportion of planners, in a sample of cities rather than organizations, who had no planning degree.[23] These statistics indicate the diversity that is subsumed under the terms *planner* and *planning*. Moreover, these results are consistent with data reported in the *AIP Newsletter* of 1974.

The last characteristic to be discussed is the job context of the sample. As is obvious from Table 3.3, the membership of the American Institute of Planners extends over a broad range of both public and private employment categories. While the majority of planners are employed by either subnational governments or are engaged in

Table 3.2
Survey of Planners Breakdown of Undergraduate Majors

Major Field*	(%)	Major Field	(%)
Architecture and design	24.7	Public administration	1.8
Landscape architecture	0.3	Urban studies	1.6
Geography	6.7	Business administration	3.0
Engineering	10.2	History	3.3
Planning	9.6	Mathematics	0.8
Economics	6.7	Natural science	1.3
Political science	11.3	Other	14.7
Sociology	3.9	Not applicable	.1

*N = 761. There were no population data available for comparison. However, for comparative sample data utilizing identical categories see *AIP Newsletter*, June 1974. See Appendices for additional information on background characteristics, sample questionnaire, scale construction, and data sources.

private consulting, many planners are employed by agencies and institutions that span a variety of different substantive concerns. This finding is also in keeping with previous findings and reflects again the diversity within the field of planning. In addition, this wide diversity of professional job contexts provides more solid criteria, we believe, for the analysis of professional planning standards than previous studies that have focused exclusively on local public planners.

Statistical Methods

The review of the literature suggested at least two important potential cleavages within the planning profession that one could expect to be statistically associated with the attitudes planners hold toward the planning process; that is, amount of formal planning education, and public versus private work context. Moreover, other behavioral-science studies, as well as conventional wisdom, led us to conclude that other variables such as age, sex, years of experience, and membership grade (which planners possess in differential proportions) are also potentially related to the way a planner may conceptualize various aspects of the planning process. Therefore, our initial endeavors were directed at examining this relationship using multivariate statistical analyses. An introduction to the general procedures employed follows directly.

This section focuses upon the prediction of certain attitudes from knowledge of a planner's educational background and agency type.

Table 3.3
Survey of Planners Breakdown of Type of Employment

Type of Organization*	(%)	Type of Organization	(%)
City	22.9	Consultant	24.0
County	9.6	Industry or business	3.4
Metropolitan and regional	13.1	University or research	8.5
State	7.5	Other	4.5
Federal	5.1	Not applicable	1.4

*N = 772. Appendix A contains a sample questionnaire. For comparative sample data utilizing identical categories, see *AIP Newsletter*, June 1974.

In that it is possible that certain extraneous variables might be contributing to this predictability, since they may be correlated with both our independent and dependent variables, statistical control was implemented using a regression-analysis approach.

We conducted a general linear test in which two regression models are formed; a full or unrestricted model, and a restricted model. The full model includes all the variables that may contribute to the prediction of our dependent variable. We fit the full model by the method of least squares and obtained a $SSE(F)$ (error sum of squares for the full model). This measures the fit of our data to this regression model. We then formulated a restricted model that contains only the variables we want to control; for example, age, experience, membership grade, and sex. We again calculated the fit of this new model to our data by calculating the term $SSE(R)$ (error sum of squares for the restricted model). We then compared the fit of our data to each model by examining $SSE(F)$ and $SSE(R)$. If these two quantities are very close it indicates that the additional information provided by adding on more independent variables does not result in a regression model which fits our data noticeably better, or improves the predictability of our dependent variable by a significant amount. On the other hand, if the $SSE(F)$ is significantly smaller than the $SSE(R)$, this indicates that the fit of our full model is significantly better, and that the inclusion of some or all of our additional independent variables adds significantly to the prediction of our dependent variable.[24]

In order to test these alternative models statistically, a null or statistical hypothesis was formed along with an alternative hypothesis, and a resulting test statistic was calculated based upon the error sum of squares terms.

H_0: Reduced model is the better model
H_1: Reduced model is not the better model

The test statistic was:

$$F = \frac{SSE(R) - SSE(F)}{df_R - df_F} \div \frac{SSE(F)}{df_F}$$

If there is a significant contribution to the prediction of our dependent variable by our proposed set of additional independent variables presented in the full model, the term to the left of the division sign will be relatively large and will result in a large value of F, which will result in rejection of our null hypothesis, and retention of our alternative hypothesis.

One specific *example* of this procedure (which was applied to all dependent variables reported in the text) involves the prediction of a planner's attitude toward the possibility of comprehensive rational planning in a pluralistic society. The independent variables that the literature would suggest are conceptually important are planning agency type (public or private) and amount of formal planning education. The potential influencing variables we would like to control are age, experience, membership grade, and sex. Our restricted model, therefore, will consist of only those variables that we want to control: age, experience, membership grade, and sex. Our full model will contain these control variables and the additional variables—agency type, and amount of formal planning education. Through this approach we can see if agency type and amount of formal planning education add a significant amount of information to the prediction of our dependent variable.

Our null and alternative hypotheses for this test were :

$$H_0: \beta_5 = \beta_6 = 0 \text{ (restricted model)}$$
$$H_1: \sim (\beta_5 = \beta_6 = 0) \text{ (not restricted model)}$$

The definition of the full model is:

$$Y_i = \beta_0 + \beta_i X_{i1} + \beta_2 X_{i2} + \beta_3 X_{i3} + \beta_4 X_{i4} + \beta_5 X_{i5} + \beta_6 X_{i6} + \epsilon_i$$

where:

Y_i is a planner's attitude toward the possibility of comprehensive planning

X_{i1} is a planner's age

X_{i2} is a planner's experience

X_{i3} is a planner's membership grade

X_{i4} is a planner's sex

X_{i5} is a planner's agency type

X_{i6} is a planner's amount of formal planning education

ϵ_i is the individual error term

The definition of the restricted model is:

$$Y_i = \beta_0 + \beta_1 X_{i1} + \beta_2 X_{i2} + \beta_3 X_{i3} + \beta_4 X_{i4} + \epsilon_i$$

where Y_i, X_{i1}, X_{i2}, X_{i3}, X_{i4}, and ϵ_i are defined as above. The test statistic for this situation is:

$$F = \frac{SSE(R) - SSE(F)}{df_R - df_F} \div \frac{SSE(F)}{df_F} = 1.05 - 1.29 = .814$$

Since the test statistic is not significant, we retain our null hypothesis that the restricted model is the better model in this situation. In other words, we conclude that the inclusion of the variables agency type and amount of formal planning education do not add significantly to the contribution of our dependent variable over and above the contribution to prediction already made by the knowledge of a person's age, experience, membership grade, and sex.

Our control variables, therefore, form the "important" set of independent variables in predicting a planner's attitude toward the possibility of comprehensive rational planning in a pluralistic society. It is important, however, to note the difference between a statistically significant relationship and one that has theoretical significance. It is true that agency type coupled with amount of formal planning education do not significantly contribute additional information to the prediction of the dependent variable. But the chosen model here— the restricted model with age, experience, membership grade, and sex—accounts for less than 1% of the variance in our dependent variable. In other words the model, although the better of the two as determined through statistical comparison, is virtually useless, since knowledge of our control variables reduces the errors of prediction by only 1%. Even with the inclusion of agency type and amount of formal planning education the model still only accounts for 2% of the variance in our dependent variable, which means that 98% of the variance is unexplained.

This same approach using full and restricted models was employed for each of the dependent variables examined in this study. The exact same models as described above were utilized with only the dependent variable changing from model to model. In almost all cases the restricted model employing only the control variables was the preferred model. Nonetheless, in all cases (whether the better model was the restricted model including only the control variables, or the full model including the control variables, agency type and amount of formal planning education) no model accounted for more than 4% of the variance in the dependent variable. Most in fact accounted for less than 1%.

The question arises then as to why such theoretically important variables in the planning literature should be so unrelated to planners' attitudes toward planning issues. One answer to this might be found in an examination of the mean-square error terms in each of the regression analyses. The mean-square error term is an unbiased estimator of the population variance of the dependent variables, and each of these terms was found to be very small (either less than one or very close to one). This suggests that planners as a group are *very homogeneous* with respect to their attitudes. There do not appear to be any overall systematic cleavages in the way planners conceptualize various aspects of the planning process which are related to the planner's age, sex, years experience, formal education, membership grade, or public versus private work context. In other words, the direction of planners' attitudes on a variety of questions under investigation does not vary as a function of differential levels of the above variables and, therefore, precludes any useful linear regression model from emerging.

However, the above considerations do not address several important questions; namely, the specific degree of homogeneity over the entire range of issues, and, more importantly, the direction of those attitudes. Are planners homogeneous on the question of national planning because virtually all planners of all ages, from both the public or private sectors, of all levels of experience and educational backgrounds, favor national planning—or, is the reciprocal true? Moreover, if planners are indeed homogeneous internally, how do they compare with a representative sample of the American public along a variety of attitudinal dimensions? We will address the foregoing concerns in a contingency table analysis in the remainder of this work. Since agency type (public or private) and amount of formal education have been identified as being theoretically important, we will employ them as vehicles to express the attitudes planners hold toward a variety of factors inherent in the planning process. Moreover, since our regression approach has identified years of experience as being highly correlated with two other variables (age and membership grade), we will also employ years of experience as a relevant variable in our tabular analyses, as a measure of the profession's attitudes over the time dimension. Finally, specific references to the construction and validation of the Guttman scales employed in later chapters, as well as more specific methodological concerns (including a sample questionnaire), may be found in the Appendices.

Planning—The Nature of the Process: An Empirical Analysis

The purpose of this section is to initiate a profile of the planner with respect to his attitudes towards factors inherent in the planning process, to focus upon the distribution, incidence, and interrelationships among those attitudes, and to begin to assess which of the two dominant strains of planning ideology is most thoroughly reflected in those attitudes.

It might be suggested, admittedly, that this dichotomy of the range of values and ideologies within planning, represented by the traditional ideology of planning and advocacy, is a dialectic more appropriate for serving the needs of the scholar than incapsulating substantive reality. However, the polarity between the two perspectives, and the value points on the continuum in between, reflect the very real cleavages apparent within the planning profession with respect to questions central to both the planning practitioner and pundit alike. Some of these questions are: What is the nature of the planning process?—that is, in what way is planning any different from politics?—or, on what basis does the planner's recommendation rest? Why should the planner's professional recommendations for a community be any more or less authoritative, legitimate, or important than those of the civil engineer or politician? Is the planner and his craft "one among equals" or is the planner a member of a profession with a privileged perspective on the public interest? For whom do planners plan and to what ends? Is the planner a technician in the service of public or private clients or an independent professional technically capable and conceptually legitimized to leave his/her impact on the mosaic of metropolitan America? It is to such questions, divisive and important, that the traditional planning ideology and advocacy speak. It is, therefore, within the framework of these two rather diverse conceptual perspectives that planners' attitudes will be compared and contrasted.

However, any analysis of professional standards initially must confront the realization that various factors influence the content and character of professional socialization and may, therefore, directly influence the relative distribution of those standards among the membership as a whole. We indicated previously that among the characteristics that planners possess which could produce cleavages in the profession, and thereby reduce professional cohesiveness or homogeneity are exposure to formal planning education and type of employment (public-agency versus private-sector employment). We will at this point elaborate further on these two characteristics.

In the case of exposure to formal planning education, it is postulated that to the extent that a core of professional values in planning exists, those values are most pronounced in planners undergoing formal training in planning rather than another academic field. Formal education in planning is a primary mechanism by which professional socialization occurs, and therefore comparison of planners with and without formal planning education provides a measure of the relationship between amount of formal planning education and specific attitudes. Moreover, empirical evidence from case studies indicates that formal planning education exerts an effect on planners' attitudes, as they relate to norms concerned with conceptions about the planner's appropriate professional role. In addition, it can also be hypothesized that public- versus private-sector work context could be expected to influence the attitudes of planners. Public planners serve at a defined range of salary that ephemeral master, the "public interest."[25] Private planners, at least ostensibly, are involved in planning for profit. Moreover, Francine Rabinovitz suggests "many public planners view private practitioners with distaste."[26] Because of the potential divergent reward structures and motivations, the dichotomy of public versus private planners will serve as an additional criterion and control group to measure what specific association this factor has on the cohesiveness of attitudes within the planning profession. Finally, while the possession of formal education as well as employment in the public versus the private sector measure important potential subgroups within the profession, an additional variable, years of experience in the field, will also be focused upon in our subsequent analyses. The reason for this is that experience measures an important source of divergent views (and therefore a point of cleavage) as well as the important dimension of time. In other words, years of experience is an index of the degree to which the profession's standards are more or less stable over time. We will begin our substantive analysis with an important element of traditional planning ideology, the presumed political neutrality of the master plan.

Judd and Mendelson note that "the notion of neutrality pervades the planning literature."[27] The concept of administrative neutrality is, again, reminiscent of the philosophy of municipal reform; that is, in order to ensure the interests of the community as whole, a disinterested nonpolitical planning commission was supposed to remove master planning from the political process and create an objective and politically neutral guideline for community development.[28] The importance of the master plan in the ideology of planning theory is expressed in Edward Banfield's contention that to planners "a plan made without reference to a master plan is a contradiction in terms."[29] Indeed, one might suggest that the emphasis on the neutrality of the planner and the planning process serves a strategic purpose in the profession's aspiration to utilize the master plan "to determine the overall framework in which urban physical development takes place."[30] Which is to say, "If an official wishes to persuade his superiors and political critics that his decisions on a wide range of subjects should be considered authoritative, his most obvious strategy is to maintain that they are technical—to maintain, that is, that public policy has been declared in a highly operational fashion and that he speaks as expert interpreter of it."[31] Such a strategy seems, in fact, imperative given the stated purpose of the master plan, which in addition to dealing with the physical form of the city attempts to "promote health, safety, morals, orders, convenience, prosperity, and general welfare."[32] One relevant point that can be drawn from the preceding definition is the inherent commonality of the objectives of the master plan and the output of the process we normally call politics.

As such, the fiction of the political neutrality of master planning provides a potential mechanism by which to avoid confrontation between planners and politicians over questions relating to legitimacy. To define a process as inherently political and then claim expertise is a poor strategy on which to build support. However, the point has been made that attacks upon traditional planning ideology have been forthcoming. Paul Davidoff's comments reflect the criticism that many advocate planners have of traditional planning ideology with respect to administrative neutrality: "Appropriate planning action cannot be prescribed from a position of value neutrality, for prescriptions are based on desired objectives."[33] Moreover, in another context, Davidoff asserts "the environment desired for the future is, in the first instance, purely a matter of values."[34] Davidoff's premise about the inability to create a value-free, politically neutral plan, leads logically to his assertion about the undesirability of unitary plans for the community; that is, those created by a single public agency. The question we will address subsequently is to what extent Davidoff's conception of the master plan dominates the attitudes of the rank and file membership. Do planners conceive of the master plan as a political instrument designed to reward some interests and deprive others or as a neutral and comprehensive assessment of community objectives? In addition, to what extent are the attitudes of planners related to formal planning education and public versus private work context, and to what extent are the foregoing relations affected by the number of years of experience in the field?

An examination of Table 3.4 reveals a striking rejection by all planners of the neutrality of plans made by public agencies. The precise statement presented to our sample of planners was: "No plan produced by a public agency is neutral but benefits some interests and discriminates against others." This statement reflects a central theme of advocacy planning—the political nature of the planning process. Consequently, the overwhelming agreement in the sample (87.7%) suggests a significant rejection of this aspect of traditional planning ideology among planners. Additionally, an examination of the responses for planners possessing formal versus no formal planning education indicates that to the extent that the statistically significant differences do exist ($p < .01$), there is a slight tendency for those planners having formal planning education to agree more with the contention that plans are not neutral assessments of community objectives, but are statements of political values that reward some interests and deprive others.

Table 3.4 also discloses the relationship between agency type and attitudes toward the neutrality of master plans. It is apparent that while there is a slight tendency for private planners to agree more (90.2% versus 86.8% among public-agency planners), the difference is not statistically significant and in itself is far less relevant than the strong support by the majority of all planners for a definition of the master plan that establishes it as essentially political enterprise.

Table 3.5 deals with another consideration—the effect of formal versus nonformal education controlling for agency type (public versus private). One factor evident from the table is that any effect introduced by the control variable will be moderated by the fact that the distribution is so heavily skewed in the direction of agreement. The introduction of agency type as a control variable manifests a continued trend for formal planning education to be associated with a rejection of the political neutrality of public-agency plans for both public and private planners. However, the relationship remains statistically significant only for public planners. The introduction of years of experience (dichotomized as ten years or less and greater than ten years) did not change the nature of the relationship. In other words, public planners possessing formal planning education at both levels of experience were (in a statistically significant sense) more likely to agree with an assessment of public plans that rejected their political neutrality. Moreover, this relationship was statistically significant only for public planners (experience data not displayed).[35]

Table 3.4

Planners' Attitudes toward Neutrality of the Master Plan

No Plan Is Neutral*	Entire Sample (%)	No Formal Planning Degree (%)	Formal Planning Degree† (%)	Public Planners (%)	Private Planners (%)
Agree	87.7	84.0	91.1	86.8	90.2
Undecided	4.8	6.8	3.3	5.3	4.1
Disagree	7.5	9.2	5.6	7.9	5.7
Total	100.0	100.0	100.0	100.0	100.0
	(767)‡	(324)	(427)	(509)	(244)
		$[\chi^2_2 = 9.20; (p < .01)]$		$[\chi^2_2 = 1.73; (p, \text{n.s.})]$	

*Source: Survey of Planners Project. The exact statement was: "No plan produced by a public agency is neutral but benefits some interests and discriminates against others." See Appendix A for the questionnaire.

†Formal planning degree includes all members of the sample possessing a bachelor's, master's, or Ph.D. in planning. Public planners are those members of the sample employed by a public agency (federal, state, local governments, and universities). Private planners include all others.

‡N sizes for this and subsequent tables are expressed within parentheses. Variations of sample N are a result of missing data for that variable.

The inference that can be drawn from these data is that any differences *between* planners on this dimension are far less salient than the cohesiveness *within* the profession. Also, the direction of professional consensus is such that most planners see public plans as inherently political; that is, they reward some interests and discriminate against others.

Given that planners define the output of the planning process in such a fashion as to equate it with a political endeavor, what is their conception of the process itself? Much debate ranges over the question, which in substance reduces to, What is planning? In chapter one the distinction between generic planning, national economic planning, and American planning was addressed. The central features of American planning were underscored: its decentralized character, its advisory status, its focus on the use of physical space rather than larger, more encompassing social concerns. However, such broad outlines fail to capture the ideological parameters that emerge from a review of the literature which attempts to delineate planning. Alan Altshuler, for example, contends that "planning is, in the final analysis, simply the effort to infuse activity with consistency and conscious

Table 3.5

Planners' Attitudes toward Neutrality of the Master Plan, Controlling for Type of Agency

	Public Planners		Private Planners	
No Plan Is Neutral*	No Formal Planning Degree (%)	Formal Planning Degree (%)	No Formal Planning Degree (%)	Formal Planning Degree (%)
Agree	81.9	91.1	88.5	91.4
Undecided	7.8	3.4	5.3	3.1
Disagree	10.3	5.5	6.2	5.5
Total	100.0	100.0	100.0	100.0
	(204)	(292)	(113)	(128)
	$[\chi^2_2 = 9.37; (p < .009)]$		$[\chi^2_2 = .80; (p, \text{n.s.})]$	

*Source: Survey of Planners Project. See Table 3.4 for exact question and operational definitions of formal planning degree and agency type.

purpose."[36] Andreas Faludi, in a recent work, states that "planning is the application of the scientific method, however crude—to policy making."[37] Charles Merriam defines planning as essentially social rationality: "Planning is an organized effort to utilize social intelligence."[38] Finally, Yehezkel Dror states that "planning is the process of preparing a set of decisions for actions in the future, directed at achieving goals by preferable means."[39]

Many of the assumptions about the nature of the planning process are apparent in the definitions presented. One central dimension apparent in all of the discussion that addresses the question What is planning? is the relative contribution of the technical or rational components versus the normative or value-laden aspects to the totality of the endeavor. Clearly, most administrative theorists today accept the inescapable interaction of facts and values in any process that involves decision making. Altshuler, for example, provides a cogent illustration of the technical versus normative interface in planning in his observation, "There is no simple or single measure of a good school, park, or library system. There can be no single measure of a good policy for regulation of land use."[40] Nonetheless, traditional planning doctrine has chosen to place planning closer, at least in theory, to the scientific/rational pole of this conceptual continuum. The question raised here is, Given a range of responses arrayed to reflect the relative content of the technical to value-laden dimensions of planning, how will planners themselves define the process?

Table 3.6 discloses that for the overwhelming majority of all planners (78.3%), the planning process is one in which value judgments loom large in the conduct of professional activity. Given an implicit continuum ranging from a primarily technical to a primarily value oriented definition of planning, all but a few (3.5%) planners reject what could be called an exclusively technical definition of the process. Moreover, scrutiny of the cells for formally and nonformally educated planners and those employed by the public versus the private sector indicate that the planning profession is very homogeneous with respect to this question. In other words, there are no major cleavages within the profession on this question between either public and private planners, or those possessing formal education in planning versus those planners trained in other academic fields. Specifically the differences between categories are not statistically significant and the majority of all planners accepted a definition of planning that rejects the conception of planning as an essentially technical endeavor. Finally, an examination of Table 3.7 illustrates that the effect of controlling for agency type in the table is of little consequence. In addition, controlling for the number of years of experience in no way altered the foregoing relationship.[41]

The conclusion which can be drawn from these data is that there are no real differences within the profession on the definition of the planning function. And the direction of professional consensus is such that most planners clearly reject an essentially technical (in favor of a more normative) definition of planning.

Table 3.6

Planners' Attitudes toward Conception of the Planning Process

Conception of the Planning Process*	Entire Sample (%)	No Formal Planning Degree (%)	Formal Planning Degree (%)	Public Planners (%)	Private Planners (%)
Strictly technical	3.5	4.4	3.1	3.5	3.7
Mostly technical	18.2	18.8	17.6	19.2	15.2
Value-oriented	78.3	76.8	79.3	77.3	81.1
Total	100.0	100.0	100.0	100.0	100.0
	(763)	(319)	(425)	(506)	(243)
		$[\chi^2_2 = 1.17; (p, \text{n.s.})]$		$[\chi^2_2 = 1.74; (p, \text{n.s.})]$	

*Source: Survey of Planners Project. See Table 3.4 for exact definitions of formal planning degree and agency type. The precise statement was:

Please indicate which one of the following statements best describes your conception of what planning is:

—Ours is strictly a technical activity of applying the profession's engineering, statistical, and design tools to a given project or problem in order to determine a feasible solution and the blueprint for its accomplishment.

—Our recommendations are mostly technical but inherent in them are some unavoidable policy judgments on how the community's physical plan should be developed.

—We purposely integrate technical advice on the proposed use of community resources and recommend choices based on value judgments, as well as technical expertise. [See Francine Rabinovitz, *City Politics and Planning*.]

Planning: The Basis of the Recommendations

One essential policy question that emerges from the foregoing is, Given the planners' real and potential impact on public policy, what serves as the basis of the professional recommendations made by planners?—or, Given that planners acknowledge that both the process and eventual outputs of planning are heavily imbued with value judgments, what criteria are available to planners to guide the value-choice aspects of their work? Among the alternatives for such a potential source of legitimacy are: planning's status as a profession, a theory of planning, and the resulting role planners believe they should play in the urban policy process. The subsequent analyses will focus on these three dimensions.

One consistent source of legitimacy for planners, at least in practice, has been planning's role as a profession with a unique perspective on comprehensive approaches to urban development.[42] Indeed, as Altshuler notes, planners stress the interrelatedness of problems, the necessity of integrative approaches, and the unique function of

Table 3.7

Planners' Attitudes toward Conception of the Planning Process, Controlling for Type of Agency

	Public Planners		Private Planners	
Conception of the Planning Process*	No Formal Planning Degree (%)	Formal Planning Degree (%)	No Formal Planning Degree (%)	Formal Planning Degree (%)
Strictly technical	5.0	2.8	3.7	3.9
Mostly technical	20.2	18.3	14.5	15.5
Value-oriented	74.8	78.9	81.8	80.6
Total	100.0	100.0	100.0	100.0
	(202)	(289)	(110)	(129)
	$[\chi_2^2 = 2.05; (p, \text{n.s.})]$		$[\chi_2^2 = .06; (p, \text{n.s.})]$	

*Source: Survey of Planners Project. See Table 3.6 for exact question. Table 3.4 contains operational definitions of formal planning degree and agency type.

planning as a profession dedicated to a comprehensive and rational perspective on the various elements related to urban development.[43] In addition, the profession's own canons indicate the membership's professional commitment to serve the "public interest primarily."[44] Whether planning is or is not a profession has both practical and theoretical parameters. In the first regard, it appears that planning may soon be subjected to the licensing, educational accrediting, and mechanisms of self-monitoring that are normally associated with a profession.[45] Moreover, planners currently have much of the paraphernalia of professionalism: graduate-school education, professional associations, and journals.

However, the theoretical questions relating to planning's professionalism appear more complex. Planning's leading theorists themselves dispute whether planning is a profession.[46] Much of this debate centers on questions of purpose rather than techniques. Some planners, such as Henry S. Churchill, reject the concept of planning as a profession because of its advisory character.[47] Others contend that planning's professionalism is contingent upon expanding the scope of planning from a primarily physical- and land-use-oriented endeavor to more encompassing social and ideological concerns. The question raised here is, Does the average planner believe planning possesses the ethical and intellectual requirements to be considered a profession, and to what degree is the membership cohesive on this question?

Table 3.8 reveals that 77.6% of all planners believe planning is a profession. In addition, there is no statistically significant difference between either public versus private planners, or those planners with or without formal education on this position. Table 3.9 indicates that controlling for type of agency does not alter the relationship. Also, controlling for years of experience did not change the foregoing relationship (data not displayed). Clearly, planners are extremely cohesive on the question of professionalism and the direction of their sentiments is toward a conception of planning as a profession in the same sense as the more traditional professions of medicine and law.[48]

Altshuler has demonstrated that questions of professionalism in planning are inherently related to questions of a theory, which itself can provide a source of legitimacy for policy recommendations. "Seen in this light, the planner's search for assurance that he is a professional surely represents more than just a striving for status and prestige. It also represents a deep longing for a body of professional theory to show him his competence, his purpose, and his duty and to give professional content to his integrity."[49] In addition, Altshuler sees that this theory must be focused on the "purpose and function rather than with unique knowledge and procedures."[50] He predicates this perspective on the observation that the generally acknowledged professions "are distinguished more clearly by their purposes than skills."[51] Moreover, while skills and procedures change over time, most professions relate and evaluate techniques with reference to their underlying purpose. As Robert Merton states, "Medicine is at heart a polygamist becoming wedded to as many of the sciences as prove their worth."[52] He goes on to note that techniques in medicine are judged relative to their utility in meeting the objectives of medicine, which are dealing with problems of the sick.

In this sense, then, it is not the sophistication of skills in a profession but the clarity of its purpose that is relevant. "It seems clear, further, that the acknowledged professions are, as a group, distin-

Table 3.8

Planners' Attitudes toward Planning as a Profession

Planning Is a Profession*	Entire Sample (%)	No Formal Planning Degree (%)	Formal Planning Degree (%)	Public Planners (%)	Private Planners (%)
Agree†	77.6	77.4	78.0	79.0	75.0
Undecided	9.7	10.3	9.4	8.6	11.7
Disagree	12.7	12.3	12.6	12.4	13.3
Total	100.0	100.0	100.0	100.0	100.0
	(764)	(319)	(427)	(510)	(240)
		$[\chi_2^2 = .21; (p, \text{n.s.})]$		$[\chi_2^2 = 2.03; (p, \text{n.s.})]$	

*Source: Survey of Planners Project. See Table 3.4 for exact definitions of formal planning degree and agency type.

†The exact question was: "A number of planners have expressed different opinions about the question of whether planning possesses the ethical and intellectual requirements to be considered a profession: in the same sense as the more traditional professions, Law, Medicine, etc. Do you agree or disagree that planning is a profession?"

guished not so much by refinement of skills as to the uses they are put. The professions differ markedly in sophistication of technique and even in the capacity to measure achievement. By both criteria, some professions are inferior to some skill groups not generally considered professional."[53]

Andreas Faludi confronts the dilemma of the relationship of theory to purpose in planning. He draws the distinction between theory *in* planning and a theory *of* planning. The former can be regarded as techniques and procedures such as economic-location theory and its application to urban residential patterns. The latter theory of planning, whether normative or positive, has more holistic dimensions, and in the final analysis has as its focus the ultimate purpose(s) of planning. It is also the theory in planning that has had the most rapid development, while a theory of planning remains far less articulated. Stated another way, there is much more consensus on the means of planning than on the ends of planning.

Table 3.10 expresses the attitudes of the membership toward this question of planning theory. Clearly, the majority of planners (65.0%) believe there exists a body of knowledge and techniques sufficient to

Table 3.9

Planners' Attitudes toward Planning as a Profession, Controlling for Type of Agency

	Public Planners		Private Planners	
Planning Is a Profession*	No Formal Planning Degree (%)	Formal Planning Degree (%)	No Formal Planning Degree (%)	Formal Planning Degree (%)
Agree	79.2	78.8	74.5	76.4
Undecided	10.4	7.8	10.0	12.6
Disagree	10.4	13.4	15.5	11.0
Total	100.0	100.0	100.0	100.0
	(202)	(293)	(110)	(127)
	$[\chi_2^2 = 1.71; (p, \text{n.s.})]$		$[\chi_2^2 = 1.26; (p, \text{n.s.})]$	

*Source: Survey of Planners Project. See Table 3.4 for exact definitions of formal planning degree and agency type.

constitute a theory of planning. In addition, the cohesiveness among planners on this question is more relevant than any divisions between various subgroups of the profession. More precisely, examination of the cell frequencies for both formally and nonformally educated planners and those employed by public and private agencies indicates about the same degree of support (66.0% versus 64.8% and 66.4% versus 62.5% respectively). Moreover, the differences are not statistically significant and indicate no cleavages with respect to education and agency type on this question.

The effect of controlling for agency type is displayed in Table 3.11. The table, again, underscores a great degree of homogeneity among planners, at least with respect to the variables under investigation. That is, for both public planners with a formal planning degree, and public planners without a formal planning degree, the proportion who believe there is a theory of planning is substantially similar and the difference is not statistically significant. The same relationship holds for private planners. Finally, controlling for years of experience did not in any way alter this relationship. In other words, there were no statistically significant differences related to the variable experience (data not displayed).[54]

Table 3.10
Planners' Attitudes toward a Theory of Planning

There Is a Theory of Planning*	Entire Sample (%)	No Formal Planning Degree (%)	Formal Planning Degree (%)	Public Planners (%)	Private Planners (%)
Yes†	65.0	66.0	64.8	66.4	62.5
No	35.0	34.0	35.2	33.6	37.5
Total	100.0	100.0	100.0	100.0	100.0
	(763)	(318)	(426)	(509)	(240)
		$[\chi^2_1 = .08; (p, \text{n.s.})]$		$[\chi^2_1 = .93; (p, \text{n.s.})]$	

*Source: Survey of Planners Project. See Table 3.4 for exact definitions of formal planning degree and agency type.

†The exact question was: "Do you think there exists today a body of knowledge and techniques sufficient to constitute a theory of planning?"

One can conclude from these data that planners are convinced planning possesses a body of knowledge and techniques sufficient to constitute a theory of planning. Clearly, the profession's response is very homogeneous with respect to this question. Also, there appears to be a great deal more support for the fact that planning is a profession with a coherent theory among the membership than exists in the theoretical literature dealing with these concerns.

The last consideration of this section deals with the role planners believe they should play in the urban policy process. The concept of role employed here refers specifically to "the behavior he (the planner) exhibits on the basis of norms that tell him what action is appropriate when he is acting as a planner."[55] Many observers of the planning profession have noted that one of the most enduring legacies of the philosophy of municipal reform has been its effect on the attitudes of planners toward the political process. Norman Beckman summarizes the political sentiments that planners have traditionally expressed as follows: "The cause of this failure to achieve rational, orderly urban development is 'politics' and politicians—the elected officials that run our local governments."[56] Beckman cautions planners about the consequences of these attitudes if they lead to an

Table 3.11

Planners' Attitudes toward a Theory of Planning,
Controlling for Type of Agency

There Is a Theory of Planning*	Public Planners		Private Planners	
	No Formal Planning Degree (%)	Formal Planning Degree (%)	No Formal Planning Degree (%)	Formal Planning Degree (%)
Yes	68.7	65.2	63.6	62.7
No	31.3	34.8	36.4	37.3
Total	100.0	100.0	100.0	100.0
	(201)	(293)	(110)	(126)
	$[\chi^2_1 = .50; (p, \text{n.s.})]$		$[\chi^2_1 = .00; (p, \text{n.s.})]$	

*Source: Survey of Planners Project. See Table 3.4 for the exact definitions of formal planning degree and agency type.

emerging role model that places the planner in competition with the elected politician. Because, as he observes, while the mass public is, indeed, cynical about politicians, their respect for civil servants is only marginally greater. He himself believes the planner's most appropriate role is that of bureaucrat.[57]

Francine Rabinovitz, on the other hand, contends that the role planners play is important, given the existing conditions with respect to metropolitan governments. Many, in effect, are no longer capable of purposeful action given their fragmented, pluralistic decision making centers.[58] Accordingly, since these political systems are weak, the plans and proposals of planners and other professionals take on additional significance. The question becomes, according to Rabinovitz and others, Do the norms of the planning community provide the incentive to play the appropriate decision-making role?[59] The nature of the role has been outlined. "In the case of the urban planner the skills required for discovering the formulating coalitions and maintaining alliances in all but the most cohesive systems are, to varying degrees, the skills of the politician."[60]

However, Rabinovitz observes that there is evidence that norms of the planning profession related to the technical competence preclude planners from assuming political/policy positions. "The preferred role is one in which the professional planner does not go beyond technical and policy advice on the use of community resources."[61] She notes there is evidence that a political role may be regarded "not only as unnecessary to truly professional planning but as inherently unprofessional."[62] Rabinovitz and others have underscored the strong technical core to the planning profession, presumably an observation generated by the propensity of planning to focus on "'comprehensive' and 'rational' rather than political solutions to urban policy questions."[63] Nonetheless, the apolitical and technical role of planners has been seriously challenged by advocacy planning. Davidoff, for example, rejects the possibility that planners can operate as value neutrals. Since there is no unified public interest to serve, he believes planners should advocate specific policy positions. "The advocate planner would be more than a provider of information, an analyst of current trends, a simulator of future conditions, and a detailer of means. In addition to carrying out these necessary parts of planning, he would be a proponent of specific substantive solutions."[64] The concept of advocacy, predicated on the legal model, envisions the planner in a relationship with a client whose interests the planner seeks to serve. Consequently, the planner espouses specific policy positions. Advocacy of course accepts political pluralism as a reality and is predicated on the assumption that public policy is legitimately the result of a bargaining process among many groups of diverse interests. As such, advocacy rejects in substance the role of the planner as a neutral participant in the policy process. "The prospect for future planning is that of a practice which openly invites political and social values to be examined and debated. Acceptance of this position means rejection of prescriptions for planning which would have the planner act solely as a technician."[65]

The distribution of attitudes toward the appropriate role planners should play has never been subjected to extensive empirical analysis. In an attempt to do so, an index was created that is conceptually organized to form a continuum reflecting two diverse poles: specifically, the traditional conception of the planner as a technician and the converse, a role definition that rejects this position for a more policy-oriented perspective. The following questions were employed in the construction of the index.

1. The urban planner should *not* openly strive to sell his plans by being an active part in the political process.

2. The urban planner in his capacity as an advisor should ultimately accept the goals submitted by the elected representatives of the voters.

3. The urban planner should base his recommendations on professional, rather than political, criteria.

4. Urban planners, by virtue of their professional training, are in the best position to be neutral judges of the public interest.

The questions were presented in Likert format, the response categories were ordinal, and the principal intensity structure among the items is designed to focus on the willingness of the planners to assume specific policy positions or conversely to accept the role of technical advisor.[66]

Table 3.12 indicates that the predominant role preference of all planners is that of technician (48.3%). Given the manner in which the variable was measured, this reflects high concurrence with the belief that the planner should not "sell" plans by being actively involved in the political process, and that the planner, in his advisory capacity, should accept the goals of elected officials and base his recommendations on professional rather than political criteria. Finally, the role of technician also indicates a strong support for the belief that planners are in the best position to be neutral judges of the public interest.

The data in Table 3.12 also indicate that there is no statistically significant difference on preference for type of role between public versus private planners.

The difference between formally educated versus nonformally educated planners is significant ($p < .01$). However, the difference indicates that planners with formal planning degrees are *less* prone to accept the technician's role and conversely *more* likely to accept that of the advocate than are planners with no formal degree.[67]

Table 3.13 illustrates the effect of controlling for agency type. The statistically signfiicant difference between planners having formal degrees and those who do not disappears. Moreover, the data show that the technician's role is not statistically related to formal planning education; that is, to the extent that the technician's role is the predominant professional norm (and the data indicate it is), that norm does not appear to be exclusively a function of the professional socialization related to acquiring a planning degree. Indeed, for both

Table 3.12
Planners' Attitudes toward the Role of the Planner

Attitudes toward the Role of the Planner*	Entire Sample (%)	No Formal Planning Degree (%)	Formal Planning Degree (%)	Public Planners (%)	Private Planners (%)
Technician†	48.3	52.4	45.2	49.1	45.4
Moderate	32.0	32.1	31.3	32.3	33.2
Advocate	19.7	15.5	23.5	18.6	21.4
Total	100.0	100.0	100.0	100.0	100.0
	(757)	(317)	(425)	(505)	(238)

$$[\chi_2^2 = 7.88; (p < .01)] \qquad [\chi_2^2 = 1.17; (p, \text{n.s.})]$$

*Source: Survey of Planners Project. See Table 3.4 for exact definitions of formal planning degree and agency type.

†Index computed utilizing questions presented in preceding text. For a discussion of the techniques, scale items, and index-to-item correlation, see Appendix B.

public and private planners those with a formal degree in planning are slightly less likely to concur with the technician's role.

Although not statistically significant, these differences seem to indicate a trend in our sample data that is contrary to the conclusion of the case-study literature which focuses on planners' roles. Nonetheless, since these differences are not statistically significant, this suggests, as do other findings of the chapter, that practitioner norms have their origin in factors other than formal planning education— for example, in the practice of planning itself, or in the self-selection that may occur among the type of people attracted to the planning profession.

The final concern is the effect of controlling for experience on the role the planner believes he or she should play. One hypothesis which could be presented is that experience is highly related to the role the planner believes he should play. Or, that the influence of the advocacy literature, and its decidedly political posture, will be most pronounced among younger planners. It is not. Table 3.14 indicates that among both public and private planners, regardless of level of experience or planning-degree background, in no case is the advocate

Table 3.13
Planners' Attitudes toward the Role of the Planner, Controlling for Type of Agency

Attitudes toward the Role of the Planner*	Public Planners		Private Planners	
	No Formal Planning Degree (%)	Formal Planning Degree (%)	No Formal Planning Degree (%)	Formal Planning Degree (%)
Technician	53.3	45.9	48.6	42.9
Moderate	31.8	32.2	34.9	31.0
Advocate	14.9	21.9	16.5	26.1
Total	100.0	100.0	100.0	100.0
	(201)	(292)	(109)	(126)
	$[\chi_2^2 = 4.37; (p, \text{n.s.})]$		$[\chi_2^2 = 3.22; (p, \text{n.s.})]$	

*Source: Survey of Planners Project. See Table 3.4 for exact definitions of formal planning degree and agency type.

role the modal preference. Moreover, for most subgroups, the preferred role is that of technician. The one interesting trend emerging is that for public planners with less than ten years of experience a statistically significant difference ($p < .04$) exists between those with, versus those without, a formal degree in planning (45.4% versus 55.6%). Degree-holding public planners with less than ten years of experience are *more* likely to be advocates and *less* likely to be technicians than their counterparts who possess no formal planning degree. Nonetheless, even for these public planners with less than ten years' experience who possess a formal planning degree (the group we would suggest most likely to be attracted to advocacy), the modal preference is for a role orientation consistent with the traditional ideology of planning; namely, that of technician.

An analysis of the private planners having less than ten years of experience, shown in Table 3.14, indicates that for this group there is also a statistically significant difference between degree- versus nondegree-holding planners. Among younger, private planners with formal degrees in the field, the majority support the role of technician. Among those planners with over ten years of experience there is no statistically significant difference between those with or without a formal planning degree in either the public or private sector. Moreover, among planners with over ten years of experience, in almost all cases the modal choice is that of technician. Also, in this subgroup the advocate role was the least preferred role definition across all categories of education and employment.

One final consideration that we felt might be relevant was that either age or experience might have an independent effect on the role the planner felt he should play if it were analyzed in direct relation with the role variable. However, neither contingency-table analyses nor correlational analyses (Pearson's r or Tau) looking at role as the dependent variable and age or experience as the independent variables showed any statistically significant relationship between the role a planner thought was most appropriate and his age or experience. In other words, planners of different ages and varying years of experience in planning are not differentially committed to any one type of role definition. This suggests there is not much support for those who would imply that the planning profession is undergoing a significant transition with respect to its preferred role definition.

Clearly, the planning profession's preferred role definition continues to remain skewed in the direction of the planner as technician.

Planners' Attitudes toward Comprehensiveness

Among the more consistent themes in the literature dealing with planning is the concern of the profession with comprehensiveness. While the term itself has been subjected to a variety of different interpretations, one essential feature has been planning's role in rationally integrating diverse elements into a more holistic outcome. As Altshuler has observed, "The 'ideal type' defender of comprehensive planning would contend that a serious effort should be made to plan in detail the future evolution of all important economic and social patterns. Others would limit their support to the planning-in-general outline of change in particular strategic variables."[68] The theoretical importance of comprehensiveness in planning doctrine is profound. In some sense the comprehensiveness to which planners aspire (as well as suggest they can provide) implies a primarily rational, as opposed to political, approach to decision making. Moreover, in traditional planning ideology it is clear that planners believe they are most qualified to provide the body politic with comprehensive solutions to society's complex problems. Altshuler, for example, observes that few planners "believe that any group of planners can achieve a total comprehensiveness of perspective on any issue. Many do believe, however, that professional planners can come closer to achieving it on numerous issues than other participants in the urban decision process."[69]

The importance of comprehensiveness in planning theory warrants a discussion of the major theoretical literature focusing on the subject. This will lay the groundwork necessary to assess the effect that various theoretical critiques of the ideal of comprehensiveness have had on planners' attitudes toward the comprehensiveness doctrine in planning. The empirical focus of this section will be on the planners' conceptions about three related elements of comprehensiveness. First, its scope; that is, what should be the legitimate subject of concern of public planning? Second, its theoretical possibility; do planners believe that comprehensive planning by the government is possible in a pluralistic society? Third, planners' support for the creation of a federal agency responsible for comprehensive planning

Table 3.14

Planners' Attitudes toward the Role of the Planner, Controlling for Type of Agency and Years of Experience

Attitudes toward the Role of the Planner	Public Planners		Private Planners	
	No Formal Planning Degree (%)	Formal Planning Degree (%)	No Formal Planning Degree (%)	Formal Planning Degree (%)
Under 10 Years Experience				
Technician*	55.6	45.4	39.6	51.9
Moderate	29.9	27.9	45.8	22.2
Advocate	14.5	26.7	14.6	25.9
Total	100.0	100.0	100.0	100.0
	(117)	(172)	(48)	(54)
	$[\chi_2^2 = 6.33; (p < .04)]$†		$[\chi_2^2 = 6.67; (p < .03)]$	
Over 10 Years Experience				
Technician*	48.2	46.5	56.4	36.8
Moderate	35.8	37.7	23.6	36.8
Advocate	16.0	15.8	20.0	26.4
Total	100.0	100.0	100.0	100.0
	(81)	(114)	(55)	(68)
	$[\chi_2^2 = .08; (p, \text{n.s.})]$		$[\chi_2^2 = 4.80; (p, \text{n.s.})]$	

*Source: Survey of Planners Project. See Table 3.4 for exact definitions of formal planning degree and agency type.

†χ^2 computed with role as the dependent variable, controlling for agency type (public or private) by experience. In addition a contingency-table analysis was performed in which experience was combined in ordinal categories of 5 years (5 years or less, 6 to 10 years, 11 to 15 years, etc.). The identical pattern observed above was replicated.

on a national basis. In order to place the planners' responses in perspective, we will begin by reviewing the major critiques of comprehensiveness emerging from the literature.

As outlined in chapter two, the philosophy of municipal reform was in many ways embraced by the planning profession and given expression in the traditional ideology of planning. The traditional model of planning, as Edward Banfield has observed, is simply another variant of the rational-choice model. "The rational selection of a course of action; i.e., the making of a rational plan, involves essentially the same procedure as any rational choice."[70] The elements of rational decision making can be expressed as follows: (1) the decision maker lists all the opportunities for action open to him; (2) he identifies all the consequences that would follow from the adoption of each of the possible actions; (3) he selects the action that would be followed by the preferred set of consequences.[71]

The traditional ideology of planning, of course, incorporates the philosophy and methodology of rational decision making in its model of comprehensive planning. The conceptual framework supporting the classical model of comprehensive planning is essentially contingent upon the existence of a unitary public interest that looms above (and is morally superior to) the political process. The features of the classical model of planning can be summarized, again, as follows: (1) a planning commission and professional staff created to assist in the formulation of the policy for the community as whole; (2) the assessment of community needs, which is predicated primarily on "rational" and technical versus "political" criteria; (3) the identification of all relevant potential development choices and consequences and the establishment of community goals or objectives, as well as the expression of these goals in a community plan whose "salient features include a map of what the pattern of land development will be at some point in the future";[72] and (4) the utilization of the master plan as criteria to evaluate short-range development choices.[73]

In a generic sense, then, the traditional model of planning seeks freedom from the irrationality of "political" constraints in order to fashion a comprehensive solution (plan) to development problems. However, it should be added that freedom from political constraints can be more correctly defined as freedom from the constraints of "particular" political interests; namely, those not in accordance with the interests of the community as a whole. This is worth noting because comprehensive rational planning logically implies a great deal of very centralized political control in order to implement goals.

As indicated previously, the comprehensive model of planning and traditional planning ideology have undergone sustained attack from both within planning (advocacy planning) and in the more generalized critique of rational decision making emerging from economics, political science, and decision theory. Among the more classic criticisms is Banfield and Meyerson's analysis of public housing in Chicago. After stipulating the criteria for rational choice, enumeration of alternatives, identification of all possible consequences, and selection of action followed by a preferred set of consequences, Meyerson and Banfield describe the ends-means relationship they observed in the practice of public housing planning in Chicago, noting that it "resembled somewhat the parlor game in which each player adds a word to a sentence which is passed around the circle of players: the player acts as if the words that are handed to him express some intention (i.e., as if the sentence that comes to him were planned) and he does his part to sustain the illusion."[74]

Banfield's own critique of the rational decision making model calls into question a variety of assumptions of the comprehensive model. To begin with, he questions the ability to establish any but the most abstract goals in a pluralistic community. In addition, Banfield states that the institutional character of American community politics, decentralized, fragmented, and pluralistic, mitigates against the very nature of comprehensive planning. Moreover, he believes that even if the enormous complexity of predicting change in future environments were resolved, there would exist significant organizational impediments to truly rationally planned change. In other words, organizations themselves may possess characteristics that work against comprehensive rational planning; namely, political constraints that prescribe the range of possible alternatives, or the simple goal of organizational survival, which usually operates in the favor of short-run rather than long-run goals.[75] He expresses the interaction of rational versus political considerations in real-world planning by noting that the considerations which finally governed the selection of sites and the type of project were generally political rather than technical.[76]

A second criticism of the rational model, and one that itself provided the conceptual infrastructure of an alternative decision making approach, is Charles Lindblom's work on incrementalism. Lindblom's own analysis begins with a delineation of the requirements of the rational comprehensive decision making model, similar to Banfield's, in which the decision maker lists all related values (in his example, those with respect to inflation). He then enumerates all potential policy alternatives. The third step is the systematic comparison, utilizing available theory, of all relevant values in an attempt to formulate a policy outcome which attains the greatest proportion of the desired values. Finally, the decision maker would seek to make the policy choice that best expresses the possibility of maximizing the decision-makers values.[77]

Lindblom's attack on the rational model is predicated on the underlying contention that the rational model is too much of a theoretical ideal to be in any sense isomorphic with reality. Or in other words, it does not conform to the behavior patterns of most administrators in practice. According to Lindblom, the rational model assumes administrators have intellectual skills and resources that in reality they do not have the time or the assets to acquire. In addition, in public administration at least, managers are precluded from practicing rational decision making because their function is constrained within certain parameters outlined by law or politics. Moreover, Lindblom observes that there is no real consensus on values in society, and in fact, there are no real measures of majority preferences on a variety of questions prior to the public discussion generated by a potential policy which focuses on the question. Therefore, it is not possible to rank values as required in the first step of the model or compare even a subjective ranking when values are found to conflict. "Suppose, for example, that an administrator must relocate tenants living in tenements scheduled for destruction. One objective is to empty the buildings fairly promptly, another is to find suitable accommodations for persons displaced, another is to avoid friction with residents in other areas in which a large influx would be unwelcome. . . . How does one state even to himself the relative importance of these partially conflicting values?"[78]

As Lindblom also contends the rational model simplifies the relationship between policy and values which is best expressed as follows: "Unable consequently to formulate the relevant values first and then choose among policies to achieve them, administrators must choose directly among alternate policies that offer different marginal combinations of values."[79]

As a result of the constraints imposed on the decision maker with respect to the resources and the nature of values in policy—that is, both shaping and being shaped by the policy itself—Lindblom concludes that policy does not evolve in a rational comprehensive fashion but in increments through successive limited comparisons, resulting in slight deviations from present policies. Policy, then, rather than being finalized is constantly in evolution. Lindblom also rejects the test of a "good" policy imposed by the rational model in which a policy is good if it meets the criterion of achieving a certain percentage of an operational goal. For the incrementalist, good policy is the result of consensus on the policy and not necessarily the values that underlie it.[80]

Alan Altshuler's seminal work, *The City Planning Process*, itself raises serious theoretical questions about the underlying assumptions of comprehensive rational planning. According to Altshuler, the most important functions of comprehensive planners are: (1) to create a master plan that can guide the deliberations of specialist planners; (2) to coordinate the planning of specialist planners in light of the master plan; and (3) to coordinate the planning of specialist agencies so as to ensure that their proposals reinforce each other to further the public interest.[81] The requirements for ideal performance of these objectives include an understanding of the public interest as it relates to the plan and a causal knowledge of the elements of the plan, which enables the planner to assess the impact of the proposed policy on the public interest. "If comprehensive planners deal with many more areas of public policies than specialists, their factual and causal knowledge in each area is bound to appear shallow—at least by comparison with the specialists in it. Hence their claims to comprehensiveness, if they are to be persuasive, must refer primarily to a special knowledge of the public interest."[82] In addition, Altshuler states that the comprehensive planner implicitly assumes community goals are measurable and can be ranked, because "it is impossible to plan without some sense of goals, call them what you will."[83] This fact, however, raises both theoretical and normative problems for the practicing planner in that it explicitly requires the assumption that planners can resolve value questions in expert fashion, and this is a source of legitimacy also claimed by the politician.[84] Moreover, Altshuler states that middle-range planning also has serious theoretical problems for the doctrine of comprehensiveness. "Men who plan to achieve operational—even though relatively general—goals are specialists, not comprehensive, planners."[85] It is clear that the doctrine of comprehensiveness in traditional planning ideology does claim to place the planner in a position to evaluate the proposals of specialist planners and does not accept a role for the planning profession which could be described as "one among equals."

However, the incrementalists, particularly Lindblom, are not without their own critics. For example, Andreas Faludi is critical of the incremental model, noting that Lindblom's critique mixes empirical and normative elements in its own presentation and produces in essence a normative prescription; that is, it suggests how planners and administrators should approach decision making. Lindblom does so because he himself produces a model that substitutes agreement on policy for the criterion of validity. "He [Lindblom] argues for replacing the search for knowledge as a basis for decisions by political or market choices. This argument is related to what he feels to be the only criterion of a good decision, i.e., agreement."[86] In addition, Faludi argues that what Lindblom calls the rational comprehensive approach is not necessarily a critique of comprehensive planning but more representative of "blueprint planning," an approach which "determines every detail of the solution to a problem, and only then proceeds unswervingly towards implementing the plan."[87] Finally, Faludi takes Lindblom to task for not stipulating those circumstances to which the incremental decision making model does not apply.

Amitai Etzioni also provides a cogent analysis of some of the oversights of incrementalism. Etzioni states, "Decisions by consent among partisans without a societywide regulatory center and guiding institutions should not be viewed as the preferred approach to decision making."[88] He outlines two reasons. First, all groups in society do not have equal power, and decisions reached exclusively through consent among partisans will be skewed in the direction of the powerful and privileged. Second, incrementalism tends to neglect social innovation by concentrating on deviations from current policy and focusing on short-range considerations. Also, Etzioni disputes that policy can only move in increments and suggests that at critical points it does, indeed, move in leaps and bounds. For example, he states that studies which uncover strong tendencies toward incrementalism in decision making, such as Richard Fenno's classic study of Congress, obscure the fact that many incremental decisions are related to and affected by fundamental decisions. While an analysis of change in the federal budget over time may show only marginal changes, such an analysis fails to grasp major fundamental policy choices such as the vast growth in defense spending after World War II or the space program, which represents a societal commitment to fundamental policy decisions and from which many incremental decisions are forthcoming.[89] Etzioni provides his own model, mixed scanning, which incorporates elements of both the incremental and rational models. He provides an illustration of mixed scanning versus the rational and incremental approaches, which is worth quoting at length.

Assume we are about to set up a worldwide weather observation system using weather satellites. The rationalistic approach would seek an exhaustive survey of weather conditions by using cameras capable of detailed observations and by scheduling reviews of the entire sky as often as possible. This would yield an avalanche of details, costly to analyze and likely to overwhelm our action capacities (e.g., "seeding" cloud formations that could develop into hurricanes or bring rain to arid areas). Incrementalism would focus on those in which similar patterns developed in the recent past and, perhaps, on a few nearby regions; it would thus ignore all formations which might deserve attention if they arose in unexpected areas.

A mixed-scanning strategy would include elements of both approaches by employing two cameras: a broad-angle camera that would cover all parts of the sky but not in great detail, and a second one which would zero in on those areas revealed by the first camera to require a more in-depth examination. While mixed-scanning might miss areas in which only a detailed camera could reveal trouble, it is less likely than incrementalism to miss obvious trouble spots in unfamiliar areas.[90]

The impact of traditional planning ideology and advocacy can be integrated into the larger debate between proponents of the comprehensive rational decision making model and those who reject this model in favor of a more incremental approach.[91] Proponents of both posit assumptions about factors inherent in the models that lead to rather diverse conclusions about the nature of the state, the status of rationality as a method, the existence of a unitary public interest, and the criteria for good policy. For example, the traditional model of comprehensive planning postulates a view of the state that is Hegelian in substance. In other words, the state is viewed as an organic whole, a body politic, metaphorically larger than the totality of its constituents. Proponents of the incremental model or advocacy, on the other hand, support a view of the state that is pluralistic. Influenced by the market model in economics, pluralists see the state as composed of individuals, aligned in groups, who produce equilibrium in a policy sense through participation in the political-bargaining process. In this regard, then, the state is merely the political and institutional framework that legitimizes the bargaining process and is not an entity apart from that process. This view rejects the almost independent existence of the state implied by the organic model. Indeed, one planning theorist has underscored the divisions related to these two diverse conceptions of the state by contending that pluralism is essentially antiplanning.[92]

Moreover, proponents of comprehensive rational planning posit a high degree of control over the decision-making process. They assume, in essence, that it can be rationalized and that resources can be allocated efficiently through centralized decision making. Also, they accept implicitly the legitimacy of centralized political control, at least over specific areas related to planning. Advocacy planning and incrementalism, on the other hand, contend that the methodology of comprehensive planning requires too much of the intellectual and capital resources available to most managers. In addition, advocates reject rationality in the first instance as a criterion for decision making, underscoring the essentially value-laden nature of choices associated with comprehensive planning. They also claim that only the marketplace of political bargaining contains sufficient information to generate efficient policy.[93] Moreover, those who favor comprehensive planning must accept a unified public interest, which assumes the existence of a criterion to be utilized in decision making. To the advocate and incrementalists in general, the public interest is merely the output of the bargaining process. Also, comprehensive planning advocates and incrementalists differ on their view of a good policy. To the advocate, a good policy is a policy that includes all participants who can affect policy outcome—in other words, consensus. Those supporting comprehensive planning see a good policy as that which is measurable, rational, and inclusive.[94] Given the substantial amount of literature on the comprehensive ideal, as well as the assault on comprehensiveness by decision theorists and the advocacy movement, what is the position of the profession as a whole? How have planners been affected by this theoretical debate? Do they believe comprehensive planning as an ideal is possible or desirable, and what does comprehensiveness mean to the planner in terms of the scope of the public planning process?

The first question related to the comprehensiveness doctrine, which we will address subsequently, is the legitimate subject of concern of public planning agencies. Melvin Webber has observed, "The city planner's responsibility relates primarily to the physical and locational aspects of development within a local government's jurisdiction."[95] While it is true that the formal power of planning in the United States has been limited to a focus on the use of physical space, it is also clear that the planning literature eschews this exclusively physical definition of planning. Social planning, however vaguely defined, has significant appeal among planning's leading theorists. Social planning is, among other things, a break from the traditional concept of city planning as an avocation concerned with the proper alignment of streets and public buildings, toward a more comprehensive type of planning that includes economic and social elements. Social planning is also a conceptual surrogate for the process of politics. The question raised here, and implicitly throughout the chapter, is where do planners at large stand vis-à-vis the theoretical debate related to these questions. Table 3.15 shows that an inordinate proportion of planners (88.1%) contend that the public planning agencies' legitimate subject of concern is the physical, social, and economic development of the community. Moreover, there is no statistically significant difference between formally educated versus nonformally educated planners.[96]

However, there is a statistically significant difference between public versus private planners on this question ($p < .03$, 90.4% versus 83.0%) with public planners more in accordance with the expanded role of the planning agencies. More important, however, is the fact that the vast majority of both public and private planners favor a role for the public planning agency in accordance with the requirements of comprehensive planning theory; namely, legitimately encompassing the physical, economic, and social development in a community.

Table 3.16 indicates that controlling for type of agency eliminates the independent effect of agency type. Moreover, the introduction of experience did not influence this relationship. Again, the clear preference among planners for a form of physical, social, and economic focus for the public planning function overwhelms any differences between subsets of planners. Any legacy of environmental determinism expressed in a preference for a purely physical focus for the planning function is clearly dead within the profession.

The second general question, the possibility of comprehensive planning in a pluralistic society, is addressed in Table 3.17. The exact statement—"comprehensive rational planning by government is virtually impossible in a pluralistic society"—must be taken into consideration in the analysis of the data. Clearly, the majority of all planners

Table 3.15

**Planners' Attitudes toward the
Legitimate Subject of Concern of Public Planning Agencies**

Subject of Concern of Public Planning Agency*	Entire Sample (%)	No Formal Planning Degree (%)	Formal Planning Degree (%)	Public Planners (%)	Private Planners (%)
Physical development exclusively†	2.5	2.8	2.3	1.4	4.6
Physical & economic development	9.4	10.9	7.8	8.2	12.4
Physical, economic, & social	88.1	86.3	89.9	90.4	83.0
Total	100.0 (767)	100.0 (321)	100.0 (427)	100.0 (203)	100.0 (294)
		$[\chi^2_2 = 2.46; (p, \text{n.s.})]$		$[\chi^2_2 = 11.13; (p < .03)]$	

*Source: Survey of Planners Project. See Table 3.4 for exact definitions of formal planning degree and agency type.

†The exact question was: "What do you think should be the legitimate subject of concern of public planning agencies?"

(53.4%) reject this position, underscoring the strong commitment within the profession to the concept of comprehensive rational planning as an ideal. In addition, there are no apparent cleavages between various subgroups of planners—those with formal planning education or employed by public versus private agencies. The majority of both groups reject the contention that comprehensive rational planning is impossible in a pluralist society.

Table 3.18 displays the results of controlling for type of agency. There are no significant differences between groups and no effective change in the nature of the relationship. The introduction of experience as a control variable did produce one statistically significant deviation; private planners with less than ten years of experience *and* possessing a formal planning degree were more likely than any other group to agree with the contention that comprehensive rational planning was impossible. Moreover, their 43.3% support for this conten-

Table 3.16

Planners' Attitudes toward the Legitimate Subject of Concern of Public Planning Agencies, Controlling for Type of Agency

Subject of Concern of Public Planning Agency*	Public Planners		Private Planners	
	No Formal Planning Degree (%)	Formal Planning Degree (%)	No Formal Planning Degree (%)	Formal Planning Degree (%)
Physical development exclusively	1.5	1.4	5.4	4.0
Physical & economic development	8.8	7.1	15.3	9.5
Physical, economic, & social	89.7	91.5	79.3	86.5
Total	100.0	100.0	100.0	100.0
	(203)	(294)	(111)	(126)
	$[\chi_2^2 = .51; (p, \text{n.s.})]$		$[\chi_2^2 = 2.25; (p, \text{n.s.})]$	

*Source: Survey of Planners Project. See Table 3.4 for exact definitions of formal planning degree and agency type.

Table 3.17

Planners' Attitudes toward Comprehensive Rational Planning in the U.S.

Comprehensive Rational Planning by Government Is Impossible*	Entire Sample (%)	No Formal Planning Degree (%)	Formal Planning Degree (%)	Public Planners (%)	Private Planners (%)
Agree†	30.3	28.0	32.0	29.5	32.5
Uncertain	16.3	19.2	14.3	17.1	14.4
Disagree	53.4	52.8	53.7	53.4	53.1
Total	100.0	100.0	100.0	100.0	100.0
	(766)	(322)	(428)	(509)	(243)

$$[\chi_2^2 = 3.83; (p, \text{ n.s.})] \qquad [\chi_2^2 = 1.24; (p, \text{ n.s.})]$$

*Source: Survey of Planners Project. See Table 3.4 for exact definitions of formal planning degree and agency type.

†The exact statement was: "Comprehensive rational planning by the government is virtually impossible in a pluralistic society."

Table 3.18

Planners' Attitudes toward Comprehensive Planning in the U.S., Controlling for Type of Agency

Comprehensive Rational Planning by Government Is Impossible*	Public Planners		Private Planners	
	No Formal Planning Degree (%)	Formal Planning Degree (%)	No Formal Planning Degree (%)	Formal Planning Degree (%)
Agree	28.6	30.0	28.5	35.9
Uncertain	20.2	15.1	17.0	12.5
Disagree	51.2	54.9	54.5	51.6
Total	100.0	100.0	100.0	100.0
	(203)	(293)	(112)	(128)

$$[\chi_2^2 = 2.27; (p, \text{ n.s.})] \qquad [\chi_2^2 = 1.91; (p, \text{ n.s.})]$$

*Source: Survey of Planners Project. See Table 3.4 for exact definitions of formal planning degree and agency type.

tion represented the only group that showed a modal support for this proposition (data not displayed). In other words, among private planners with less than ten years of professional experience, possessing a formal planning degree is associated with a rejection of the comprehensive-planning ideal.[97]

The overall conclusion evident in the data is that the support for the possibility of comprehensive rational planning exhibits a great theoretical tenacity among planners. Also, this tenacity persists in spite of very compelling assaults by both the incrementalist model in general and the advocacy movement within planning itself, on the ideal of comprehensive rational planning in a pluralist society. Such a finding demonstrates a majority dominance within the profession of at least one central theoretical perspective of the classical model of planning; that is, the ability of government to plan in a comprehensive and rational fashion.

The final consideration addressed in this chapter will be the desirability of having a federal agency responsible for comprehensive planning on a national basis. The question raised here is, Do planners see the need to establish a federal government agency to carry out such planning?

However, in order to address this question, some considerations relevant to national planning must be explored—the environment for planning in the United States and the requirements of political control implicit in comprehensive ideal. Specifically, in the first instance, the ideological environment for planning in the United States is not favorable. A very fundamental assumption of the government's role in planning in this country is that some failure exists in the ability of the private market to allocate land use in the interests of the entire community. Planning's generic origins in this country can be traced to municipal beautification and the nuisance control. In the case of the latter, planning has been equated with zoning, which itself was perceived as a mechanism by which the dysfunctions of the market as it relates to nonconforming land uses could be addressed (the proverbial glue factory in a residential neighborhood). As Altshuler observes, the principal justification for American planning for many years has been simple businesslike foresight.[98] In other words, in the United States planning emerged as a mechanism by which externalities could be controlled and municipal efficiency achieved, and planning was forced to justify itself in a political atmosphere dominated by a laissez faire economic philosophy. Ernest Erber provides an interesting commentary on the essential tension between the American political culture and the requirements of planning.

America's historical dedication to unfettered freedom in private exploration of resources made it anti-planning in its basic philosophy, both as institutionalized dogma and as popular mores. We hero-worshipped the "rugged individualist." The entrepreneur was at the top of the status index; the civil servant way down on the list. Teachers were rated by the quip that "those who can—do; those who can't—teach." Private enterprise was cloaked with a scantity [sic] given no other secular institution, and government was viewed as a necessary evil with that government governing best which governed least. This hardly constituted favorable soil for the growth of a profession based on the concept that the utilization and allocation of our resources would benefit from establishment of deliberate goals by public authority to be achieved through systematic control of development by governmental agencies.[99]

Clearly, such is not an ideal environment for the growth of philosophy supporting deliberate planning of societal objectives by the national government.

The second major consideration is the requirement for political control implicit in the comprehensive rational planning model. In order to implement the comprehensive community plan, some degree of political control is implicit. In order to organize and implement a national plan, a great deal of political control is required. It has been observed that opponents of planning have asserted that planners have a bias toward the centralization of political authority reflected in their support for an expanded role for government. Indeed, some planners contend that planning is the one function of government least conducive to decentralization. Rexford Tugwell, for example, advocated a fourth branch of government status for planning to pursue a factual or empirical basis for social policy "dictated by contemporary resources, techniques and circumstances, rather than political expediency."[100] Also, it appears clear that planning theorists understand the dynamic tension between the American political system and any attempt at national planning. "Certainly if a planning agency is subject to endless participatory consultation, undue scrutiny by the mass media, and group veto (in a country known for the group veto)—and there is little doubt to me it would—the planning which results might very well be no more daring than the holding pattern it was meant to replace."[101]

Nonetheless, in spite of some very real political (if not theoretical) problems, there is much evidence in the literature of planning to suggest that planners support some form of national planning for the United States. Table 3.19 indicates they do; 65.1% of all planners believe the United States should establish a federal agency responsible for comprehensive planning on a national basis. In addition, there is no statistically significant difference between planners on the basis of formal planning education or type of employment. The latter is worthy of a brief comment; on a priori grounds, one might have assumed that private planners would have showed less support for national planning. What this suggests is that norms prevail within the planning community which override the attitudes normally associated with private sector employment; that is, comprehensive national planning by the federal government is not normally supported by private enterprise.

In addition, Table 3.20 displays again a high degree of cohesion within planning on the basis of characteristics that have been under-

Table 3.19
Planners' Attitudes toward National Planning

Should U.S. Have National Planning Agency?*	Entire Sample (%)	No Formal Planning Degree (%)	Formal Planning Degree (%)	Public Planners (%)	Private Planners (%)
Yes†	65.1	62.7	66.8	67.1	61.0
No	34.9	37.3	33.2	32.9	39.0
Total	100.0	100.0	100.0	100.0	100.0
	(762)	(322)	(422)	(507)	(241)
		$[\chi_1^2 = 1.17; (p, \text{n.s.})]$		$[\chi_1^2 = 2.38; (p, \text{n.s.})]$	

*Source: Survey of Planners Project. See Table 3.4 for exact definitions of formal planning degree and agency type.

†The exact question was: "Do you think the United States should establish a federal agency responsible for comprehensive planning on a national basis?"

scored as most conducive to cleavages among planners. Examination of the cells expressing support for a national planning agency manifests very similar levels of support between planners possessing formal versus no formal planning degree, controlling for agency type. Moreover, controlling for years of experience did not alter the nature of the foregoing relationships (data not displayed).[102]

Conclusions

The chapter has explored the attitudes of planners toward factors related to the nature of the planning process, the basis of the recommendations made by planners, and planners' attitudes toward the ideal of comprehensiveness. Planners' attitudes were evaluated in relation to two general objectives. First, we endeavored to assess the influence of the traditional planning doctrine versus advocacy planning on the attitudes of the planning profession, as well as to determine the direction of planners' attitudes; for example, the majority opinion on the status of planning theory. Second, we sought to determine the degree to which the planning profession is homo-

Table 3.20
Planners' Attitudes toward National Planning, Controlling for Type of Agency

	Public Planners		Private Planners	
Should U.S. Have National Planning Agency?*	No Formal Planning Degree (%)	Formal Planning Degree (%)	No Formal Planning Degree (%)	Formal Planning Degree (%)
Yes	63.4	69.7	60.2	61.6
No	36.6	30.3	39.8	38.4
Total	100.0	100.0	100.0	100.0
	(202)	(290)	(113)	(125)
	$[\chi^2_1 = 1.86; (p, \text{n.s.})]$		$[\chi^2_1 = .01; (p, \text{n.s.})]$	

*Source: Survey of Planners Project. See Table 3.4 for exact definitions of formal planning degree and agency type.

geneous internally with respect to the attitudes of various subgroups of the membership—public versus private planners and those with and without formal planning degrees.

In the first regard, the assessment of the influence of traditional planning doctrine versus advocacy on the questions addressed in this chapter can be best expressed as a "mixed bag." Planners accepted and rejected aspects of both the traditional doctrine of planning and advocacy; for example, planners clearly rejected the political neutrality of plans made by public agencies. They accepted in effect a definition of the master plan that equated it with any political policy output; namely, one that rewards some interests and discriminates against others. Such a position is very compatible with the essentially normative conception of the planning process postulated by advocacy planning. Moreover, given a range of responses arrayed along a continuum to reflect the relative content of the technical versus value-laden dimensions of planning, the vast majority of planners defined planning as a process in which they integrate advice and recommend choices based on value judgments, as well as technical expertise. This is very much at variance with the tendency of traditional planning doctrine to define planning as a function much closer to the rational/technical end of the continuum.

However, as for the contention that planning is a profession with a theory capable of providing a legitimate basis for professional recommendations, the majority of planners expressed strong support, indeed far more support than exists within the theoretical literature focusing on these concerns. Moreover, the predominant role preferences for planners are in accordance with dictates of the traditional model of planning, that is, the planner as technical/staff advisor rather than policy advocate.

The faith in the ideal of comprehensiveness is still viable among planners. This concept, which underscores the traditional ideology of planning's commitment to its ability rationally to integrate diverse elements into a more holistic outcome, still has strong support. The vast majority of planners believe that the legitimate subject of concern of public planning agencies is the physical, economic, and social development of the community. Moreover, the majority of planners insist that comprehensive rational planning by government is possible in a pluralistic society. Such a position is clearly in opposition to the pluralists' contention that good policy is the result of the rational choice of allowing the political system, rather than comprehensive planning, to produce policy equilibrium by including all relevant interest groups in the policy process, and by assuming that most policy decisions will be slight deviations from existing courses of action. Finally, the majority of all planners support the establishment of a federal government agency whose responsibility would be to implement comprehensive planning on a national basis. The political feasibility aside, such a position implies a strong commitment to the ideal that the society can achieve a rational utilization of resources through comprehensive planning and public authority.

With respect to the second consideration, the degree to which the planning profession is homogeneous or cohesive with respect to the attitudes of various subgroups, the data indicate that the profession is overall very cohesive. There was a statistically significant tendency for public planners and those possessing formal planning degrees to reject the neutrality of master plans. In addition, formally educated planners were less likely to be supportive of an exclusively technical role for the planner. Also, public planners were more supportive of an expanded role for public planning agencies.

The introduction of experience as a control variable had a specific effect on the following areas. Public planners with a formal planning degree (at both levels of experience) were more likely than private planners to agree that no plan is ever politically neutral. Also, public planners with a formal planning degree and less than ten years of experience were more likely than any subgroup to express a preference for the advocate role, and less likely to accept an exclusively technical role. However, among all groups the modal preference was for the role of technician. One final difference related to experience was that private planners with a formal planning degree and less than ten years of experience were more likely to agree that comprehensive rational planning by the government is virtually impossible in a pluralistic society.

Yet, these exceptions are far less relevant than the commonalities that exist between planners in the public and private sectors, between those who possess formal planning degrees versus those who do not, and among those possessing varying degrees of experience. In other words, our contingency-table analyses substantiated what our multivariate statistical analysis had initially indicated; namely, there are very few systematic cleavages within the planning profession related to variables such as age, sex, membership grade, formal education, and public or private work context. Moreover, those which do exist and which we have explicated in this chapter are subsumed by the fact that on most of the questions we explored, a vast majority of planners have a clear and defined direction in their attitudes.

Finally, in this chapter we have focused on a within-group comparison by looking at planners in relation to subgroups within the profession. There is much to suggest that planners are, indeed, in many ways attitudinally cohesive, or in statistical terms they do not display a great deal of within-group variance. However, there is also much evidence to suggest that planners are very different if compared to other groups of similar socioeconomic profiles. The subsequent chapter will focus on a between-group comparison. Specifically, we will focus on a comparison of planners and the U.S. public in order to measure the influence of professional standards on the attitudes planners hold toward the political process.

Chapter 4

Planners and the Public

Introduction

The objective of this chapter is to compare and contrast planners both with themselves and with a representative sample of the U.S. public on the dimensions of subjective political ideology, political party identification, and on various measures of political participation. With respect to these considerations much speculation and some empirical evidence suggest that planners as a group are oriented toward the liberal end of the political spectrum, particularly in their commitment to the role of government as an active agent in the private marketplace.[1] In addition, the same evidence suggests that planners are more likely to identify themselves with the Democratic party or as Independents and less likely to identify themselves as Republicans than the mass public. Also, planners have presumably inherited a strong reformist tradition characterized by high levels of political cynicism presumably affecting their desire to engage in political activity.[2] It will be the purpose of this section to test empirically these assumptions and to integrate the findings within a larger theoretical context that relates to the influence of planners on the urban policy making process.

Ideology: Planners and Social Reform

In order to embark on any analysis of ideology one must in some manner address the question of how to operationally define the concept. Indeed, as Philip Converse has observed, ideology has often served as the primary exhibit of the doctrine that "what is important to study cannot be measured and that what can be measured is not important to study."[3] In order to avoid the conceptual and methodological pitfalls inherent in the implications of Converse's assertion we shall define ideology "as a configuration of ideas and attitudes in which the elements are bound together by some form of constraint or functional interdependence."[4]

Two components of the foregoing definition require some elaboration. First, the definition of ideology employed can, of course, imply a more holistic set of attitudes perhaps more appropriately called a belief system. However, we shall utilize the term with the understanding that the focus is on those attitudes whose objects are political. In addition, ideology can be understood to possess constraint, which can be summarized as "the success we would have in predicting, given initial knowledge that an individual holds a specific attitude, that he holds certain further ideas and attitudes."[5] Or, in a simplified sense, the extent to which a person is cognizant of "what goes with what" in ordering the political world, that is, the extent to which the attitudes in a belief system are ordered into some integrated whole.[6] Constraint is, therefore, implicitly dependent upon levels of information. Philip Converse provides an excellent illustration of the lack of constraint in the example of the avowed socialist who professes a strong commitment to the belief that private enterprise and not government should have the dominant role in matters relating to the control of electric power and housing.[7] Obviously, some factor of interrelatedness or constraint is absent in the sense of being able to predict this person's attitudes toward public control of the economy on the basis of his professed adherence to socialist doctrine.

In addition, ideology may be understood as having both an abstract and an operational domain. For example, Lloyd Free and Hadley Cantril found distinct differences in the response patterns of Americans to abstract statements about political beliefs, as compared with more concrete or operational statements. Specifically, they concluded that Americans are ideologically conservative and operationally liberal.[8] James W. Prothro and Charles M. Griggs, utilizing sampling data from both a Northern and a Southern city, also discovered distinctions between adherence to abstract principles of democracy and their specific application. However, they concluded that there was greater ideological consensus in the liberal direction at the abstract level or, in other words, that their sample appeared to be abstractly liberal and operationally conservative.[9] Herbert McClosky, utilizing a sample that consisted of both political influentials and the general electorate also found greater support for abstract principles of democracy than in the application of those principles to a concrete context.[10] In addition, McCloskey found that the political influentials were

decidedly more democratic in their attitudes than the general electorate. Also, he found the political influentials more likely than the
general electorate to express opinions, to be ideologically oriented,
and to be more internally consistent in the views that they did
express over a broad range of political stimuli.[11]

In addition to the abstract and operational domains of political
ideology and the clear elite-mass differences, there is the expression
in American politics of ideology with respect to some point on the
liberal and conservative continuum. Indeed, few concepts in political
theory have the ambiguity that is associated with an attempt to
delineate the terms *liberal* and *conservative*. One could suggest several
reasons for this. First, the positions associated with each term have
changed over time. Classical liberalism, for example, was characterized by commitment to protection of the individual against encroachment by the state and by strong support for a system of checks
and balances. On the economic plane, classical liberalism became
closely associated with laissez faire economics.[12] This definition of
liberal, of course, has little resemblance to the concept of positive
government associated with twentieth-century liberalism and exemplified by the New Deal commitment to the legitimacy of public
authority as an agent of social amelioration.[13] Second, there is some
question as to whether a liberal or conservative ideology, seen as a
logically interrelated set of attitudes about the political world, has
any real application to the mass of the American body politic.[14] Philip
Converse, utilizing national sample data, concludes that fewer than
4% of Americans can be classified as ideologues with respect to
any well-defined liberal-conservative orientation. The results also
suggest that for most people, constraint among attitudinal elements
is low, and that political issues are not evaluated by the public against
some generalized standard of performance but as discrete, isolated
matters.[15] Indeed, the nonideological character of American parties
and politics for a while appeared almost axiomatic.[16] However, there
is some indication of a growing awareness of issues and ideology
among the American public since the election of 1964.

Finally, there is the question of dimensionality, that is, the concepts of liberalism and conservatism implicitly suggest a unidimensional continuum along which most objects in the political world can
be arrayed. Scholars have questioned this unidimensional construct

with some suggesting a distinct dichotomy between those issues primarily viewed as economic versus those concerned primarily with civil liberties.[17] Others have suggested a wide divergence between those questions subsumed under the substantive domains of domestic versus foreign policy. However, in spite of the very real considerations of the operational versus abstract, the foreign versus domestic, and the economic versus civil-libertarian dimensions of ideology, the liberal-conservative continuum, in the words of Converse, "has been highly serviceable for simplifying and organizing events in most Western politics for the past century."[18] In addition, the concept of the liberal-conservative continuum has served as a theoretically valid and quantitatively reliable discriminating device in isolating opposing orientations to politics.[19] Finally, the sheer prominence of the liberal-conservative dimension as a reference point in American politics and journalism has engendered some, admittedly difficult, attempts at operationalization.

Indeed, while consensus is not clear, the broad outlines of liberalism and conservativism in contemporary American politics have been richly elaborated.[20] Among the latter are a commitment to "experience (tradition), stability, and the prudent use of power."[21] Liberalism, on the other hand, has been characterized as valuing "imagination, change, and the broad distribution of power."[22] One of the more pivotal distinctions between liberalism and conservatism centers on the use of public authority in the form of the federal government to achieve domestic social objectives. "The general disposition of the liberal is to approve of such use, and that of the conservative is to disapprove."[23] Indeed, contemporary liberalism is epitomized in a real sense by the desire to strengthen the powers of government in pursuit of the public welfare. This distinction based on the desire for positive rather than passive government has been described as follows: "The liberal favors the use of government to ameliorate the ills of society; the conservative looks upon the growth of government as an unnatural and even malignant phenomenon. To the liberal, government is good; to the conservative, good government is limited."[24]

It is one of the explicit hypotheses of this research that planners are more likely to identify themselves as politically liberal than the U.S. public as a whole and that this liberalism is a function of professional values and norms inherent within the planning profession.[25] For example, planner Melvin Webber states that the contemporary planner inherits a "pragmatic orientation to betterment as old as the early social reform movements that spawned the profession."[26] Others have suggested that the planning profession possesses a distinct heritage which influences both the formal training of planners and the character of planning policy formulation.[27] Presumably, part of this tradition is the planning profession's commitment to a liberal ideology of governmental intervention in the interest of societal change.[28] As Anthony James Catanese states, "The people attracted to the planning profession have been liberal in general in their attitudes toward the role of government and dubious of a free market that had no constraints."[29] In some sense the very fundamental orientation of planning, "a profession based on the concept that the utilization and allocation of our resources would benefit from establishment of deliberate goals by public authority,"[30] is one which can be considered liberal in the context of the American political spectrum. Ernest Erber contends that the basic philosophy of America, its respect for rugged individualism and santification of private enterprise, is decidedly antiplanning in orientation.[31] A review of the literature suggests that planners do possess a liberal bias in their orientation, at least with respect to their advocacy of governmental involvement. It also is evident that critics of planning have recognized this orientation among planners. Alan Altshuler notes: "Those who oppose planning have generally asserted that planners have a professional bias in favor of bigger and bigger government, less and less subject to pressures from interest groups. Planners, they say, are in the business of creating new proposals which call for governmental activity."[32]

Planners' biases toward the expansion of government are clear in the call that emerges from planners for some form of national planning. One work in planning theory goes as far as creating the generalized outline for a graduate-degree program in the field of national planning.[33]

The foregoing analysis engenders the working hypothesis that a significantly larger proportion of planners when compared to the U.S. public will identify themselves as liberals. It is evident from Table 4.1 that this hypothesis is supported. The proportion of planners who identify themselves as liberals is considerably greater than that of the mass public. The 20% difference is both substantial and statistically significant. Conversely, the opposite is true at the conservative end of the continuum; planners are decidedly less conservative by self-identification than the U.S. population at large.

The magnitude of the foregoing differences, since they are in the expected directions, suggests a strong bias within planning toward identification with the liberal end of the political spectrum. However, two considerations are relevant. First is the degree to which the magnitude of the differences between planners and the public is real and not the function of additional, uncontrolled variables that are themselves producing the observed differences. The second consideration is the extent to which subjective political ideology among planners is tied to some measure of concrete attitudes. Empirical research suggests that at least three potential intervening variables

Table 4.1

Comparison of Planners and U.S. Public on Subjective Political Ideology

Subjective Political Ideology‡	Planners (%)	Public* (%)
Liberal	50.5	30.5
Moderate	40.3	40.0
Conservative	9.2	29.5
Total	100.0	100.0
	(772)	(1410)

$[d_{max} = .203; (p < .001)]$†

*Source: NORC, *National Data Program for the Social Sciences, Spring 1974 General Social Survey*. Original variable format collapsed for presentation. See Appendix D, Data Sources.

†Kolmogorov-Smirnov Two Sample Test. The test statistic (two-tailed) employs the maximum absolute difference between two cumulative distributions as a criterion for determining the probability that two samples have been drawn from populations with the same theoretical distribution. See Myles Hollander and Douglas A. Wolfe, *Nonparametric Statistical Methods*.

‡The exact question was: "Generally, how would you characterize your own political beliefs?"

are associated with variations in political attitudes and behavior: education, income, and subjective social class.[34] There is substantial evidence of elite/mass differences in political attitudes and behaviors which are themselves some function of the variations between groups in society on the very factors that produce elite/mass dichotomies in the first place, i.e., variations in income and educational levels and social class differences.[35] Since planners as a group are middle-income professionals possessing nonrepresentative levels of education, social class status, and income, all three factors are relevant to any controlled comparison of planners with the public at large.[36]

In essence, the original working hypothesis must be modified to incorporate these considerations. While part of the variance between planners and the U.S. public on the dimension of subjective political ideology may be due to the differential levels of education, income, and social class among planners, we contend statistically significant differences will persist after controlling for all potential intervening variables.

Table 4.2 compares planners with the U.S. public controlling for level of education. The differences between planners and the public are replicated after the introduction of the control variable. Since virtually all planners have at least a bachelor's degree (99.9%), only one level of education appears for them. As might be anticipated on a priori grounds, planners share a certain commonality with that segment of the population possessing a college education. However, all planners are significantly more liberal and conversely less conservative than the U.S. public controlling for *any* of the three levels of education. Nonetheless, as Table 4.2 indicates, while controlling for education minimizes the magnitude of the differences between planners and the college-educated public with respect to the proportion who perceive themselves as liberals to 8.8% (50.5% versus 41.7%), the converse is also true. Planners are decidedly less conservative (9.2% versus 35.5%) than that segment of the population sharing similar educational levels. The foregoing indicates that the variance between planners and the public on subjective political ideology is not the simple effect of the obvious differences in educational levels that exist between planners and the public. Moreover, rather than being the simple function of education, the differences between planners and the public remain statistically significant after controlling for education.

Table 4.3 presents a comparison of planners and the U.S. public controlling for income.[37] Again only one level of the control variable appears for planners. Statistically significant differences between planners and the public persist after controlling for level of income. Planners are more likely to identify themselves as liberal and decidedly less likely to identify themselves as conservative than Americans of *all* three income levels.

The last control variable to be examined is subjective social class. Subjective social class identification, like education and income, has been isolated as a useful predictor in voting behavior, and is found generally to correlate with other forms of political behavior as well.[38] For these reasons, it is imperative to assess the independent effect of

Table 4.2

Comparison of Planners and U.S. Public on Subjective Political Ideology by Level of Educational Attainment (Degrees)

		U.S. Public*		
Subjective Political Ideology	Planners (%)	Bachelor's or Graduate (%)	H.S. and Junior College (%)	Less than H.S. (%)
Liberal	50.5	41.7	28.0	29.3
Moderate	40.3	22.8	42.8	43.4
Conservative	9.2	35.5	29.2	27.3
Total	100.0	100.0	100.0	100.0
	(772)	(211)	(772)	(477)

$[d_{max} = .263; (p < .001)]$†

*Source: NORC, *National Data Program for the Social Sciences, Spring 1974 General Social Survey.* Original variable format collapsed for presentation.

†Kolmogorov-Smirnov Two Sample Test (two-tailed) calculated employing a comparison of the cumulative distributions of planners with that segment of the U.S. public possessing a bachelor's degree or greater. Since 99.9% of all planners possess at least a bachelor's degree and over 80% have some graduate work completed, planners act as their own control for this variable.

subjective social class on political ideology, as presented in Table 4.4.[39] Again, only one level of the control variable appears for planners. Clearly an examination of the proportion of liberals, moderates, and conservatives for those elements of the U.S. public identifying themselves as middle or upper class lends substance to the contention that the cleavages between planners and the public on political ideology are, again, not the simple effects of differences in perceived social class.

The last consideration of relevance to the comparison of planners and the U.S. public is the combined effect of all three characteristics—education, income, and subjective social class. Each of the previous comparisons has been of planners with a specific segment of the U.S. population, those possessing a certain level of education or income, or those identified with a specific social class. Table 4.5 addresses the question of the additive effect of all three characteristics in combina-

Table 4.3

**Comparison of Planners and U.S. Public
on Subjective Political Ideology by Income**

Subjective Political Ideology	Planners (%)	U.S. Public*		
		Over $25,000 (%)	$10,000–24,999 (%)	Under $9,999 (%)
Liberal	50.5	31.5	28.9	33.2
Moderate	40.3	32.5	40.9	40.3
Conservative	9.2	36.0	30.2	26.5
Total	100.0	100.0	100.0	100.0
	(752)	(114)	(623)	(566)

$[d_{max} = .219; (p < .001)]$†

*Source: NORC, *National Data Program for the Social Sciences, Spring 1974 General Social Survey*. Original variable format collapsed for presentation.

†Kolmogorov-Smirnov Two Sample Test (two-tailed) calculated employing a comparison of the cumulative distributions of planners with that segment of the U.S. public having incomes of $10,000 or greater. Planners are middle-income professionals. The American Institute of Planners reports a median income between $15,000–$20,000 and that over 90% of the profession made $10,000 or more in the sample year. See *AIP Newsletter*, June 1974.

tion. Examination of the table indicates that planners are more liberal and less conservative than either of the two U.S. public subgroups, and indeed, the addition of the control variable, socioeconomic status, does not alter the relationship.

The foregoing analysis and the literature suggest that the professional values of planning play some role in the manifest differences between planners and the public with respect to political ideology. There are a number of potential mechanisms by which these professional norms are transmitted and sustained. One could postulate in the case of planners a process of shared professional norms engendered initially by a process of self selection; that is, the attraction of particular types of individuals to planning—those with a strong commitment toward the preservation of the environment by public authority.[40] Additionally, one could suggest a process of shared

Table 4.4

Comparison of Planners and U.S. Public
on Subjective Political Ideology by Subjective Social Class

Subjective Political Ideology	Planners (%)	U.S. Public*		
		Upper Class (%)	Middle Class (%)	Working Class (%)
Liberal	50.5	29.5	31.8	29.5
Moderate	40.3	40.9	37.0	42.8
Conservative	9.2	29.6	31.2	27.7
Total	100.0	100.0	100.0	100.0
	(752)	(44)	(660)	(698)

$[d_{max} = .220; (p < .001)]$†

*Source: NORC, *National Data Program for the Social Sciences, Spring 1974 General Social Survey*. Original variable format collapsed for presentation.

†Kolmogorov-Smirnov Two Sample Test (two-tailed) calculated employing a comparison of the cumulative distributions of planners with that segment of the U.S. public identifying themselves as middle class. The statistic ($d_{max} = .265$; $p < .001$) was calculated comparing planners with the U.S. public identifying themselves as middle or upper class combined. Planners, because of income and education, were assumed to be middle class; however, comparison of the cumulative distribution functions of the middle- and upper-class public with planners did not alter the relationship.

professional norms initially inculcated through exposure to formal planning education and later reinforced through organizational membership and interaction. Finally of course, there is the possible interaction of all of the preceding. Nonetheless, there is evidence to suggest that exposure to formal planning education itself exerts an independent influence on professional planning values. However, the question of ideology introduces an additional consideration. Unlike the traditional ideology of planning and advocacy whose philosophies produce very diverse perspectives on other issues, there is a general consensus that both strains of planning doctrine are liberal in the context of American politics. Consequently, exposure to any type of formal planning education can be expected to exert an ideological influence that is essentially liberal. One hypothesis which emerges

Table 4.5

**Comparison of Planners and U.S. Public
on Subjective Political Ideology by Socioeconomic Status**

| | | U.S. Public* | |
Subjective Political Ideology	Planners (%)	Upper Socioeconomic Status (%)	Lower Socioeconomic Status (%)
Liberal	50.5	43.4	29.6
Moderate	40.3	20.6	42.3
Conservative	9.2	36.0	28.1
Total	100.0	100.0	100.0
	(772)	(136)	(1162)

$[d_{max} = .268; (p < .001)]$†

*Source: NORC, *National Data Program for the Social Sciences, Spring 1974 General Social Survey*. Upper socioeconomic status included those members of the U.S. population possessing a college or graduate degree and who were middle or upper class by self-identification and reported income. Lower socioeconomic status included all others. Also see Appendices A and B.

†Kolmogorov-Smirnov Two Sample Test (two-tailed) calculated employing a comparison of the cumulative distributions of planners with that segment of the U.S. public classified as upper socioeconomic status. Planners are self-defined "middle income professionals." For a statistical profile of planners for the sample year, see *AIP Newsletter*, June 1974.

from this reasoning is that if the professional values of planning play a particular role in the observed disparity between planners and the public, those values would be most manifest among those planners possessing exposure to formal planning education. Consequently, it can be expected that the proportion of liberals among planners would be largest among those planners exposed to formal planning education. Table 4.6 expresses this within-group comparison of planners. Clearly, the hypothesis is supported; the magnitude of the difference is over 20% and statistically significant ($p < .0005$). Evidently, exposure to formal education in planning is highly related within the planning profession to subjective political ideology.

However, in order to provide some substantiation for the independent effect of formal planning education on political ideology, it is necessary to interpret the relationship within the context of any additional variables that themselves may be potential confounding factors. As we have done previously, we focus on public versus private work context, as well as years of experience in the field.

Table 4.7 expresses the relationship between formal planning education and political ideology controlling for whether the planner is employed in a public or private agency. The relationship that was

Table 4.6

Comparison of Planners with Formal and No Formal Planning Education on Political Ideology

Subjective Political Ideology	No Formal Planning Education (%)	Formal Planning Education* (%)
Liberal	33.3	53.4
Moderate	53.2	38.1
Conservative	13.5	8.5
Total	100.0	100.0
	(111)	(626)

$[\chi_2^2 = 15.34; (p < .0005)]$

*Exposure to formal planning education was operationally defined as having an undergraduate degree, graduate course work, or a graduate degree in planning. No formal planning education included all others.

apparent between ideology and formal planning for the total sample is modified somewhat by the introduction of the type of agency as an intervening variable. For public plannners the relationship remains both strong and statistically significant. Public planners who have been exposed to formal planning education are consistently more liberal and less conservative than those possessing no formal education.

Among private planners, however, the relationship, while not statistically significant, is nonetheless consistent with hypothesized expectation. Among planners employed in the private domain, the proportion of planners identified as liberals is greater among formally educated planners and the opposite is true among conservatives. Clearly, exposure to formal planning education is related to subjective political ideology among all planners.[41]

Finally, Table 4.8 illustrates the effect of controlling for years of experience. The table reveals that a further specification of the nature of the relationship between exposure to formal planning education and ideology is required. Clearly, among all subgroups in the table

Table 4.7

**Planners with Formal and No Formal Planning Education
on Political Ideology by Type of Agency**

Subjective Political Ideology	Public Planners		Private Planners*	
	No Formal Planning Education (%)	Formal Planning Education (%)	No Formal Planning Education (%)	Formal Planning Education (%)
Liberal	33.3	53.1	34.9	53.4
Moderate	54.0	40.1	51.1	34.7
Conservative	12.7	6.8	14.0	11.9
Total	100.0	100.0	100.0	100.0
	(63)	(424)	(43)	(193)
	$[\chi_2^2 = 9.23; (p < .009)]$		$[\chi_2^2 = 5.04; (p, \text{n.s.})]$	

*Public planners are those members of the sample employed by a public agency (federal, state, local governments, and universities). Private planners include all those employed in the private sector. See Table 4.6 for exact definition of formal planning education.

there is a relationship between exposure to formal planning education and ideology. The nature of that relationship is such that overall
exposure to formal education is associated with a tendency to be
more liberal and less conservative. However, the relationship is statistically significant only for public planners with less than ten years
of experience. Among this group the association is most apparent.
Clearly, the relationship between exposure to formal planning educa-

Table 4.8

**Planners with Formal and No Formal Planning Education
on Political Ideology by Agency Type and Experience**

Subjective Political Ideology	Public Planners*		Private Planners	
	No Formal Planning Education (%)	Formal Planning Education (%)	No Formal Planning Education (%)	Formal Planning Education (%)
Under 10 Years' Experience				
Liberal	28.9	55.4	40.0	64.4
Moderate	57.9	38.6	46.7	27.6
Conservative	13.2	6.0	13.3	8.0
Totals	100.0	100.0	100.0	100.0
	(38)	(249)	(15)	(87)
	$[\chi_2^2 = 9.86; (p < .007)]$		$[\chi_2^2 = 3.19; (p, \text{n.s.})]$	
Over 10 Years' Experience				
Liberal	41.7	49.1	30.8	42.0
Moderate	45.8	42.8	53.8	43.0
Conservative	12.5	8.1	15.4	15.0
Totals	100.0	100.0	100.0	100.0
	(24)	(173)	(26)	(100)
	$[\chi_2^2 = .76; (p, \text{n.s.})]$		$[\chi_2^2 = 1.19; (p, \text{n.s.})]$	

*Public planners are those members of the sample employed by a public agency
(federal, state, local government, and universities). Private planners include all those
employed in the private sector. See Table 4.6 for exact definition of formal planning
education.

tion and a planner's political ideology is most strong among the younger members of the profession.

The second consideration with respect to political ideology is the question referred to as "constraint," the extent to which one is aware of what goes with what in ordering the political world. In this particular case we will examine the degree to which a planner's subjective political ideology is correlated with specific attitudes toward national priorities. One consistent theme emerging from voting behavior studies of the American body politic is the relative lack of consistency among issue positions, and the differences between elites and masses in levels of conceptualization. Indeed, differences in attitude constraint in the ability to sense "what goes with what" in the political world prompted one scholar to note: "The common tendency to characterize large blocks of the electorate in such terms as 'liberal' or 'conservative' greatly exaggerates the actual amount of consistent patterning one finds."[42]

However, very real differences emerge in the capacity of various subsets within the mass public in their ability to deal with the ideas and images of the political world. Herbert McClosky remarked concerning this elite mass cleavage: "The political views of influentials are relatively ordered and coherent. As liberals and conservatives, Democrats and Republicans, they take stands on issues, choose reference groups, and express preferences for leaders that are far more consistent than the attitudes and preferences exhibited by the electorate. The latter's opinions do not entirely lack order but are insufficiently integrated to meet the requirements of an ideology."[43]

It can be demonstrated that planners by virtue of their education, income, and occupational status are by any objective criteria an elite group. The hypothesis then follows that planners will manifest elite levels of constraint; or, that in some sense, planners like other elites are cognizant of what goes with what in ordering their political world. One test of this hypothesis is the examination of the relationship (correlation) between planners' subjective political ideologies and their preferences with respect to some objective policy alternative. It is hypothesized that those planners who identify themselves as, for example, liberals will choose expected liberal preferences for particular policy positions. It becomes necessary, however, to operationalize those expected policy positions.

One congressional voting study found distinct evidence of ideological voting when legislation was divided into specific policy domains. Among those domains of potential relevance to this analysis are government management, social welfare, and spending on arms and defense. Subsumed under social welfare were legislative proposals dealing with "public housing, urban renewal, labor regulation, education, urban affairs, and employment opportunities and rewards."[44] Legislation included under the policy domain of government management was "regulation of business activities, distribution of the tax burden, conservation, setting of interest rates, and balancing the budget."[45] Aage Clausen operationalized a liberal by an activistic or high support position for legislation subsumed under both the social welfare and government management domains. Conservatives were operationalized as those members who expressed low support or opposition to legislation incorporated under the social welfare and government management domains. Other studies have suggested a similar dichotomy on the domain of spending for national defense with liberals tending to manifest low levels of support and conservatives high.[46]

One measure of support, or the lack of it, for a particular policy is the desire to increase or decrease expenditures. Indeed, it can be assumed that the desire to increase or decrease expenditures on a particular policy is some measure of the relative importance of the policy to the individual. Table 4.9 expresses the correlations between the subjective political ideology of both planners and the public on specific policy domains.

In all cases the association between the subjective political ideology and spending priorities is higher for planners than for the public at large. In addition, the sign of the coefficients of both planners and the public on the spending for the environment, blacks, and welfare is in the expected direction with liberals expressing preferences for increased spending and conservatives for decreased spending. On the question of arms and defense the inverse is true. Liberal planners express a preference for decreased spending, while conservative planners indicate a preference for increased spending.

However, as before, the question of the independent effects of certain variables on any comparison of planners with the public must be considered. First of all, the concept of a patterned or integrated set of ideas about the political world is one usually associated with very select elements of the body politic. "The shaping of belief systems . . . into apparently logical wholes that are credible to large numbers of people is an act of creative synthesis characteristic of only a miniscule proportion of the public."[47]

Consequently, any comparison of planners and the public must control for variations in any characteristics which might, themselves, explain variations in the data. In Table 4.10 the public is broken down by an index of socioeconomic status composed of measures including education, subjective social class, and income. It is evident that the magnitude of the associations for that segment of the U.S. population classified as lower socioeconomic status are clearly smaller than for planners or for that segment of the U.S. population classified as upper socioeconomic status. In addition the associations are in the expected direction across all policy domains with liberals expressing a preference for increased expenditures on the policy domains of the environment, the problems of big cities, blacks, and welfare and for decreased expenditures on arms and defense. Conservatives manifest exactly the opposite preferences. Interestingly, the associations on the last three policy domains—blacks, arms and defense,

Table 4.9

Associations (Gamma) between Expenditure Priorities and Political Ideology for Planners and U.S. Public

Priorities†	Planners	U.S. Public*
Environment	.43	.24
Problems of big cities	.31	.09
Blacks	.54	.18
Arms and defense	(−).55	(−).23
Welfare	.52	.21

*Source: NORC, *National Data Program for the Social Sciences: Spring 1974 General Social Survey.*

†Correlation Coefficients were computed for variables with national priorities arrayed in the direction of preference for decreased (low) through increased (high) spending for each specific policy domain. Subjective political ideology was arrayed in ascending order on a scale ranging from conservative (low) to liberal (high).

and welfare—are essentially similar for both planners and the upper socioeconomic public with associations between political ideology and expenditures on blacks and arms and defense actually larger for planners than the public. However, the associations on the environment and the problems of big cities are lower for planners than that segment of the U.S. population classified as upper socioeconomic status. Examination of the contingency tables indicates a tendency among conservative planners to favor increased expenditures on these domains. One possible explanation, rather than a lack of ideological consistency, is the obvious professional self-interest in additional expenditures in these areas. In conclusion, it seems reasonable to state that planners, like Americans of similar socioeconomic status, share a sense of "what goes with what" in ordering their political world. A relationship exists between planners subjective political ideology and their preferences for expenditures on particular policies.

Table 4.10

**Associations (Gamma) between Expenditure Priorities
and Political Ideology for Planners and U.S. Public by Socioeconomic Status**

		U.S. Public*	
Priorities†	Planners	Upper Socioeconomic Status	Lower Socioeconomic Status
Environment	.43	.51	.21
Problems of big cities	.31	.59	.04
Blacks	.54	.48	.16
Arms and defense	(−).55	(−).47	(−).23
Welfare	.52	.55	.18

*Source: NORC, *National Data Program for the Social Sciences: Spring 1974 General Social Survey*. For criteria utilized in the establishment of socioeconomic-status index see Table 4.5.

†Coefficients were computed for variables with national priorities arrayed in the direction of preference for decreased (low) through increased (high) spending for each specific policy domain. Subjective political ideology was arrayed in ascending order on scale ranging from conservative (low) to liberal (high). The χ^2 between socioeconomic levels was significant for all policy domains ($p < .01$ minimum) with the exception of the welfare domain. Planners are assumed to be an upper socioeconomic status group for purposes of comparison.

Planners and the U.S. Public: Party Identification

This section will deal with the hypothesis that planners are more likely to identify themselves as Democrats or as Independents, and less likely to identify themselves as Republicans than the U.S. public and that this relationship will persist after controlling for some potentially influencing variables. Much of the foregoing discussion suggests that planners when compared to the mass U.S. public constitute a distinct reference group. Planners were more likely to identify themselves as liberals than the general public, and this relationship remained statistically significant after controlling for confounding factors. In addition, we concluded that a relationship exists between a planner's subjective political ideology and his or her expenditure priorities. In effect, our implicit assumption is that planners constitute an elite group, a group willing to pay the higher "information costs" associated with political sophistication.[48] Planners' professional biases toward the liberal end of the political spectrum and their strong professional heritage with respect to a commitment to social welfare values should be essentially incompatible with the policy positions of the Republican party and should essentially predispose planners to identify themselves as Democrats or as Independents.

This, of course, implies that a partisan cleavage exists on questions of relevance to planners and that planners are aware of such divisions and can distinguish between them and act accordingly. In the first regard, available evidence suggests the Democrats and Republicans are most divided on the dimension of government management, a dimension that subsumes legislation dealing with government intervention in areas relating to economics and natural resources, or more generally the use of public authority as an active agent in the private marketplace. A quantitative analysis of party voting in Congress over a twelve-year period found that Democrats and Republicans had the greatest systematic between-group variance and the least within-group variance on questions relating to government management. This high cleavage between the parties, and high cohesion within the parties, was in the direction of Democrats expressing high support for government management with Republicans expressing high opposition. As noted previously, planning almost by definition is committed to the deliberate use of public authority toward the establishment of an environment conducive to the optimal use of resources. In some sense, the very need for planning is, in effect, an implicit admission of some inherent deficiency in the philosophy of laissez faire. Consequently, it is assumed that planners will identify least with the political party with which they share the least opinion congruence on this essential matter. The second greatest partisan division found by Clausen in his study of Congress was on legislation subsumed under the social-welfare dimension. The party cleavage was in the direction of Democrats manifesting high support and Republicans high opposition to such legislation.

Table 4.11 examines the first hypothesis, that planners are more likely to identify themselves as Democrats or as Independents, and less likely to identify themselves as Republicans. First of all, although the absolute percentage of the U.S. public identifying with the Democratic party is slightly higher than it is for planners, as one moves down the table to the Independent and Republican cells, planners begin to deviate; that is, planners are more likely to perceive themselves as Independents and less likely to perceive themselves as Republicans than the mass U.S. public. In addition, the differences are both statistically significant and in the expected directions.

As indicated previously, certain intervening variables are inextri-

Table 4.11

Comparison of Planners and U.S. Public on Political Party Identification

Party Identification	Planners (%)	U.S. Public* (%)
Democratic	43.6	44.1
Independent	44.1	32.6
Republican	12.3	23.3
Total	100.0	100.0
	(759)	(1402)

$[d_{max} = .110; (p < .001)]$†

*Source: NORC, *National Data Program for the Social Sciences: Spring 1974 General Social Survey*. Original variable format collapsed for presentation.

†Kolmogorov-Smirnov Two Sample Test (two-tailed) calculated employing a comparison of the cumulative distribution of planners with that of U.S. public.

cably related to variations in political behavior, particularly party identification. For example, upper socioeconomic groups, the well educated, white collar, and the moderately affluent are more likely to identify with the Republican party.[49] Consequently, such variables must be held constant in order to make valid comparisons. Table 4.12 compares planners with the public on party identification controlling for level of educational attainment. The first observation which can be underscored is that planners when compared to the public possessing similar levels of education, a bachelor's or greater, are substantially more Democratic and decidedly less Republican than Americans of comparable education. Indeed, planners constitute the smallest proportion of Republicans of any of the educational levels examined, a finding which is at variance with the national tendency of the well educated to identify with the Republican rather than the Democratic party.[50]

Table 4.13 presents the second control variable, income. The role of

Table 4.12

Comparison of Planners and U.S. Public on Political Party Identification by Level of Educational Attainment (Degrees)

Party Identification	Planners (%)	U.S. Public*		
		Bachelor's or Graduate (%)	H.S. and Junior College (%)	Less than H.S. (%)
Democratic	43.6	29.3	41.5	54.5
Independent	44.1	44.7	34.6	24.6
Republican	12.3	26.0	23.9	20.9
Total	100.0	100.0	100.0	100.0
	(759)	(208)	(706)	(487)

$[d_{max} = .143; (p < .005)]$†

*Source: NORC, *National Data Program for the Social Sciences: Spring 1974 General Social Survey*. Original variable format collapsed for presentation.

†Kolmogorov-Smirnov Two Sample Test (two-tailed) calculated employing a comparison of the cumulative distributions of planners with that segment of the U.S. public possessing a bachelor's degree or greater.

economics in political theory is a persistent theme in both normative and empirical scholarship. The relationship of income to party identification that could be expected on the basis of existing empirical evidence would associate low income with Democratic-party identification. The data support this contention. Moreover, planners are more consistently aligned with the Democrats or Independents and less aligned with the Republicans, and such differences remain statistically significant after controlling for income.

Table 4.14 expresses the comparison of planners and the U.S. public controlling for subjective social class. Examination of the table presents the relationship between subjective social class and party identification for the general public. Clearly, the largest proportion of the working class identifies with the Democratic party, while the largest single proportion of those in the upper class with the Republican party. Moreover, planners identify less with the Republican party than do any of the self-identified social classes, including those in the working class. Again, planners are more likely to identify with the

Table 4.13

Comparison of Planners and U.S. Public on Political Party Identification by Income

Party Identification	Planners (%)	U.S. Public*		
		Over $24,999 (%)	$10,000– 24,999 (%)	Under $9,999 (%)
Democratic	43.6	28.6	43.3	49.7
Independent	44.1	38.4	37.1	28.0
Republican	12.3	33.0	19.6	22.3
Total	100.0	100.0	100.0	100.0
	(759)	(112)	(612)	(561)

$[d_{max} = .095; (p < .01)]$†

*Source: NORC, *National Data Program for the Social Sciences: Spring 1974 General Social Survey.* Original variable format collapsed for presentation.

†Kolmogorov-Smirnov Two Sample Test (two-tailed) calculated employing a comparison of the cumulative distribution of planners with that segment of the U.S. public with incomes of $10,000 or greater.

Democratic party, or with Independents, and are less likely to identify with the Republican party. In addition, the differences are statistically significant and consistent with hypothesized expectations.

Table 4.15 presents a comparison of planners and the U.S. public controlling for all three control characteristics in combination; education, income, and subjective social class. The addition of these combined controls does not alter the significance of the foregoing relationship. Indeed, one fact that appears clear is that planners are distinctly less Republican and more Democratic than that segment of the U.S. public classified as upper socioeconomic in status. In addition, planners are less Republican than either of the two socioeconomic groupings. It can be concluded that after controlling for certain variables such as education, income, and socioeconomic status—both individually and collectively—the relationship between political party identification for planners and the public persists as hypothesized.

Table 4.14
Comparison of Planners and U.S. Public
on Political Party Identification by Subjective Social Class

Party Identification	Planners (%)	U.S. Public*		
		Upper Class (%)	Middle Class (%)	Working Class (%)
Democratic	43.6	22.2	40.6	48.9
Independent	44.1	31.1	31.5	33.5
Republican	12.3	46.7	27.9	17.6
Total	100.0	100.0	100.0	100.0
	(759)	(45)	(641)	(707)

$[d_{max} = .156; (p < .001)]$†

*Source: NORC, *National Data Program for the Social Sciences: Spring 1974 General Social Survey.* Original variable format collapsed for presentation.

†Kolmogorov-Smirnov Two Sample Test (two-tailed) calculated employing a comparison of the cumulative distribution of planners with that segment of the U.S. public identifying themselves as middle class. The statistic calculated comparing planners with U.S. public identifying themselves as middle or upper class combined is: $(d_{max} = .170; p < .001)$.

An additional consideration, however, remains. Since Independents constituted the largest single category of planners (44.1%), an alternative hypothesis to the very low identification with the Republican party is that it is an artifact of the tendency of Republican planners to identify themselves as Independent, while in reality leaning toward the Republican party. Indeed, the phenomenon of the "hidden partisan" necessitates some analysis of the party identification preference, if any, of those initially identifying themselves as Independents.[51]

Our secondary working hypothesis consistent with the foregoing analysis suggests that of those planners who identify themselves as Independents, the largest single proportion lean toward the Democratic and not the Republican party. In order to have some bench mark of comparison we again employ the U.S. public. Table 4.16 expresses the responses of Independents for both planners and the U.S. public, with respect to which of the two parties they were more

Table 4.15

Comparison of Planners and U.S. Public
on Political Party Identification by Socioeconomic Status

Party Identification	Planners (%)	U.S. Public* Upper Socioeconomic Status (%)	U.S. Public* Lower Socioeconomic Status (%)
Democratic	43.6	30.8	46.4
Independent	44.1	41.4	32.3
Republican	12.3	27.8	21.3
Total	100.0	100.0	100.0
	(759)	(133)	(1146)

$[d_{max} = .155; (p < .05)]$†

*Source: NORC, *National Data Program for the Social Sciences: Spring 1974 General Social Survey.*

†Kolmogorov-Smirnov Two Sample Test (two-tailed) calculated employing a comparison of the cumulative distributions of planners with that segment of the U.S. public classified as upper socioeconomic status.

sympathetic toward. The data are consistent with our working hypothesis and statistically significant. Clearly, of those planners identifying themselves as Independents, 60.3% report leaning toward the Democratic party. The data indicate that there is an even greater tendency for planners to identify with the Democratic party than the original analysis reveals. Table 4.16 also indicates a clearer partisan split for planners than for the public in the sense that only 11% of the planners profess to being closer to neither of the parties, versus 31.5% of the public who profess no allegiance to either of the parties.

Planners and the Public: Political Participation

The purpose of this section is to compare and contrast planners and the public on various measures of conventional political participation. One generalization emerging from the literature on political participation is indicative of the findings in this field. "Citizens of higher socioeconomic status participate more in politics. This generalization

Table 4.16
Comparison of Planners and U.S. Public on Independent Party Identification

Independent Identification	Planners (%)	U.S. Public* (%)
Independent close to Democratic	60.3	45.3
Independent	11.0	31.5
Independent close to Republican	28.7	23.2
Total	100.0 (335)	100.0 (457)

$[d_{max} = .205; (p < .001)]$†

*Source: NORC, *National Data Program for the Social Sciences: Spring 1974 General Social Survey*. Original variable format collapsed for presentation.

†Kolmogorov-Smirnov Two Sample Test (two-tailed) calculated employing a comparison of the cumulative distributions of planners with that segment of the U.S. public identifying themselves as independents.

has been confirmed many times in many nations. And it generally holds true whether one uses level of education, income, or occupation as the measure of social status."[52]

Moreover, the relationship between socioeconomic status and increased levels of political participation has a variety of explanations. Some focus on the greater resources of higher status individuals, others on the greater consequences of political decisions for upper-status individuals.[53] However, as with all generalizations, there are admitted deviations from the overall pattern. Indeed, as Sidney Verba and Norman H. Nie contend, "If the socioeconomic model 'works' and there are no additional forces that cause deviations from it, the result is that citizens of upper social status participate more than those of lower social status. The consequences of such a situation would, of course, be significant in terms of the governmental response to participation."[54]

The general relationship between socioeconomic status and political participation has been expressed in terms of providing a baseline for analysis. Verba and Nie, employing national sample data, found that "the relationship between socioeconomic status and overall participation is linear and fairly strong."[55] This is another way of saying that socioeconomic status explains a great deal of the variance in political participation. Nonetheless, other factors—race, organizations, place of residence, age, and political partisanship—interact with socioeconomic status, in some cases accelerating participation and in other cases moderating the tendency of upper socioeconomic groups to participate. One such factor, organizational membership, was found to exert an independent effect over and above socioeconomic status on the likelihood of engaging in political activity.[56]

One hypothesis that emerges from the foregoing is that on the basis of existing empirical evidence, the a priori expectation would be that planners by virtue of their socioeconomic characteristics and organizational membership would participate politically more than a representative sample of the U.S. public. However, certain considerations suggest an alternative hypothesis. First, there are various norms associated with the planning profession that indicate an organizational effect which would depress political participation among planners. One of the most consistent themes in the literature dealing with planning is the high degree of political cynicism within the profession. Indeed, Deil Wright states that two complementary themes appear in the findings of this research: "First, a distinct anti-political bias exists among planners. Second, and closely related to the first, is the observation that as professional planning norms become more pervasive there is a consequent atrophy in planners' capacity to affect public policy."[57] This antipolitical bias, manifested in a general aversion to politics, has been identified as an important element in the planner's heritage. Presumably this legacy of political cynicism is a manifestation of the planner's reformist opposition to "political" rather than "rational" solutions to public policy questions.[58] Indeed, Francine Rabinovitz contends that a strong professional bias exists which identifies various aspects of political participation as inherently unprofessional.[59] Others have reiterated the strong reluctance of planners to assume policy positions.[60] In addition, political cynicism has been associated empirically with political inactivity among the well educated.[61] Consequently, it is hypothesized that active organizational membership for planners, i.e., belonging to the planning profession, will depress political participation among planners such that there will be no significant difference between the participation rates among planners and the public. In order to test the hypothesis, a standard political participation scale was employed as the measure of political activity with particular emphasis on the inclusion of items not in violation of provisions of the Hatch Act, since the sample includes both public and private planners.[62]

Table 4.17A presents a comparison of planners and the public on measures of political participation. Clearly, the hypothesis is rejected; in fact, an examination of both the frequencies and the means of Table 4.17A and of the results in the ANOVA table in Table 4.17B indicate strong support for almost the reciprocal position. Planners report involvement in conventional political activity at a frequency far in excess of the mass public and more in accordance with the expected levels of participation of a group with their socioeconomic profile. From voting through party work the percentages for planners greatly exceed the mass public in conventional political participation.

The results of the analysis of variance, reported in the ANOVA table, using the political participation scale as the dependent variable indicates that the difference between the groups is statistically significant. Planners obviously participate in conventional political activity at a rate far greater than the literature suggests:

$$(F_{1,704} = 24441.5; p < .0001)$$

It was stated previously that the empirical research on political participation indicates that the socioeconomic characteristics which planners possess as middle income professionals would lead to expectations of high levels of political participation among planners. However, it was assumed that professional planning norms would exert a negative effect on participation rate among planners. Since this hypothesis was rejected, an alternative hypothesis, that planners participate at essentially the same rate as that segment of the U.S. population possessing similar levels of education, income, and socioeconomic status can be tested. Table 4.18A examines this hypothesis; obviously it also is rejected. Planners participate at a rate in excess of

Table 4.17A

Comparison of Planners and U.S. Public on Political Participation

Political Participation	Planners* (%)	(N)	U.S. Public† (%)	(N)
Voting	98.7	(761)	83.8	(2447)
Persuade others how to vote	68.9	(760)	14.7	(2523)
Attend political meetings	58.2	(763)	5.8	(2523)
Contribute money	60.5	(762)	8.3	(2516)
Party work	44.1	(760)	4.6	(2522)
Group mean‡	3.302		1.182	
Group N		(775)		(2523)

*Percentages are based upon respondents who answered yes to the question presented. The questions on voting for both groups included those responding that they had voted in all, most, or some of the elections. See Appendix A for exact questions.

†Source: Inter-University Consortium for Political Research (ICPR) of the Institute for Social Research, the University of Michigan. CPS 1974 American National Election Study.

‡Scores ranged from a minimum of zero to a maximum of five.

the mass public even after controlling for socioeconomic status, as is demonstrated in the ANOVA summary table in Table 4.18B. Therefore, planners report political participation at a rate that exceeds the expectations for a group possessing their socioeconomic profile. Clearly, the foregoing indicates a reevaluation of the literature with respect to planners and political participation. In effect, alternative conclusions are suggested by the data. Namely, the high degree of political cynicism supposedly associated with the planning profession may not exist, or it does not act as a mechanism which decreases political participation among planners. Another alternative is that since existing literature focuses on the attitudes of select members of the profession, for example agency heads, perhaps the broad-based membership of the profession is to some extent at variance with the reputed positions of the leadership.

Conclusions

The purpose of this chapter was to compare and contrast planners with a representative sample of the U.S. public on the dimensions of subjective political ideology, political party identification, and on various measures of political participation. Planners were found to be more liberal and less conservative than a representative sample of the U.S. public. In addition, this relationship remained statistically sig-

Table 4.17B

ANOVA Summary Table on Participation Index

Source*	D.F.	SS	MS	F
Between groups—planners versus public	1	2593.79	2593.79	2441.5
Within groups (error)	3193	3392.65	1.06	
Total	3194	5986.44		

*The ANOVA table was designed using an index of political participation as the dependent variable ($p < .001$). The index was created by summing the answers to the questions in Table 4.17A (i.e., yes = 1, no = 0), for each individual index value:

$$score = \sum_{i=1}^{5} x$$

The maximum score value was five. Also see Appendix B.

nificant after controlling for education, income, and subjective social class, indicating that the differences between planners and the public were not the simple effects of failing to hold these variables constant in the comparisons. In addition, a statistically significant relationship between the possession of a formal planning degree and the dimension of political ideology was established.

Planners were also found to be inordinately Democratic in partisan self-identification, and this relationship also remained statistically significant after controlling for various socioeconomic characteristics closely associated nationally with political party identification. The examination of those planners initially identifying themselves as In-

Table 4.18A

**Comparison of Planners and U.S. Public
on Political Participation by Socioeconomic Status**

| | | | U.S. Public† | | | |
Political Participation	Planners* (%)	(N)	Upper Socio-economic Status (%)	(N)	Lower Socio-economic Status (%)	(N)
Voting	98.7	(761)	97.7	(218)	82.5	(2229)
Persuade others how to vote	68.9	(760)	35.8	(218)	12.8	(2305)
Attend political meetings	58.2	(763)	16.5	(218)	4.8	(2305)
Contribute money	60.5	(762)	26.7	(217)	6.6	(2299)
Party work	44.1	(760)	12.4	(218)	3.8	(2304)
Group mean‡		3.302		2.060		1.109
Group N		(775)		(218)		(2305)

*Percentages are based upon the respondents who answer yes to the question presented. Socioeconomic index was computed by including in the upper socioeconomic group those possessing a bachelor's or graduate degree and those identified as middle or upper class by social status and income.

†Source: Inter-University Consortium for Political Research (ICPR) of the Institute for Social Research, the University of Michigan. CPS 1974 American National Election Study.

‡Scores ranged from a minimum of zero to a maximum of five.

dependents indicated an even greater proportion of planners leaning toward the Democratic party and away from the Republican party than was originally established. With respect to political participation, planners were found to participate politically at levels far in excess of the mass public or of those members of the U.S. public possessing similar levels of education, income, and social class.

At this point it seems appropriate to repeat some points previously established and to reevaluate them in light of the present analysis. The conceptual framework of this study established the inherently normative character of the planning function by attempting to establish the commonality between planning and politics. Indeed, the paucity of planning theory was emphasized as well as the reliance of decision making in planning upon professional standards, most of which were normative in content and many of which were rooted in the history and development of the planning movement in the United States.

In addition, the available evidence suggests that planning is highly discretionary in nature; one of the largest empirical studies of this question reports a great deal of nonprogrammed activity or deviations from prescribed procedure among planners.[63] All the foregoing raises the question of the planner's representativeness. Planners are obviously not representative, in the statistical sense, of the U.S. public. However, the evidence suggests that planners are also not representative of the U.S. public in an attitudinal sense with respect to various political beliefs and behaviors. Indeed, a substantial case can be made to the contrary; that is, as the literature suggests, planners constitute a distinct professional or reference group with particu-

Table 4.18B
ANOVA Summary Table on Participation Index

Source*	D.F.	SS	MS	F
Between groups— planners versus public	1	344.92	334.92	186.11
Within groups (error)	980	1816.30	1.85	
Total	981	2161.22		

*See Table 4.17B for construction of the participation index ($p < .0001$).

lar values and objectives at stake in the implementation of public policy. The implications from a policy perspective seem clear. The planner's role as expert should be reevaluated. The planner is, perhaps, best regarded as a member of an interest group with a specific value-laden focus on the direction and content of public policy.

We suggest these data indicate that planners, by the very nature of their discipline, are predisposed to favor positive government and that they are astute enough to realize the position of such sentiments within the context of American politics. What these data do not address is the legacy of municipal reform on the attitudes of planners toward other aspects of their political world—for example, the very real political question so important to planning theory: Is there indeed a unitary public interest? In order to expand our profile of the planner with respect to the attitudes he holds toward the political process, we will again return to our within-profession focus in the next chapter. We will again focus on planners, employing the variables of formal education, agency type, and years of experience. It is hoped we will shed some light on the intriguing question of the relationship of the planner's political liberalism to the political reformer's "outlook," which he has presumably inherited.

Chapter 5

The Roots of Reformism

Introduction

In the previous chapters the influence of the municipal reform movement on the development of various planning standards and ideologies was explored. It was stated that the literature suggests that the ideology of municipal reform is an important element of the contemporary planner's heritage. Among the major tenets of reformism that were emphasized as having exerted an influence on traditional planning ideology were the municipal reform movement's distinct antipolitical bias and its commitment to the concept of a solitary public interest. Also, the reform movement's support for the political neutrality of expertise and rationality, and the tendency to centralize executive influence in the interest of efficiency were identified as important influences on planning doctrine. The purpose of this chapter is to measure empirically planners' attitudes relating to these concerns to see whether or not they do indeed reflect the various positions that have been imputed to them.

Implicitly we are seeking to discover the nature of the relationship between a planner's demonstrated political liberalism and the political-reformer outlook he presumably possesses. In other words, if planners do exhibit a strong commitment to the ideology of municipal reform, are they aware that the reform movement represented a very conservative force in American politics? Do planners still believe (as their traditional ideology suggests they must) in a unified public interest? Moreover, do they remain convinced that they, as professional planners, are most capable of being neutral judges of that public interest? How, if at all, has the ideology of municipal reform influenced the planner's conception about the preferred structure of local government? What is the one best form of local government necessary to produce effective planning? How has the reformist tradition of deference to the expert influenced the planner's attitudes toward the citizen-participation group in the public planning process? Does the professional planner formally educated in the discipline manifest the high levels of political cynicism or support for positive government that the case-study literature implies? These are the questions to which we will address ourselves. In addition, we will retain our focus on the cohesiveness within the profession by examining the influence of formal planning education, public-agency versus private-agency employment, and years of experience on various relevant variables.

Also, since the traditional ideology of planning received so much of its theoretical structure from the ideology of municipal reform, we will use the former as an index of the strength of the latter. If the planner rejects important elements of the municipal-reform ideal—for example, the existence of unitary public interest—he calls into question important elements of traditional planning doctrine, and at the same time suggests strong support for important elements of advocacy.

The dependent variables employed in this chapter include scales and measures of attitudes toward concepts and factors whose origins are in the philosophy of municipal reform, and which were outlined in chapter two. The independent variables, as stated previously, are formal planning education, agency type, and years of experience in the field. We will begin our analyses with the question of political cynicism.

Political Cynicism

The planner's disdain for the political process is presumably an important legacy of the ideology of municipal reform. Indeed, a distinct antipolitical bias among planners is one of the principal findings of research in this area.[1] This antipolitical bias, expressed in a general aversion to politics, is reputedly a manifestation of the planner's political-reformer outlook, which places a higher value on "rational" as opposed to "political" solutions to policy problems. There is empirical evidence to suggest that the degree to which planners are effectively socialized into traditional professional norms is associated with their willingness to engage in overt political activities.[2] Indeed, one case study found the most politically oriented planner to be one without formal planning education.[3]

In order to address the question of political cynicism it was important to determine the relative importance of political cynicism within the context of the entire domain of attitudes that planners hold, and to establish a quantitatively reliable measure of political cynicism.

The dependent variable measure employed is a standard political cynicism scale consisting of six modified Likert items, which constitute a Guttman type scale.[4] Guttman scaling procedures were utilized and a composite cynicism score ranging from zero through six was assigned to each person.[5] An evaluation of the items for their scalability indicated that they meet the requirement for the establishment of a valid Guttman Scale. The coefficient of reproducibility for the scale equaled .9354, and the coefficient of scalability was .6419. Consequently, the scale possesses the properties inherent in Guttman type scales, that is, unidimensionality (the measurement of the relative position of an individual vis-à-vis an underlying concept, in this case political cynicism) and cumulativeness (the component items can be arrayed by their relative degree of difficulty).[6] In addition, the composite cynicism scores provide a functional metric to be utilized as the dependent variable measure in this analysis. The political cynicism scale itself was constructed utilizing the pattern of the sample responses. Each respondent was assigned a scale score value based on the number of items passed. Those scoring zero and one were identified as politically cynical, those scoring two and three as politically neutral, and those scoring four, five, or six as politically trusting.

The first objective was to determine if political cynicism would emerge as one of the most important dimensions in planners' attitudes. The lack of comparable national sample data for this variable dictated that the best procedure was to subject all the responses in our data set (many of which themselves produced validated scales) to a factor analysis. Factor analysis is a statistical technique that isolates interdependencies among items and attempts to express the common dimensions underlying the items in terms of a smaller number of factors. Moreover, since the mathematical algorithm employed in factor analysis extracts factors in the order of greatest explanatory power, we can utilize factor analysis as a convenient technique for examining the importance of our political cynicism scale.[7]

Specifically, it is hypothesized that political cynicism will load on the first factor and, therefore, be a part of the dimension in our data set that accounts for the single largest percentage of the total variance.

Indeed, this was found to be true; the political cynicism scale did load on the first factor, and in fact represented the only variables that did load significantly on factor one.[8] This indicates its relative importance among a varied array of issues ranging from national priorities to attitudes toward comprehensiveness.[9]

However, our real purpose was to isolate the impact of professional planning norms on political cynicism. In this regard, it was hypothesized that levels of political cynicism would be different among different subgroups of the profession. Therefore, we tested the independent and interactive effects of formal planning education (degrees) and agency type (public or private) on the level of political cynicism among planners. The working hypothesis was that planners possessing a formal planning degree would be more politically cynical than those planners not possessing such a degree. In addition, planners employed by public agencies should reflect the profession's bias more completely and should be more politically cynical than those employed by private agencies. Finally, the interactive effect of both variables should be such that those planners who are formally educated and employed by public agencies will be the most cynical of all the subsets investigated. Table 5.1A contains the proportional breakdown of planners on the political cynicism scale.

A two-factor analysis of variance was performed on a subset of the variables using the composite scores of the political cynicism scale as the criterion variable. The two factors employed were agency type and formal planning education.[10] The levels of the first factor were public and private and the levels of the second factor the presence or absence of a formal planning degree. Because of the nonexperimental nature of the research, all factors are considered to be classification factors since they are impossible to manipulate by the researcher. Therefore, the ANOVA model has fixed rather than random effects. Because of this, generalizations made from the results of the analysis are extended only to those levels of the factors which were present in the research study. Any resulting differences between the means of the factor levels are, of course, to be interpreted in light of the quasi-experimental nature of the design.[11]

However, as seen in Table 5.1B the results of the two-way ANOVA indicate no significant interaction between agency type (public or private) and formal planning education (degree) with respect to the mean level of political cynicism. In addition, the main effects of both factors are nonsignificant, which indicates there is no significant difference between either public or private planners with respect to level of political cynicism, and there is no significant difference between planners with formal degrees in planning and those without formal degrees.

It could, however, be postulated that the presence or absence of a formal planning degree may be only one operational measure of exposure to professional values. Nonetheless, the role of formal planning education in the literature is that of a mechanism for the transmission of professional norms. However, professional socialization can occur through exposure to formal planning education, even though that education may not lead to a degree. In order to address this potential criticism, a second two-way factor analysis of variance was performed

Table 5.1A

Planners by Level of Political Cynicism, Controlling for Type of Agency

		Public Planners*		Private Planners	
Scale Score	Entire Sample (%)	No Formal Planning Degree† (%)	Formal Planning Degree (%)	No Formal Planning Degree (%)	Formal Planning Degree (%)
Cynical‡	20.0	18.5	21.8	20.7	18.4
Neutral	66.4	67.5	63.3	69.4	68.0
Trusting	13.6	14.0	14.9	9.9	13.6
Total	100.0	100.0	100.0	100.0	100.0
	(758)	(200)	(289)	(111)	(125)

*Public planners are those members of the sample employed by a public agency (federal, state, local governments, and universities). Private planners include all those employed in the private sector.

†Formal planning degree includes all members of the sample possessing a bachelor's, master's, or Ph.D. in planning.

‡The items constituting the scale and the presentation of the cutoff points and the inter-item correlation matrix are discussed in Appendix B. The coefficient of reproducibility = .9354. Minimum marginal reproducibility = .8195. The coefficient of scalability = .6419.

utilizing measures of those planners having any exposure to formal planning education as the first factor in the form of coursework versus those who have none. The second factor remained the same—agency type (public or private). The results of this second ANOVA, in effect, replicated the first ANOVA. Neither the interaction term ($F_{1,704} = .097$; $p < .999$) nor either of the main effects, agency type: ($F_{1,704} = .186$; $p < .999$) or formal education: ($F_{1,704} = .168$; $p = .999$) was significant (data not displayed).

Our final consideration was the introduction of years of experience as a control variable. Since the results of the second ANOVA replicated those of the first, the initial definition of formal planning education was used. Planners were classified into two groups—those possessing a formal planning degree versus those who did not have such a degree. A three-factor analysis of variance was performed with experience, agency type, and formal education as the independent variables. Only the main effect of experience was significant ($F_{1,680} = 16.40$; $p < .001$) (data not displayed).[12] Planners with ten years or less of experience were more cynical than those with greater than ten years of experience (20.6% versus 14.8%, or a mean of 2.71 on the cynicism scale versus a mean of 2.44). What this implies is that political cynicism among planners is far more directly related to such factors as age or experience than it is to the professional socialization

Table 5.1B
ANOVA Summary Table on Political Cynicism Scale

Source*	D.F.	SS	MS	F	p
Main effects	2	.443	.222	.174	.999
Formal education	1	.239	.239	.188	.999
Agency type	1	.177	.177	.139	.999
Interaction	1	2.185	2.185	1.716	.187
Error	704	896.362	1.273		
Total	707	898.991	1.272		

*The dependent variable measure was the composite cynicism scores ranging from one through six. For a discussion of scaling techniques and computer program employed see Appendix B. Since the results were not significant, the means are not reported.

†The use of analysis of variance with a Guttman Scale is justified due to the interval level of the scale values. See Allen L. Edwards, *Techniques of Attitude Scale Construction*.

inherent in planning education or to the work context of a public or private agency.

It can be concluded then that exposure to formal planning education and agency type were found to have no statistically significant independent or interactive affect upon the mean level of political cynicism among planners. Clearly, these findings are at variance with many of the conclusions based on the case-study literature in planning. We will return to the implications of our own findings in our conclusions section of this chapter. At this point, however, we turn our focus to perhaps the central theoretical pillar of both the municipal-reform movement and the traditional ideology of planning, namely, the existence of a unitary public interest.

The Public-Interest Doctrine

It has been asserted previously that one fundamental commonality between traditional planning doctrine and the ideology of reformism is in the commitment of both to the concept of a solitary public interest. Indeed, the pursuit of the public interest is, in some sense, at the very foundation of what Richard S. Bolan calls the classical model of planning.[13] According to this model, the planning commission with its professional staff assumes its role as guardian of the whole public interest by representing a comprehensive (rather than particularistic) perspective on community development. The general plan is an expression of this comprehensive perspective and serves the function of a yardstick against which short-range development decisions can be measured. According to Bolan, "The master plan would essentially eliminate debate on goals and on general means so that debate could focus on relatively narrow grounds of particular means."[14]

In addition, the rhetoric associated with the master plan indicates that this "public interest" is superior to other particularistic or pluralistic interests. Clearly, the assumptions of the comprehensive model of planning like those of reformism are predicated on the doctrine of the "community as a whole." This doctrine of course represents a de facto rejection of political pluralism as a precept. As Alan Altshuler states, "Those who contend that comprehensive planning should play a large role in the future evaluation of societies must argue that the common interests of society's members are their most important interests and constitute a large proportion of all their interests. They must assert that conflicts of interest in society are illusory, that they are about minor matters, or that they can be foreseen and resolved in advance by just arbiters (planners)."[15]

In many ways the public-interest doctrine has been the edifice of the planning profession's source of legitimacy or the philosophical justification for the intervention of public authority in the private marketplace.[16] This philosophy along with its "public-regarding" implications has presumably wide appeal among planners. Dennis Judd and Robert Mendelson contend that "even those planners who stress the complexity of the city—as most planners do—often speak of one public interest."[17]

The concept of a solitary public interest has been associated in traditional planning ideology with the presumption that planners have a special knowledge of the public interest. As Judd and Mendelson argue, "In traditional planning doctrine, one of the most sacred assumptions has been that planners represent and have a unique knowledge of the public interest."[18]

Clearly, the basis of this unique perspective on the public interest is predicated upon the technical competence of the planner and the planning profession's more "comprehensive" perspective. Traditional planning doctrine, like reformism, has been heavily imbued with elements of scientific management, particularly with respect to the role of the value-free technician expressed in the belief that planners were "politically neutral and that planners did not take sides in community conflicts, but rather worked for something we sometimes call the community as a whole."[19] In traditional planning doctrine the planning staff represented both "a comprehensive viewpoint and a scientific approach."[20] Indeed, as Altshuler states, "The case for efforts at genuinely comprehensive planning has generally rested heavily on the thought that planners can resolve conflicts among goals in expert fashion."[21]

The conception of the expert's ability to resolve such a dispute has its origin in the philosophy of municipal reform. To the reformers the city was a nonpolitical entity in pursuit of governmental efficiency. To the reformer politics was employed pejoratively and the concept of politics or political parties, which tended to divide rather than pursue the public interest, had no place.[22] In fact, the entire concept of interest-group pluralism, with its focus on separate demands by various elements of the body politic, was at variance with government by the "community as a whole and a solitary public interest."[23]

The foregoing suggests the working hypothesis that the majority of planners will express agreement with the contention that there is a solitary public interest in which all social and political groups hold a share. Indeed, as stated previously, much of the theoretical foundation of the comprehensive model of planning indicates that planners must accept the public-interest doctrine. As Ernest Erber has remarked, "The implications of the challenge to the public interest doctrine are clear, direct and serious—and, if true, shattering. If there is no unifying public interest to be served, if the science and art of planning is to be placed in the service of each special interest group in a pluralistic society, what happens to the concept of comprehensiveness?"[24]

However, Table 5.2 indicates a great deal more diversity within the planning profession with respect to the public-interest doctrine than the literature suggests. Clearly, the majority of planners do not accept the existence of a solitary public interest, and a significant minority (40.2%) reject its existence altogether.

Table 5.2
Planners' Attitudes toward the Public Interest

There Is a Solitary Public Interest	Entire Sample* (%)	No Formal Planning Degree (%)	Formal Planning Degree (%)	Public Planners (%)	Private Planners (%)
Agree	43.3	49.5	38.3	45.5	40.2
Uncertain	16.5	15.7	17.4	17.8	14.2
Disagree	40.2	34.8	44.3	36.7	45.6
Total	100.0	100.0	100.0	100.0	100.0
	(752)	(319)	(418)	(501)	(239)

$$[\chi_2^2 = 9.69; (p < .007)] \qquad [\chi_2^2 = 5.50; (p, \text{n.s.})]$$

*Source: Survey of Planners Project. The exact statement was: "There is a solitary public interest in which all social and political groups hold a share." Table 5.1A contains the exact definitions of formal planning degree and agency type.

As indicated previously, the advocacy movement within planning has engaged in a sustained attack on the vital assumptions of traditional planning ideology. None of these assumptions could be more vital to the traditional ideology of planning than the public-interest doctrine. One could suggest (and we do) that if advocacy planning itself possesses one central and enduring value premise, it is the rejection of a solitary public interest in which all social and political groups hold a share. What our data indicate is that advocacy planning's rejection of the existence of a public interest has significant support within the planning profession.

However, it has been stated that formal planning education has been underscored as exerting an independent effect on planning norms.[25] In addition, it has been emphasized that one major dichotomy within the planning profession is between those planners employed by the public versus those employed by the private sector. On an a priori basis, both of these variables can be assumed to be related to attitudes about factors inherent in the planning process and will be employed in all subsequent comparisons.

In the first regard, it can be hypothesized that professional values would be most thoroughly inculcated in those planners possessing a formal degree in the field. Indeed, if planners do possess a political reformer's outlook as the literature indicates, the expression of that philosophy as it relates to the public-interest doctrine should be most manifested in those planners having formal planning degrees. With respect to the second consideration, it is hypothesized that planners employed in the public versus the private domain, because of the different reward structure and motivations in each sector, will express divergent attitudes. Consequently, it is hypothesized that public planners, because of their involvement in the public sector and its programs, will be more committed to the belief in a solitary public interest than planners employed in the private domain. In addition, it is hypothesized that the interactive effect of both formal planning education and public employment will produce among this group the highest commitment to the concept of a solitary public interest.

Table 5.2 examines the first hypothesis. In the case of formal planning education there is a clear statistical relationship between planners having formal degrees in the field and attitudes toward the public interest ($p < .007$). However, the relationship is not in the hypothesized direction. In fact, the converse is true. Approximately thirty-eight percent of those planners possessing formal planning degrees—bachelor's, master's, or doctor's—accept the contention that there is a solitary public interest. On the other hand, 49.5% of those planners not possessing formal planning degrees agree with the contention that there is in fact a solitary public interest. In addition, a comparison of planners with and without exposure to formal planning education elicited a similar finding: while no statistically significant difference was found ($p < .08$), the distribution for those exposed to formal planning courses was not in the hypothesized direction.

The evidence suggests that the legacy of the philosophy of municipal reform expressed in the pivotal question of the existence of a solitary public interest is clearly not related to formal planning education in the direction suggested by the literature. There is indeed a relationship; however, the data indicate that exposure to formal planning education is associated with the rejection of the proposition that a solitary public interest exists.

The next consideration is the relationship between agency type and attitudes toward the public interest doctrine. Table 5.2 indicates that there is no statistically significant difference between the two groups with respect to this variable. Indeed, while there is a slight tendency for public planners to agree more than private planners (45.5% versus 40.2%) and conversely, a slight tendency for private planners to disagree with the contention that there is a solitary public interest, planners appear more homogeneous with respect to this variable than was hypothesized.

Table 5.3 deals with the consideration of the effect of formal education on attitudes toward the public-interest doctrine controlling for agency type. Examination of Table 5.3 indicates that the relationship apparent between formal planning education and the public-interest doctrine is modified somewhat by the introduction of the control-variable agency type. Support for the working hypothesis, that public planners possessing formal planning education would be most likely to express belief in the concept of a solitary public interest, is clearly absent. Examination of the proportions within the cells across all levels of the control-variable agency type indicates that formally educated planners are more likely to disagree with the contention that a solitary public interest exists irrespective of type of agency.

Conversely, both public and private planners not possessing formal degrees in planning are more likely to accept the public interest doctrine. Finally, the introduction of experience as a control variable in no way altered the nature of the relationship (data not displayed).[26] Specifically, while not statistically significant, for both public and private planners—regardless of level of experience—possession of a formal planning degree was associated with a greater tendency to reject the existence of a solitary public interest. More specifically, in no instance did the majority of formally educated planners—controlling for both public- and private-sector employment as well as experience, support the contention that there was indeed a unitary public interest in which all social groups held a share.

The second aspect of the entire public-interest question is the planner's role as the guardian of the public interest. Indeed, Altshuler contends that a special knowledge of the public interest is implicit in the scale of comprehensiveness inherent in planning theory.[27] As Judd and Mendelson contend, "Planners have usually viewed themselves as guardians of the public interest, contrasting themselves with other professionals who owe their allegiance to narrower and more clearly defined clients."[28]

Table 5.3

**Planners' Attitudes toward the Public Interest,
Controlling for Type of Agency**

There Is a Solitary Public Interest*	Public Planners		Private Planners	
	No Formal Planning Degree (%)	Formal Planning Degree (%)	No Formal Planning Degree (%)	Formal Planning Degree (%)
Agree	51.5	40.9	47.7	33.3
Uncertain	16.8	18.9	13.6	15.1
Disagree	31.7	40.2	38.7	51.6
Total	100.0	100.0	100.0	100.0
	(202)	(286)	(111)	(126)
	$[\chi_2^2 = 5.55; (p, \text{n.s.})]$		$[\chi_2^2 = 5.30; (p, \text{n.s.})]$	

*Source: Survey of Planners Project. See Table 5.2 for exact question. Table 5.1A contains the exact definitions of formal planning degree and agency type.

It can be assumed, therefore, from the perspective of a working hypothesis that planners will agree with the position that they are in the best positions to be neutral judges of the public interest by virtue of their professional training. This position is obviously unsubstantiated by the data in Table 5.4. In fact, the majority of planners reject the contention altogether. As indicated by the previous discussion, it can be assumed that this position would acquire greatest support from planners having formal degrees in the field and employed by public agencies. Examination of Table 5.4, however, expresses a pattern similar to that evident in the case of the public-interest doctrine. Planners having formal degrees in the field are most likely to reject and least likely to accept the contention that they are capable of assuming the role of neutral judges of the public interest. In addition comparison of planners having formal exposure to planning education, rather than degrees, versus those without formal exposure was also statistically nonsignificant ($p < .607$) (data not displayed).[29]

With respect to the consideration of type of agency, clearly, it has no statistically significant effect on attitudes relating to the planner's neutral role. In fact, the largest proportion of both public and private planners, 48.2% and 53.9% respectively, rejects the contention that

Table 5.4

**Planners' Attitudes toward the Planner
as Neutral Judge of the Public Interest**

Planner Is Neutral Judge of the Public Interest*	Entire Sample (%)	No Formal Planning Degree (%)	Formal Planning Degree (%)	Public Planners (%)	Private Planners (%)
Agree	27.2	29.6	25.2	28.2	25.1
Uncertain	22.6	26.3	19.8	23.6	21.0
Disagree	50.2	44.1	55.0	48.2	53.9
Total	100.0	100.0	100.0	100.0	100.0
	(769)	(324)	(429)	(512)	(243)

$$[\chi_2^2 = 9.06; (p < .01)] \qquad [\chi_2^2 = 2.12; (p, \text{n.s.})]$$

*Source: Survey of Planners Project. The exact statement was: "Urban planners, by virtue of their professional training, are in the best position to be neutral judges of the public interest." Table 5.1A contains the exact definitions of formal planning degree and agency type.

the planner is capable, by virtue of his professional training, to assume the role of neutral judge of the public interest.

The interactive effect of formal planning degree controlling for agency type (see Table 5.5) expresses again that if formal education is associated with attitudes toward the role of the planner as a neutral evaluator of the public interest it is related in a fashion not in conformity with hypothesized expectations. In the case of both public and private planners, the proportions of planners with formal planning degrees, in opposition to the contention that the planner is a neutral judge of public interest, is higher than for those planners possessing no formal planning degrees. In the case of the private planners the differences are statistically significant ($p < .02$). The introduction of the control-variable experience produced a more complete specification of the nature of the relationship. The one statistically significant relationship that endured was for private planners having over ten years of experience (data not displayed). For this group there was a clear and statistically significant ($p < .03$) tendency for formal planning education to be associated with a rejection of the contention that the planner is a neutral judge of the public interest.

Table 5.5

**Planners' Attitudes toward the Planner
as Neutral Judge of the Public Interest, Controlling for Type of Agency**

Planner Is Neutral Judge of the Public Interest*	Public Planners		Private Planners	
	No Formal Planning Degree (%)	Formal Planning Degree (%)	No Formal Planning Degree (%)	Formal Planning Degree (%)
Agree	30.4	26.4	27.4	22.8
Uncertain	25.5	22.1	27.4	15.8
Disagree	44.1	51.5	45.2	61.4
Total	100.0	100.0	100.0	100.0
	(204)	(295)	(113)	(127)
	$[\chi_2^2 = 2.65; (p, \text{n.s.})]$		$[\chi_2^2 = 7.30; (p < .02)]$	

*Source: Survey of Planners Project. See Table 5.4 for exact question. Table 5.1A contains the exact definitions of formal planning degree and agency type.

Among all other subgroups there was no statistically significant difference related to years of experience. Moreover, for all planners in both the public and private sector, with and without formal education and at both levels of experience the modal tendency was to reject the contention that the planner by virtue of his professional training is in the best position to be a neutral judge of the public interest. Moreover, an analysis of the independent effect of experience showed a statistically significant difference. On the question of the neutrality of the planner, planners with over ten years of experience were more likely to *disagree* that the planner possessed the capacity to be neutral judge of the public interest (54.8% to 46.1% respectively).[30]

Citizen Participation

Sherry R. Arnstein has said it well—"The idea of citizen participation is a little like eating spinach: no one is against it in principle because it is good for you."[31] We concluded initially that any assessment of planners' attitudes toward citizen participation would by necessity have to avoid asking whether or not planners agreed with citizen participation in principle. We believed that—like free speech—everyone would be for it in principle, and that any opposition would emerge only in questions aimed toward the actual practice of citizen participation, as it emerges in the practice of free speech. The specific phrasing of the question was designed to assess the planner's conception about the representativeness (subjectively defined) of the citizen-participation groups in the public planning process. Its specific format was: "Citizen participation groups involved in the public planning process are representative of the interests of their communities."

Clearly, as Table 5.6 indicates, the majority of planners reject the contention that citizen-participation groups are representative of the interests of the communities they serve.

This may indeed suggest an enduring legacy from municipal reform which places much greater legitimacy in the opinions of the expert than in the opinions of the uninformed body politic. However, it could also represent the fact that citizen-participation groups are not generally representative of the interests they serve, and that planners are correct in their assessment. These data cannot distinguish between the two alternatives. They do suggest, however, that after being exposed for years to planning literature which focuses on the importance of citizen-participation groups, the profession's overall assessment of these groups' primary function—namely, to represent the interests of the community at large in the planning process—is essentially that they do not represent the interests of the community they serve. Moreover, clearly there is very little cleavage on this question between public and private planners and those with and without formal planning degrees. As Table 5.7 indicates, the effect of controlling for agency type did not alter this relationship. The same remained true when we controlled for years of experience.[32] The overall assessment of the data indicates planners are very cohesive on this question and the direction of their opinions is such that they clearly reject the representativeness of the citizen-participation group in the public planning process.

Planners and Governmental Structure

In the discussion of the municipal-reform movement, it was underscored that the philosophy of reform found its institutional expression in a preference for particular forms of local government. It was

Table 5.6

Planners' Attitudes toward Citizen-Participation Groups in the Public Planning Process

Citizen-Participation Groups Are Representative*	Entire Sample (%)	No Formal Planning Degree (%)	Formal Planning Degree (%)	Public Planners (%)	Private Planners (%)
Agree	27.5	27.2	27.4	26.6	30.5
Uncertain	23.2	24.1	23.4	23.6	22.6
Disagree	49.3	48.6	49.2	49.8	46.9
Total	100.0	100.0	100.0	100.0	100.0
	(757)	(319)	(423)	(504)	(239)

$$[\chi_2^2 = .05; (p, \text{n.s.})] \qquad [\chi_2^2 = 1.27; (p, \text{n.s.})]$$

*Source: Survey of Planners Project. Table 5.1A contains the exact definitions of formal planning degree and agency type.

stated that the prevailing assumption of the reformers that politics denoted illicit demands in opposition to the public interest or the interests of the community as a whole, understandably led to their proposals for removing "politics" from government.

The reformers attempted to remove politics from government by advocating changes in the structure of local government and the manner of electing public officials. Among the changes of relevance to the subsequent analysis were the council-manager form of government and nonpartisan and at-large elections. In addition, master planning itself, conducted under the direction of an independent planning commission designed to remove "politics" from planning, was a part of the reform package.[33]

The council-manager form, like the independent planning commission, was predicated on the structural assumption that politics and administration could and should be separated.[34] In many ways, the council-manager plan expressed a prevailing view among reformers that "the interests of the community as a whole should be

Table 5.7

Planners' Attitudes toward Citizen-Participation Groups
in the Public Planning Process, Controlling for Type of Agency

Citizen-Participation Groups Are Representative*	Public Planners		Private Planners	
	No Formal Planning Degree (%)	Formal Planning Degree (%)	No Formal Planning Degree (%)	Formal Planning Degree (%)
Agree	26.2	26.3	30.0	31.5
Uncertain	24.3	24.2	24.5	21.3
Disagree	49.5	49.5	45.5	47.2
Total	100.0	100.0	100.0	100.0
	(202)	(289)	(110)	(127)
	$[\chi_2^2 = .00; (p, \text{n.s.})]$		$[\chi_2^2 = .36; (p, \text{n.s.})]$	

*Source: Survey of Planners Project. The exact statement was: "Citizen-participation groups involved in the public planning process are representative of the interests of their communities." Table 5.1A contains the exact definitions of formal planning degree and agency type.

determined in disinterested ways and then carried into effect expeditiously and efficiently by technicians."[35] Local government was
perceived as a business, and the manager form was an expression of
the business model of corporate organization.[36] The implicit assumption apparent in the council-manager plan—that efficiency was the
principal goal of government and expertise the foremost mechanism
for its realization—is a philosophy even today commonly associated
with "good government" advocates."[37]

The council-manager plan was advocated in conjunction with nonpartisan elections. The proposed intent of nonpartisanship was to
remove local politics from the control of national politics and to
insulate the local community from the national-party framework.[38]
Since there was no Democratic or Republican way to administer a
city, the presence of the Democratic or Republican party in local
elections was extraneous to good government. In order to insure
further the interests of the community as a whole, the removal of
party labels from ballots was advocated in conjunction with at-large,
rather than ward, representation.[39] However, it must be underscored
that the wards represented not only a grass roots political organization in the urban community but also its racial and ethnic pluralism.
The reformers objected to this "structure of government which enabled local and particularistic interests to dominate."[40] The nature of
those "particularistic interests" has caused some scholars to suggest
that the stated objectives of the reform movement obscure its real
intent, which is to establish an environment more favorable to the
interests of some elements of the community than to others.[41] Recent
empirical studies have indicated variations in public policy and voting turnout associated with the adoption of reform type structures.[42]
Robert Lineberry, for example, has found that reformed cities tend to
tax and spend less than unreformed cities.[43] Terry Clark, in an analysis of decision making in fifty-one American cities, contends political
influence is more centralized in reformed than unreformed cities.[44]
Political scientists have found lower voting turnout associated with
nonpartisan elections.[45] In addition, the removal of the cue-giving
function of political party labels combined with the general tendency
of certain groups to disenfranchise themselves more than others, has
led to the contention that nonpartisan elections tend to favor upper-
echelon groups.[46] Among the groups whose influence is most en-

hanced are those who normally vote Republican.[47] In effect, the combined result of the structural reforms advocated by the municipal-reform movement tends to strengthen the influence of middle-class voters.[48]

One hypothesis emerging from the foregoing is that planners, because of their political reformer outlook, will contend that planning functions most effectively under reformed rather than unreformed structures of local government. Table 5.8 supports this contention. In all cases the majority of planners equate effective planning with reformed rather than unreformed structures of local government. Planners equate effective planning with manager-council/commission and nonpartisan elections by a very significant majority, 68.0% and 70.1%, respectively. In terms of representation schemes, a slight majority of planners favor at large over districts or wards. With respect to formal planning education there are no statistically significant differences except in the case of formal planning degree and manager-council government. In that particular case planners possessing no formal degree are more supportive of the position that effective planning will result from businesslike government.

The relationship between public-agency employment versus private and preferences of types of local government are also presented in Table 5.8. Interestingly, public planners are more supportive than private planners of nonpartisan electoral schemes (76.1% versus 66.2%). The relationship is also statistically significant ($p < .006$).

Table 5.9 presents the effect of formal planning education controlling for agency type. The one statistically significant relationship which is evident is among private planners. Those without formal planning degrees are more likely to support manager-council and commission forms of local government. In addition, while not statistically significant there is a slight tendency for those without formal planning degrees to express a stronger preference for reformed rather than unreformed structures of local government.

The introduction of experience as a control variable (data not displayed) did produce an additional specification. The only group for whom the relationship remained statistically significant was private planners with under ten years of experience. For this group, those without formal planning degrees were most likely to express a preference for manager-council or commission government. The only significant independent effect related to experience was found in the decided preference among planners with over ten years of experience for at-large versus district or ward elections (60.6% versus 41.4% respectively).[49]

Table 5.8

Comparison of Entire Sample, Planners with Formal and No Formal Education (Degree), and Agency Type on Preference for Local Government Structures

Structures	Entire Sample* (%)	No Formal Planning Degree (%)	Formal Planning Degree (%)	Public Planners (%)	Private Planners (%)
Form of government					
Manager-council/ commission	68.0	72.6	64.1	68.4	66.9
Mayor council	32.0	27.4	35.9	31.6	33.1
Total	100.0	100.0	100.0	100.0	100.0
	(746)	(318)	(412)	(493)	(239)
		$[\chi^2_1 = 5.64; (p < .01)]$		$[\chi^2_1 = .09; (p, \text{n.s.})]$	
Type of election					
Nonpartisan	70.1	74.6	71.8	76.1	66.2
Partisan	25.9	25.4	28.2	23.9	33.8
Total	100.0	100.0	100.0	100.0	100.0
	(744)	(315)	(415)	(493)	(237)
		$[\chi^2_1 = .58; (p, \text{n.s.})]$		$[\chi^2_1 = 7.32; (p < .006)]$	
Representation					
At large	50.1	51.3	48.1	50.9	47.9
District or ward	49.9	48.7	51.9	49.1	52.1
Total	100.0	100.0	100.0	100.0	100.0
	(735)	(318)	(403)	(485)	(236)
		$[\chi^2_1 = .57; (p, \text{n.s.})]$		$[\chi^2_1 = .47; (p, \text{n.s.})]$	

*Source: Survey of Planners Project. The exact question was: "In order for planning to function most effectively: . . . Which *one* of the following forms of *local* government, . . . *local* election schemes, . . . *local* representation types do you think is most desirable?" Table 5.1A contains the exact definitions of formal planning degree and agency type. See Appendix A for question format.

Domestic Social Welfare

Opponents of planning have contended that planners have a bias toward an expanded role for public authority in the private market-place.[50] Indeed, the legacy of support for positive government and a concern for its role in addressing the problems of the underprivileged,

Table 5.9

Comparison of Planners with Formal and No Formal Education (Degree) on Preference for Local Government Structures

Structures	Public Planners*		Private Planners	
	No Formal Planning Degree (%)	Formal Planning Degree (%)	No Formal Planning Degree (%)	Formal Planning Degree (%)
Form of government				
Manager council/ commission	70.0	67.0	77.5	57.1
Mayor council	30.0	33.0	22.5	42.9
Total	100.0	100.0	100.0	100.0
	(200)	(279)	(111)	(126)
	$[\chi_1^2 = .35; (p, \text{n.s.})]$		$[\chi_1^2 = 10.08; (p < .002)]$	
Type of election				
Nonpartisan	77.8	75.3	68.2	64.0
Partisan	22.2	24.7	31.8	36.0
Total	100.0	100.0	100.0	100.0
	(198)	(283)	(110)	(125)
	$[\chi_1^2 = .28; (p, \text{n.s.})]$		$[\chi_1^2 = .29; (p, \text{n.s.})]$	
Representation				
At large	52.0	49.1	49.6	45.6
District or ward	48.0	50.9	50.4	54.4
Total	100.0	100.0	100.0	100.0
	(198)	(275)	(113)	(121)
	$[\chi_1^2 = .29; (p, \text{n.s.})]$		$[\chi_1^2 = .25; (p, \text{n.s.})]$	

*Source: Survey of Planners Project. See Table 5.8 for exact question. Table 5.1A contains the exact definitions of formal planning degree and agency type.

in addition to a support for larger social welfare goals, are emphasized by contemporary planners as a part of their professional heritage.[51] Moreover, some planning theorists suggest that of "all the functions of government, the one least conducive to decentralization is planning."[52] The purpose of this section is to test the independent and interactive effects of formal planning education and agency type on the support for an expanded role for the national government. The working hypothesis is that planners possessing formal planning education (degrees) will be more supportive of govermental involvement in domestic social welfare that planners not formally educated. In addition, planners employed by public agencies will be more supportive than those employed by private agencies. Finally, the interactive effects of both variables will be such that planners formally educated and employed by public agencies will be the most supportive of all the subsets investigated.

The dependent variable measure was the Domestic Social Welfare Scale, consisting of five modified Likert items, which constitute a Guttman type scale.[53] Guttman-scaling procedures were utilized and a composite cynicism score ranging from zero through five was created. The scale meets the criteria of validity established for Guttman Scales. The coefficient of reproducibility for the scale was equal to .9240. The coefficient of scalability was .6398. The composite scale scores were utilized as the dependent-variable measure. A percentage breakdown of the planners is presented in Table 5.10A. A two-way ANOVA was performed using the identical factors employed in the political cynicism scale: formal planning education and agency type. Again, the fixed-effects model in which the factors were classification factors was employed. The independent variables in this ANOVA were not orthogonal because of the unequal N size within the treatment cells. Although this condition was present in the previous ANOVA, the topic of nonorthogonality was not expanded upon because none of the treatment effects were significant. In Table 5.10B, however, certain effects were found to be significant, and therefore the nonorthogonality of the factors must be taken into consideration in the interpretation.

No significant interaction was found to exist between agency type and formal education with respect to the mean level of support obtained by planners on the Domestic Social Welfare Scale. This indicates that the relationship which exists between the means on the dependent variable at each level of agency type remains the same with respect to the order across both levels of formal planning education. Also, the relationship between the means on the dependent variable for each level of formal education remains the same with respect to order across both levels of agency type. It also, of course, leads to the rejection of the hypothesis that public planners having formal planning degrees would be most supportive of governmental involvement as measured by the scale.

The second step in the analysis was the examination of the significance of the main effects. Both main effects were found to be significant; the main effect for agency type was significant at $p < .007$ ($F_{1,704} = 7.243$) and the main effect for formal education was found to be significant at $p < .001$ ($F_{1,704} = 14.673$). Because the interaction was found to be nonsignificant, the main effects can be interpreted directly. Because of the nonorthogonality of the factors, however, the mean squares for agency type and formal planning education are not independent, and therefore the effects of each of them upon the dependent variable cannot be considered totally independent.[54] Table

Table 5.10A

Planners by Level of Support for Domestic Social Welfare, Controlling for Type of Agency

		Public Planners*		Private Planners	
Support Level†	Entire Sample (%)	No Formal Planning Degree (%)	Formal Planning Degree (%)	No Formal Planning Degree (%)	Formal Planning Degree (%)
Low	16.5	20.2	10.3	25.2	16.8
Medium	65.3	63.6	68.9	66.7	61.6
High	18.2	16.2	20.8	8.1	21.6
Total	100.0	100.0	100.0	100.0	100.0
	(753)	(198)	(289)	(111)	(125)

*Table 5.1A contains the exact definitions of formal planning degree and agency type.

†The items constituting the scale and the presentation of the cutoff points and the inter-item correlation matrix are discussed in Appendix B. The coefficient of reproducibility = .9240. Minimum marginal reproducibility = .7891. The coefficient of scalability = .6398.

5.11 illustrates, however, that regardless of agency type, those planners who have a degree in planning have a higher mean score on the Domestic Social Welfare Scale than do those planners without a formal degree, suggesting an independent effect of this variable on attitudes toward the role of government.

As stated previously, it could be suggested that the presence or absence of formal planning education may not be adequately measured by the simple presence or absence of a formal planning degree. In order to refine the measurement more precisely, a second two-way-factor analysis was performed dichotomizing planners into those who had exposure to planning coursework versus those who had not. The results of the ANOVA, in effect, replicated the first. The interaction was nonsignificant ($F_{1,704}$ = .327; $p < .999$). Both main effects were significant: agency type ($F_{1,704}$ = 6.607; $p < .01$), and formal education ($F_{1,704}$ = 22.128; $p < .001$). Thus, exposure to formal planning education is related in a statistically significant sense to positive attitudes toward domestic social welfare. A three-factor analysis of variance was performed including years of experience as an additional independent variable (data not displayed). None of the interaction terms was significant, and all of the main effects were significant, including years of experience. The findings of the two-factor ANOVA were replicated, since the mean of public planners was significantly higher than that of private planners, and the mean for formally educated planners was significantly higher than that of

Table 5.10B

ANOVA Summary Table on Government Management Scale

Source*	D.F.	SS	MS	F	p
Main effects	2	29.027	14.514	11.647	.001
Formal education	1	18.285	18.285	14.673	.001
Agency type	1	9.025	9.025	7.243	.007
Interaction	1	1.850	1.850	1.485	n.s.
Error	704	877.308	1.246		
Total	707	908.186	1.285		

*The dependent variable measure was the composite Domestic Social Welfare Scores. For a discussion of scaling techniques and computer program employed see Appendix B.

nonformally educated planners. The main effect for experience was also found to be significant ($F_{1,680} = 8.62$; $p < .003$). The mean for planners with less than ten years of experience was significantly higher than the mean for the more experienced planners (2.71 versus 2.44). Therefore, experience was found to have an independent effect upon support for domestic social welfare. The nature of the relationship is such that planners with less than ten years of experience are more likely than those with over ten years of experience to manifest high support for domestic social welfare measures.

Conclusions

This chapter has explored the influence of the municipal-reform movement on the attitudes of planners toward a variety of issues whose origin is in the philosophy and ideology of municipal reform. The literature suggests that the ideology of municipal reform was largely adopted by the planning profession and that, in effect, the planner possesses a political reformer's outlook. The foregoing analysis indicates there is far more diversity within the planning profession than the literature suggests. In addition, it appears the contention that the planner possesses a political reformer's outlook must, on the basis of these data, be called into question. Specifically, while planners in the aggregate express a preference for the structures of municipal reform (manager-council government, at-large and nonpartisan elections), the philosophy of municipal reform with respect to the public-interest doctrine and the neutral competence of the planner has far less

Table 5.11

**Comparison of Means of Planners with Formal
and No Formal Education (Degree)
on Domestic Social Welfare Scale by Type of Agency**

Agency Type	No Formal Planning Degree	Formal Planning Degree
Public	2.53*	2.78
Private	2.13	2.62

*Composite Scale Scores ranged from zero through five.

appeal within the profession. Indeed, a very significant minority of planners reject altogether the concept of a solitary public interest. Moreover, the majority of planners reject the contention that the planner by virtue of his technical competence is in the best position to be a neutral judge of the public interest. Both points, philosophically, have been very important in the ideology of municipal reform and in the development of the classical model of planning. The planner's attitude toward citizen participation groups is most interesting. In spite of the influence of advocacy and maximum feasible participation, the overall assessment by the majority of planners is that citizen-participation groups involved in the planning process are not representative of the interests they serve. This obviously suggests avenues for further research. It may well be that while planners in principle support citizen participation their opinion of the citizen-participation group's utility to the planning function in practice is really quite negative. At any rate, the profession's assessment of citizen-participation groups is clear. To the majority of planners, they are not representative of the interests of the community they serve.

In addition, planners as a group were found to be very cohesive with respect to certain characteristics that potentially provide points of cleavage within the planning profession. In the first regard, formal planning education measured by both degrees in planning or simple exposure to planning coursework was found to manifest no systematic independent or interactive effect on political cynicism. In other words, political cynicism among planners is not, as the literature indicates, related to formal planning education. Also, this relationship remains consistent when controlling for the type of agency in which the planner is employed. Formal planning education was associated statistically with a rejection of—rather than support for—certain key elements of reformism, and the introduction of the control variable (type of agency) did not statistically modify this relationship. Formal planning education was not associated with preference for reform structures of local government. The one statistically significant relationship found indicated planners without formal planning education expressed a greater support for council-manager government than those planners possessing formal education in planning. Indeed, across the entire range of factors relating to elements of the municipal-reform movement—that is, both preferences for governmental structures and philosophy—formal planning education either had no systematic effect or was associated with attitudes that rejected, in essence, aspects of reformism. The one dimension on which planners with formal planning education expressed a systematic difference was on support for governmental involvement in domestic social welfare. Those planners who had a formal degree in planning or exposure to planning education exhibited a greater support for domestic social welfare, regardless of agency type.

One conclusion that emerges from the foregoing is that if planning education acts as a mechanism for the transmission of professional values, much of what has been called traditional planning doctrine is no longer associated exclusively with exposure to formal planning education. The one exception is with respect to the decided preference planners have for positive government. In addition, the data reveal a strong tendency toward the philosophy of pluralism among all planners and a rejection of many elements of traditional planning ideology. Various central tenets of advocacy-planning doctrine, which embraces pluralism and rejects the neutral competence of the planners in questions of policy, appear to have significant support among the members of the profession.

Our findings with respect to public-agency versus privately employed planners are similar to those outlined in chapter three. Those who hypothesize significant cleavages between the public and private sectors of the profession will find little solace in these data. Moreover, those convinced of a clear ideological dichotomy among planners possessing differential levels of experience in the field will find little support for their position in this research. In totality over the entire domain of issues we have studied the profession is quite cohesive.

Admittedly, questions of cohesion are open to various interpretations of the degree of homogeneity necessary for cohesiveness to, in fact, be present. I have stated my own position. However, I stand by my analysis. In the aggregate there are very few areas of attitudinal cleavage among planners related to formal education, public versus private work context, or differential amounts of experience. Moreover, those cleavages that do exist appear far less relevant than the substantial agreement among these subsets of the profession about so many of the factors inherent in the planning process. Moreover, our initial multivariate analysis in which we entered variables such as experience (in both a continuous and ordinal format), in addition to such variables as sex, age, and membership grade, gives us the assurance that the cohesion we find evident is not a simple artifact of the variables we chose to explore in our contingency-table analysis.

Finally, with respect to the influence of the traditional ideology of planning versus advocacy on the attitudes of the membership at large, the overall assessment is far less definitive. Planners appear committed to the symbols and expressions of *both* advocacy and the traditional ideology of planning. The implications of this finding warrant a far more extensive elaboration, which will be pursued in the final chapter.

Chapter 6

Planners, Politics, and Public Policy

Introduction

It seems appropriate at this juncture to summarize the foregoing analysis and to integrate the findings of this research with that of existing research for the purpose of providing a conceptual and normative analysis of prevailing planning ideology or doctrine. At the onset of this work it was contended that the process of planning and the planner's involvement in it is inherently political. Planners do much to establish the patterned mosaic of metropolitan America. We have observed that part of their impact is through routine decisions that have, in effect, enduring social consequences. Moreover, planners do much to establish the agenda of decision making through the evolution of an ideology in their profession which places great faith in the belief that politics is the art of the possible. As a consequence, planners participate in a process which exercises power because planners can limit the scope of political alternatives to those that meet the criteria of political pragmatism. In this regard, even the intern planner is aware that public-housing projects have clear geographical boundaries whose limits are determined by unarticulated, yet very precise, political performance standards.

In addition, we observed that the bases of many recommendations made by planners are not predicated on a positive theory of planning, but are based, in part, on professional standards whose origins are in the history and heritage of the profession itself. These factors, and the additional concern that planning is characterized by a high degree of administrative discretion, underscore the importance of understanding the planner's conceptions and attitudes toward factors that effect the planning process.

Planners—Their Ideology, Party Identification, and Political Participation

The political profile of the planner emerging from the data indicates that planners are a distinct reference group, compared to the U.S. public, at least with respect to variables of considerable significance to the policy process: ideology, party identification, and political participation. Planners were consistently more liberal and less conservative than a representative sample of the U.S. public. Planners were inordinately Democratic or Independent in partisan self-identification, and both of these relationships remained statistically significant after controlling for education, income, and subjective social class. Finally, planners were found to participate politically at far greater levels than the mass public or those members of the U.S. public possessing similar levels of education, income, and social class.

Such a political profile of planners is sufficient to underscore the fact that planners do, indeed, meet many of the criteria of a political-interest group. Planners are a reference group with specific interests in matters related to public policy. Moreover, they possess the organizational mechanism to state their goals and seek their implementation through the political process. Also, planners are clearly distinct from both the body politic at large, and those subsets that have the most similar socioeconomic profile—at least with respect to considerations of ideology, party preference, and political participation.

Planners' ideology and political-party identification warrant some additional elaboration. Planners manifest the political liberalism imputed to them in the case-study literature. Moreover, they, like other elites, are aware of "what goes with what" in ordering their political world. Planners reflect their liberal idealism in the commitment to the idea that society can control its future evolution in both a rational and equitable fashion through the medium of public authority in the form of positive government. One expression of this support for positive government is manifested in the fact that planners, when compared with the U.S. public, constituted the smallest proportion of conservatives of *any* educational, income, or socioeconomic status group investigated. This fact, however, underscores the dynamic tension between planners and the prevailing American political culture. Yet, one cannot help speculating about the political disadvantage of the planner's liberalism, given the context in which he may find himself; namely, at the state- and local-government level—an environment where the philosophy of laissez faire exercises a clear monopoly in the marketplace of political ideas. Planners, however, appear to recognize this ideological tension and the origins of a more sympathetic forum in the Democratic party. In fact, when compared with the U.S. public, planners constituted the smallest proportion of Republicans of any category of social class, income, or educational level. Indeed, this suggests a cognizance among planners of the fact that their professional standards and essential purposes are inherently incompatible with the policy positions of the Republican party.

The analysis of the political activity of planners indicates that any residual effects on the philosophy of municipal reform, with respect to pejorative attitudes toward political behavior, are not evident in my measures of planners' political activity. Planners can be described as possessing high political consciousness, at least with respect to such activities as voting, persuading others how to vote, attendance at political meetings, and contributions of time and money to political parties. In fact, planners participate at a rate in excess of the U.S. public, controlling for socioeconomic status. Or, in effect, planners report political participation at a greater rate than that of corresponding groups of Americans of upper socioeconomic status.

The second general set of objectives of my study is related to the profile of the attitudes of the planner with respect to the relative influence of the traditional ideology of planning and advocacy. The subsequent section will seek to analyze the extent to which these two strains of planning doctrine or ideology are reflected in the conceptions and attitudes of planners and the extent to which these attitudes constitute the elements of a professional doctrine of sufficient conceptual and logical integrity to provide practicing planners with a clear definition of their function and purpose.

Advocacy and Traditional Planning Doctrine: An Interaction

An analysis of the data from this research suggests that there is a significant discrepancy between either existing planning doctrine or ideology and the attitudes of the planning profession. This discrepancy is manifested in a series of conceptions, adhered to by the membership, about the planning process and the role of the planner. These attitudes suggest a conceptual synthesis produced by the interaction of the traditional ideology of planning and advocacy. In order to substantiate this contention and to lay the framework for my own critique of planning's professional doctrine we will reiterate the central features of both traditional planning ideology and advocacy.

The logic of comprehensive rational planning includes a variety of conceptual linkages, which gives the model not only its viability but its logical consistency. Proponents of comprehensive planning, for example, "must argue that the common interests of society's members are their most important interests and constitute a large proportion of all their interests."[1]

In addition, the comprehensive planner must assume that these interests, expressed as community goals, "can somehow be measured at least roughly as to importance and welded into a single hierarchy of community objectives,"[2] because "it is impossible to plan without some sense of community goals, call them what you will."[3] As noted previously, proponents of the comprehensive-planning model have always believed in the existence of a solitary public interest in which all social groups hold a share. Indeed, assaults by advocacy planners on the existence of a solitary public interest have been equated by one planner with a theoretical question of the magnitude of the "God is Dead" controversy in theology.[4]

The reason for this, of course, is that the public-interest doctrine has served as the foundation, in a conceptual sense, of the planning profession's source of legitimacy; that is, the philosophical justification for the intervention of planning into the domain of what is presumed by laissez faire economics to be the self-correcting efficiency of the market mechanism. The special place of the public-interest doctrine in the traditional ideology of planning is expressed as follows: "Planners have usually viewed themselves as guardians of the public interest, contrasting themselves with other professionals who owe their allegiance to narrower and more clearly defined clients often found in the private sector."[5]

Indeed, according to Alan A. Altshuler comprehensive planners must assume not only the existence of a public interest but the planning profession's "special knowledge of the public interest." To do less, to plan for "the achievement of goals that are general, but still operational,"[6] places the comprehensive planner in the category of a specialist planner, a conceptual contradiction in both fact and form with the ideal of comprehensiveness. The importance of the public-interest doctrine in traditional planning ideology is best expressed in the unique function that the planning profession traditionally has claimed for its practioners. Planners have rejected a definition of their function that limits it to a status of "one among equals." Planning's traditional ideology upholds, in no uncertain terms, the contention that the planner's recommendations are more legitimate, integrative, and comprehensive than those of the subject specialist: "Comprehensive and integrative approaches are the unique quality of the planning profession. It is clear that neither the housing specialist, nor the land-use specialist, nor the transportation specialist, nor the health specialist, nor the education specialist, can be considered urban planners [sic] in situations where a broad strategy involving some or all of these specialties is called for."[7]

In addition, this logically implies that planners' claims to a truly comprehensive perspective, and their ability to integrate the plans of other subject specialists, are the result of some "unique ability" to fashion solutions to development problems in accordance with the requirements of the overall public interest. Also, by implication this unique ability is *not* possessed by other professionals involved in urban development; for example, the landscape architect, civil engineer, or professional city manager. Therefore, the theoretical importance to the comprehensive-planning model of the public-interest doctrine cannot be overemphasized. For example, one planner states, "Professional planners had always noted that their services were pro bono publico. The planners' code of ethics differs from that of the design profession's from which it stemmed because its point of departure is the public interest while the ethics of other professions stress fidelity to the client's interests, usually in the private domain."[8] In the traditional ideology of planning, the client is the public at large and it is the planner who has the special responsibility of protecting the public interest.

The unique ability of the planner to provide a comprehensive perspective on the community's development through his or her special ability to understand the public interest is given theoretical credibility, if not empirical validity, by the assumption that planners can maintain a value-neutral stance in relation to the variety of public-policy choices they must make in order to engage in comprehensive planning. Indeed, this is a logical requirement of the comprehensive-planning model. As Altshuler observes, the justification for comprehensive planning has "generally rested heavily on the thought that planners can resolve conflicts among goals in expert fashion."[9] This is a claim that planners have traditionally been willing to make. "An assumption closely related to the comprehensiveness—coordination—efficiency doctrine poses the planner as the only neutral participant in decision making. If planners are uniquely comprehensive in their outlook and if they seek rational solutions to problems, it follows logically that they simply amalgamate the values of others."[10]

In a previous chapter, the structural and philosophical dimensions of the classical model of planning were established and its association with the philosophy of municipal reform was explored. The linkage between various aspects of the model clearly explicates its implicit and explicit political assumptions. For example, in order for the planning commission to exercise its function as guardian of the public interest there must, by definition, be a public interest. In addition, the rhetoric associated with the master plan indicates that this public interest is superior to other particularistic or pluralistic interests. Accordingly, the master plan exemplifies a comprehensive perspective on community development. The master plan, as such, becomes the medium of expression for long-range goals and the criteria by which short-range-development proposals are evaluated for their conformity to this physical expression of the "public interest."[11] Putting the philosophical assumptions or the political success of the model aside, the model is clearly logical with respect to its assumptions, and provides the practicing planner with an appropriate role definition, as well as a theoretical foundation of sufficient intellectual quality to provide a source of legitimacy for the planning function.

However, as we have observed, the events of the 1960s called into question many of the assumptions of traditional planning doctrine and the classical model of planning. These events helped influence the development of advocacy planning, which is in essence an alternative professional doctrine. The advocacy movement in planning clearly rejected planning's rational technical core, and its comprehensive perspective, as well as the unique ability of the profession to understand and protect the public interest. The advocacy movement replaced a faith in comprehensiveness with a faith in pluralism. Advocacy deemphasized rational technical competence and reemphasized the political-bargaining process and the importance of citizen participation. Advocacy's position with respect to the political neutrality of the planner was to negate even the possibility by insisting that the most relevant questions in planning are those of values, and not those of facts. Moreover, advocacy rejected the reformist ethos of traditional planning ideology in which planning is a kind of bounded rationality within the fixed parameters of a closed system. Advocacy planning also emphasized the importance of engaging in a more encompassing form of social planning. This new form is very distinct from the prevailing American conception in which "planning" is equated with a necessary evil, a form of externality control—for example, a community's commitment to keeping its streets aligned and its suburban areas free of "undesirable influences, nonconforming land uses or people."

In advocacy doctrine, there simply is no unitary public interest in which all social groups hold a share. Therefore, no plan can be politically neutral because the planning function by its nature is inherently value-laden. As such, politics can never be eliminated from the planning process. On the contrary, it should be incorporated into the process by extensive use of citizen input, as well as the planner's willingness to reject the role of technician in favor of that of policy advocate for a given set of opinions. Finally, in advocacy doctrine comprehensive rational planning is held suspect. Advocacy, in effect, rejects vital elements of both comprehensiveness and rationality, and substitutes in their place a preference for a pluralism of both opinion and expertise. Yet, advocacy, like the traditional ideology of planning, is a logical and coherent doctrine that also contains the elements of a professional ideology of sufficient intellectual integrity to provide a role definition for the practicing planner, as well as a theoretical justification for the planner's function.

In a very fundamental sense then, both the traditional ideology of planning and advocacy speak to the central questions of planning. Moreover, each displays the elements of a professional doctrine of sufficient intellectual integrity to provide a theoretical framework that is conceptually sound or logical with respect to its assumptions. This is not to say, of course, that the traditional ideology of planning and advocacy do not offer decidedly distinct conceptions of the appropriate professional world view. Indeed, a professional doctrine that stresses planning's comprehensive focus, its rational core, its value-neutral perspective on the public interest, is at great variance with a conception of planning that underscores its essentially value-laden, as well as political, nature. Unfortunately, the attitudes of planners appear to indicate they believe planning doctrine can and should reflect either or both of these rather diverse realities. The following sections will seek to qualify this contention.

First of all, the acceptance of two central features of advocacy planning has significant support within the planning profession. The majority of planners either disagree or are uncertain as to the existence of a solitary public interest in which all social groups hold a share. Moreover, the majority of planners disagree with the contention that planners, by virtue of professional training, are in the best position to be neutral judges of the public interest. These two contentions, in one sense, manifest a sophistication among planners with respect to the political process. Specifically, if planning does indeed share the commonality with "politics" that this study has sought to establish, then the concept of the "neutral expert" in the allocation of values in accordance with some ephemeral public interest is, indeed, a contradiction in terms. Nonetheless, this substantial challenge to the public-interest doctrine by planners requires some response to Ernest Erber's eloquently phrased question: "If there is no unifying public interest to be served, if the science and art of planning is to be placed in the service of each special interest group in a pluralistic society, what happens to the concept of comprehensiveness?"[12]

If there is no solitary public interest to be served, planners cannot, obviously, claim a unique ability to coordinate the various physical, social, and economic elements of development into a comprehensive plan that accords with an overriding public interest. Moreover, the attitudes that planners express have a variety of implications for the logical coherence of *any* planning doctrine. For example, since only a minority accept the contention that planners, by virtue of their professional training, are in the best position to be neutral judges of the public interest, how can planners legitimately claim the function of evaluating the plans of other specialists? Such claims have, by definition, been predicated on the presumed ability of the planner to maintain a comprehensive focus, one that could more objectively integrate the various elements of a community's plan, so as to serve the "public interest."

Clearly, the planning profession's traditional defense of its position has rested on the existence of this overriding public interest and its ability to fashion objectively plans in accordance with it. If planners do not accept this role, they are reduced to the status of an interest group with specific policy preferences. They are, in effect, "one among equals." Without an overriding public interest or the ability to be objective in the integration of the specialist's plans, planners *are* specialists. And, while that speciality may be at the most generalized level of the impact of land uses, by default only the politician can legitimately claim a comprehensive perspective on the public interest.[13]

In addition, the planner's conception of the planning process rejects the very positive (i.e., rational/technical) definitions of the endeavor evident in much of traditional planning ideology. Planners in an overwhelming proportion accept a conception of the planning process that underscores its value-laden nature. Given an implicit continuum ranging from a primarily technical to a primarily value-oriented definition of planning, all but a small minority of the profession define planning as a process in which planners *purposely* integrate technical advice on the proposed use of community resources and recommend choices based on value judgments, as well as technical expertise. While such a contention is hardly surprising to administrative theorists who have traditionally accepted the inescapable interaction of facts and values in any form of decision making, it is, however, significant that planners are so skewed toward the acceptance of such a value-laden conception of the planning process. It is significant because so much of the planning movement's philosophical justification of itself was as a "rational" alternative to the vulgarities of the political process where values and special interests rather than reason dominated public policy.

Planners' conception of the planning process clearly manifests the rejection of another important element of their municipal reform heritage; namely, the belief in the essentially rational/technical core of the planning function. What is also clear, of course, is that since most planners concur with a conception of the planning process in which value judgments loom significantly, they must admit that their public-policy recommendations are based on general evaluative rationality, "the capacity to evaluate means in the absence of clear and unambiguous knowledge of ends."[14] This is not to suggest surprise at the notion that planners, or any other group, working in a multivariate environment characterized by imperfect knowledge and bounded by a fragmented political system could function otherwise. It does, however, create a problem for the planner seeking to influence public policy in accordance with some comprehensive objective. Referring to those who practice general evaluative rationality, Altshuler observes: "Like any goal generalist he will rarely be able to base his ultimate defense of any proposal on reasoning as tight as one would expect from an engineer defending recommendations within his specialty."[15]

The planner's ability to produce a direct impact on public policy is some function of his capacity to demonstrate, in at least a logical fashion, the elements of a professional doctrine which bear upon the justification for accepting the planner's contention that he is not "one among equals" but rather possesses some unique ability, absent in other urban specialists, to integrate the proposals of those specialists in a comprehensive fashion and in accordance with the public interest. The inability of the profession to evolve such a framework places the planner at a very real disadvantage—given the function the profession continues to prescribe for him, that of a comprehensive planner.

In addition, the impact of advocacy planning can also be recognized in the conceptions of planners with respect to the output of the planning process, that is, the master plan. Planners have apparently taken to heart the contention that planning, in the first instance, is a statement about some future desired state of affairs or objectives. As such, of course, it is simply a synonym for public policy and primarily a question of values. Indeed, the overwhelming majority of the profession reject the political neutrality of master plans equating them instead with any public-policy output, namely, one that rewards some interests and deprives others. This is at great variance with the neutral and comprehensive assessment of community objectives, fashioned in a rational manner, and expressive of the whole community's interests propagated by the traditional ideology of planning. It is also another expression of a central theme in advocacy, the inherently political rather than rational or technical nature of the planning process.

Nonetheless, planners cling tenaciously to elements of their traditional ideology. Specifically, the majority of all planners reject the role of the planner as a policy advocate, accepting instead the role of technical staff advisor. This is more in accordance with the profession's traditional role definition, one in which the planner offers technical and policy advice but does not advocate specific policy positions. It is, in substance, a rejection of the more political role envisioned by advocacy planning in which the planner openly espouses particular policy preferences on behalf of specific public or private clients. While the term *client* was originally intended generically, it has, in fact, become associated with those groups traditionally excluded from both the planning and the political process. The fact that planners, as a majority, reject the role of advocate is, perhaps, not surprising. The mobilization of bias at the state and local level, particularly in public organizations, does not generally support such endeavors.

However, there appears to be another side to this very practical matter. As Francine Rabinovitz contends, the role of the professional planner is vital in the fragmented metropolitan governmental arena. Her observations of the planning process lead her to argue that the skills required of the planner in all but the most cohesive political systems are "to varying degrees, the skills of the politician."[16] One could suggest, and we do, that planners who bemoan the lack of effective planning should reflect carefully on the utility of the role of technician in a process which, by the planner's own analysis, is essentially political.

In addition, planners still profess strong commitment to the ideal of comprehensiveness. Indeed, it appears that the concept is very ingrained in the consciousness of the profession. The majority of planners, as the literature suggests, are clearly convinced that comprehensiveness dictates that *all* features of a community's development—the physical, economic, and social—should be the legitimate subject of concern of public planning agencies. This suggests a deviation from the early foundations of the profession based on a design orientation and reputedly characterized by environmental determinism. Planners, it seems, have become cognizant of the inseparability of the elements of the city. They are aware that planning based exclusively on a design or land-use criterion is not comprehensive in the very sense that planners themselves employ the term.

Moreover, the majority of planners express a strong commitment to the establishment of a federal agency responsible for comprehensive planning on a national basis. In some respects these attitudes are not surprising. Planners have traditionally been accused of supporting larger grants of power to public authority and advocating proposals that expand the size of government and remove certain planning considerations from the ordinary influence of interest groups.[17] However, it must be underscored that all political systems in their authoritative allocation of values engage in national planning, either through intent or by default. The question, then, is not whether such a function as national or social planning exists, but rather, how adequately it is performed.[18] Some planning theorists realize this and describe the failures of social planning in such a fashion as to express their own normative preferences. "There are very grave inequities resulting from the way we perform our social planning: the social needs of some groups go unmet; social goods are inequitably distributed."[19] In addition, it is also clear, as indicated previously, that planners contend they can come closer to achieving comprehensive and rational solutions to planning problems than any other profession. It seems, therefore, that planners' overwhelming support for the creation of a comprehensive planning agency at the federal level can be best understood as an expression of their opposition to the existing participants in that process—special-interest groups and politicians—and, given planners' demonstrated liberalism, to the distributional outcomes of American social planning.

The last aspect of planners' faith in comprehensiveness is expressed in the majority of the profession's belief that comprehensive rational planning by government *is* possible in a pluralistic society. We suggest these attitudes are another manifestation of the contradictory influence on planning doctrine that has emerged as a result of the interaction of strong tendencies toward pluralism engendered by the advocacy movement, and the essentially incompatible philosophy dictated by the traditional ideology of planning. Indeed, the theoretical basis of advocacy planning is predicated on pluralism, and as we shall see, the philosophy of pluralism is essentially incompatible with the assumptions of comprehensive rational planning.

Ernest Erber, for example, has observed that pluralism is essentially "antiplanning."[20] In many respects he has isolated the dynamic tension evident in the attitudes of planning practitioners, that is, the inherent contradiction between the ideal of comprehensive rational planning and the realities of American pluralism. Pluralism, or interest-group liberalism, as a doctrine is, according to Theodore J. Lowi, the "amalgam of capitalism, statism, and liberalism."[21] Primary in this synthesis is the belief in the automatic or self-correcting society. Predicated on the economic concept of equilibrium, pluralism postulates a cosmology incompatible with the doctrine of comprehensive planning. As Lowi observes, "It should thus be evident that pluralist theory today militates against the idea of separate government. Separate government violates the basic principle of the automatic political society."[22] In this sense, then, pluralism reacts against the deliberate establishment of social goals, which is a clear prerequisite of comprehensive planning: "Liberal governments cannot plan. Planning requires law, choice, priorities, moralities. Liberalism replaces planning with bargaining."[23] Pluralism as both a normative ideal or as an expression of empirical reality mitigates against the ideal of comprehensive rational planning. Indeed, pluralism and comprehensive rational planning are based on assumptions about the nature of political reality that are clearly bipolar. As mentioned previously, pluralism and advocacy planning envision a political system composed of interest groups that produce equilibrium, in a policy sense, through the interaction of various self-interests in the political process. As Lowi observes, in a fashion reminiscent of Adam Smith, the presumed policy equilibrium that emerges from the process is a pluralist version of the public interest. What is also clear by implication is that a society which automatically achieves perfect policy equilibrium (i.e., a society which is self-correcting) does not need to engage in comprehensive planning, particularly in the sense that planners use the term. Moreover, the pluralistic concept of the state or public authority is one that rejects the concept of separate and purposeful government, regarding power and control as properties of the state to be held suspect and resisted rather than to be looked upon as a mechanism for providing rational planning.

Proponents of comprehensive rational planning, on the other hand, postulate a conception of the state as an organic whole with a public interest that is, metaphorically, larger than the sum of the individual interests of the body politic. From the comprehensive rational planning perspective the public interest is an operational criterion to which specific policy alternatives can be compared. To the pluralist, the public interest is merely an expression of the policy equilibrium produced by the political process. Interest-group pluralism, as Lowi notes, replaces planning with bargaining and the establishment of deliberate goals with the evolution of policy. Pluralism is, in effect, the political expression of laissez-faire economics.[24]

In addition, pluralism and advocacy reject the faith that proponents of comprehensive rational planning have in the ability of centralized political control to rationalize the resource-allocation process. They do so on two counts. First, as noted previously, their view of separate government suggests that governmental power is to be both feared and resisted. Secondly, pluralism contends that the methodology of comprehensive planning requires too much of the intellectual and capital resources available to most human beings. They reject rationality in the first instance, as the appropriate criterion for decision making, underscoring the essentially value laden nature of choices associated with comprehensive planning. They claim, in effect, that only the marketplace of political bargaining contains sufficient information to generate efficient policy. Even the respective positions on policy between the proponents of comprehensive rational planning versus pluralism are essentially divergent. To the pluralist, good policy is that which includes all participants capable of affecting the success of the policy—in other words, consensus. As such, policy does not follow a rational decision-making model (i.e., it is not comprehensive), but is incremental in that it reflects slight deviations from currently existing policy. This is at great variance with the comprehensive rational planning model, which envisions policy as measurable with respect to some criterion. This criterion is usually some conception of the public interest that is rational in the means-versus-ends sense, and inclusive in that it is based on a calculus which includes all relevant alternatives.

Planning Ideology and Public Policy: An Empirical and Normative Critique of the New Professional Doctrine in Planning

The implications of the assumptions of pluralism for comprehensive rational planning doctrine are clear. Pluralism both as a normative ideal or as an empirical reality is predicated on assumptions that negate or operate in opposition to the requirements of comprehensive rational planning. As such, the impact of advocacy, which *accepts* and is *predicated* on many of the same assumptions as pluralism, has produced contradictions in planning doctrine that sap it of the capacity to be logical, given the assumptions all theoretical systems must make. The dynamic tension introduced into planning doctrine by the assaults on traditional planning ideology by advocacy are reflected in the attitudes of the planners themselves. These attitudes are the result of a theoretical synthesis, which itself represents the origins of a new professional doctrine in planning, one that we suggest is less coherent and less useful than either of the original doctrines alone.

Moreover, we also contend that the attitudes of planners manifest the existence of some very severe conceptual gaps in the professional doctrine of planning. More specifically, what we have called the new professional doctrine within planning—an amalgam of traditional planning ideology and advocacy—really lacks the logical rigor necessary to be considered a professional doctrine at all. While the traditional ideology of planning and advocacy are based on a series of normative assumptions that are more or less tenable to various schools of thought, each possesses the characteristic of being logical with respect to its assumptions. An evaluation of the attitudes of planners in the aggregate indicates that planners are committed to conceptions of the planning process, which in a holistic sense fail to reinforce each other logically.

For example, since the overwhelming majority of planners agree that the outputs of the planning process, and that process itself, are inherently value-laden, and since only a minority of planners believe in a solitary public interest that they as professional planners can objectively assess, in what logical manner can they justify comprehensive rational planning as an alternative to the pluralist political process? If there is no solitary public interest to serve as a criterion for individual policy choices, does it not follow that the pluralistic concept of policy equilibrium is clearly superior to any deliberate planning of policy objectives by any particular interest or professional group?

Moreover, in what meaningful way are the comprehensive rational planners' recommendations for a community likely to be taken as credible, when such planners accept central components of an ideology—pluralism—which contends that the "best planning" is the result of policy formulated by various interest groups and evolved from the self-correcting pluralist bargaining process, rather than through the deliberate establishment of social goals?

In addition, the planning profession has traditionally eschewed the status of "one among equals" in the development process and supported this contention with a professional doctrine that indicated a special ability to assess the public interest objectively. In what logical manner, given the rejection of this doctrine by all but a minority of planners, can planners justify their special status as comprehensive planners vis-à-vis any other urban specialist? In other words, if planners are really specialists, there is no theoretical or logical reason to assume that their public-policy prescriptions are any more comprehensive than, for example, that of the land-use economist from whose methodology planners have borrowed extensively, if not at times exclusively. Moreover, if such is the case, is it not better to stipulate it rather than to claim for planners a comprehensive and rational focus predicated on an emerging professional doctrine which has, by virtue of incorporating elements of both traditional planning ideology and advocacy, been rendered logically inconsistent?

And, if planners have been convinced of the validity of central aspects of advocacy as a normative ideal, why the continued emphasis on comprehensive rational planning? What can comprehensive rational planning mean in a pluralist framework, outside of the attempt to minimize market externalities? It seems clear that planners must either forsake the ideal of comprehensive rational planning or adjust their professional doctrine to more adequately reflect it. Again, we suggest that the consequence of the interaction between the traditional ideology of planning and the normative assumptions of advocacy is a new and emerging planning doctrine reflected in the attitudes of planners, which has through its very lack of logical consistency (to say nothing of its normative or empirical quality) produced a type of theoretical cognitive dissonance that provides the practicing planner with very little in the way of a coherent professional role definition or an ideological framework capable of addressing specific policy dilemmas.

The practical importance of this theoretical issue is exemplified in an article focusing on ethics and values in planning. Peter Marcuse describes the curious dilemma associated with the construction of the Pam Am building in New York, which "added two million square feet of office space to one of the most congested business areas of the world."[25] The building won both a condemnation for land speculation and praise for good design by the American Institute of Architects. Marcuse utilizes the example heuristically to raise the question of the planning profession's own hypothetical response to the issue of the Pan Am building, given the ethical standards that emerge from professional planning doctrine. Referring to a hypothetical group of young planners seeking condemnation of the city-planning director, he states:

The Young Turks argued that the planners should not only have refused to work on the Pan Am project but should also have appeared before the city planning commission to point out its dangers. Expulsion from AIP was asked as the very least penalty for failure to do so.

Evidence presented included a statement from the director of the city planning commission. He himself had recommended approval of the project because he knew that at least four of the five members of the commission favored it. However, citing reasons of congestion, pollution, and inefficiencies of scale, as well as unfair competition to other developments elsewhere in the city, he felt it was against the public interest.

Amid substantial newspaper publicity, the executive committee ruled against the complainants. It found that neither the canons nor the "Guidelines on Social Responsibility" were part of the "Rules of Discipline" of the profession or intended to be enforced by it. For AIP to attempt to arrogate to itself the decision as to whether a given building should be built would be a usurpation of the democratic decision-making process which the committee could not condone.

An editorial in the leading New York newspaper the following day commented on the hypocrisy of the planning profession's claim to serve the public interest and suggested that honesty might dictate repeal by AIP of all references to the public interest anywhere in its canons.[26]

At the heart of this dilemma, of course, is the answer to the question, What is the public interest? As Melville Branch observes, identifying the public interest, as well as giving it an operational definition, is a vital concern for the planning profession.[27] Without an operational definition of the public interest, democratic theory clearly stipulates that elected public officials are the only group legitimately entrusted to determine the public interest.

This is not to suggest a sincere commitment of politicians toward the pursuit of the public interest in practice, but rather that democratic principles, as well as political pragmatism, demand that planning justify claims with respect to any unique abilities in evaluating the overall public interest. This is required because the politician's claim to a unique ability to understand the overall public interest is ex officio, and must, in a democratic political system, remain superior to that of any other group of interests without some compelling logic to the contrary. Planners' attitudes toward the public-interest doctrine suggest that logic may not be forthcoming. While the notion of leaving the determination of the public interest to the politician might strike certain planners as essentially unacceptable, it remains incumbent on the planning profession itself to suggest why this should not be the case.

Indeed, if the local political systems are inherently dominated by special interests (and pluralism as a philosophy not only accepts this, but attributes to it a type of legitimacy), and the planning profession rejects the ideal of a unitary public interest in which all groups hold a share, then planners have by default left the determination of the public interest to special-interest groups, of which planners are but one of many. For example, without an operational definition of the public interest, how can a planner justify to any constituency that a given piece of land is best left in its natural state rather than developed to its highest and best use? Such questions are essentially normative and the relative merits of each alternative cannot be logically compared to each other without some public-interest standard. Clearly, such a standard will implicitly require weighting of particular values in some priority scheme, because the most important features of the public-interest question are normative, and will always remain normative.

The interaction between traditional planning ideology and advocacy, and the inconsistencies and contradictions it has created with respect to any emerging professional doctrine, have and will continue to produce consequences similar to that described by Marcuse. Indeed, the case-study literature abounds with planners' own laments about the failure of planning to be comprehensive, rational, or effective. Moreover, this is not surprising since, as we have seen, planners themselves are committed to conceptions of the political process that preclude any real progress toward comprehensive planning.

The theoretical dualism evident among planners may explain why so many American master plans are expressive of two rather diverse conceptions of reality. The first is the logical elegance of the brightly colored plan that is comprehensive in conception, utopian in substance, apparently rational in its delineation of the use of land by subject-matter categories, and generally imbued with some muted reference to the plan's conformity with the "public interest." The second conception is the actual development of the community, which evolves according to the demands of the market, and which is for the most part independent of the designs of the plan.

The results of our analysis suggest two dominant prescriptions. One is clearly that the planning profession should endeavor to address the very real deficiencies inherent in a professional doctrine, which Judd and Mendelson contend has traditionally "extolled the profession more than it described the tasks and roles of its practitioners."[28] The ideal of comprehensive rational planning and the realities of the assumptions of pluralism are one obvious starting point. Resolving this question is important, we suggest, not only because of some quest for theoretical symmetry, but because the current situation is such that planners are inculcated with and empirically committed to an ideal of comprehensiveness and rationality *in theory* that tends to have very little relationship to their experience *in practice*.

Secondly, we suggest that the practical importance of good theory has been very well stated by Lord Keynes: "The ideas of economists and political philosophers, both when they are right and when they are wrong, are more powerful than is commonly understood. . . . Practical men, who believe themselves to be quite exempt from any intellectual influences, are usually the slaves of some defunct economist. Madmen in authority, who hear voices in the air, are distilling their frenzy from some academic scribbler of a few years back."[29] Indeed, it is not the unassailable empirical "truths" of either Marxism or laissez faire economics that have resulted in their respective influence and popularity. It is rather that both are coherent theoretical systems which are logical with respect to their assumptions. Moreover, both presume to explain and justify the present, as well as to predict the future.

Clearly, one important element in the planning profession's ability to shape public policy in the future will reside in its capacity to provide a sufficient justification of both an empirical and normative character to convince others that recommendations for a community, made by the planner, are truly more legitimate and more likely to produce a "better planned" environment than the recommendations of the civil engineer, economist, or politician.

In this regard, we reiterate the call of Altshuler for a normative theory of planning that focuses on the purposes of planning. Planners seem to have taken to heart Davidoff and Reiner's contention that "there is nothing in the factual side of the planner's work which in the first instance can reveal to him the desired nature of the future."[30] This contention is not only abundantly clear, but in accordance with the conceptual framework of this research. However, we contend that while planners are cognizant of this fact, the dynamic tension evident in planning doctrine has obscured another extremely important reality to them; that is, there is nothing in the factual side of *anyone's* work which in the first instance can determine the preferred nature of the future; or, that the value-laden aspects of planning are not the unique burden of the planning profession.

Moreover, there are precedents in the planning experience of other nations to justify the evolution of a normative theory of planning. Donald L. Foley in his discussion of British town planning, outlines the manner in which the British have approached the dilemma of values in the planning process. He outlines the main elements of town planning ideology, which are, in effect, statements about the purposes of planning that are not in the first instance subject to exclusively empirical resolution. For example,

1. Town planning's main task is to reconcile competing claims for the use of limited land so as to provide a consistent, balanced and orderly arrangement of land uses.
2. Town planning's central function is to provide a good (or better) physical environment; a physical environment of such good quality is essential for the promotion of healthy and civilized life.
3. Town planning, as a part of a broader social program, is responsible for providing the physical basis for better urban life.[31]

However, rather than avoid the implications of these rather general objectives he goes on to observe, in the case of the first objective: "It reflects the distinct suspicion that the land market has not worked for the public interest."[32] In regard to the third: "This ideological view accepts, and seems to relate town planning to, the conviction that small, or at least most middle-sized, communities of houses with gardens are to be encouraged. It sees the continued growth of the very large city clusters or conurbanizations as a distinct threat to various British held values."[33] These statements express a view of city life and urban spatial arrangements which are, in the first instance, simply an expression of values or the elements of a normative theory of planning.

The critique by Duncan MacRae, Jr. of the tendency of the social sciences in general to eliminate ethical or normative propositions from their discourse is extremely relevant to planning.

This de-emphasis on the discussion of values has been furthered by an emulation of certain aspects of natural science. According to this view, the advances in the natural sciences have resulted not merely from precision of language and symbolism, but also from elimination of propositions not testable by scientific procedures. Thus sentences inadmissible to observational test were considered meaningless and dismissed from "positive" social science. It was proper to eliminate propositions that purported to be testable empirically, but could not conceivably be tested. But the dismissal of other sentences—particularly ethical sentences—from the recognized discourse of most of the social sciences has left these disciplines without sufficient guidance in dealing with valuative problems or resolving conflicts of values.[34]

MacRae goes on to outline the elements of a model of ethical discourse which can guide the conduct of actors in the social policy process: "Central to them will be the requirement for that particular realm of interdisciplinary communication within the social sciences, that before anyone enters into ethical argument he render his own ethical system clear, consistent and general—modifying it in detail if necessary."[35]

We suggest that a normative theory of planning, which is clear with respect to its assumptions, is vital to the planning profession. Such a professional doctrine would not seek to avoid values, but rather would stipulate them in an a priori fashion. Such a set of normative principles could provide planning with a framework in which more specific concerns related to general questions of the trade-offs between efficiency and equity could be addressed. For example, simple economic efficiency justifies the traditional practice of American strip mining, which results in a scarred and ravaged landscape. It is only the introduction of social-equity concerns which generates questions of social cost that lead to alternative policy considerations. A clear normative theory, stipulated on well-clarified and logcially consistent principles, could provide the profession with a criterion by which to respond to dilemmas such as the Pan Am building, or the call for regional government as a mechanism for achieving rational and equitable planning. It is our contention that the formulation of such principles in planning is a necessary, if not sufficient, condition for the evolution of a planning doctrine which possesses the theoretical integrity to have a directive impact on public policy, rather than legitimizing foregone conclusions.

Finally, it is no doubt important for planners to resolve these concerns under existing structures of planning; that is, a planning function which is primarily local in character, physical in focus, and advisory with respect to its formal political power. However, it becomes imperative that planners resolve these concerns in a political climate in which even corporate presidents glibly speak of national planning for the United States. Because if planning is elevated in terms of formal authority and jurisdiction, the nature of many of the political concerns raised in this book will change only in degree and not in essence. For example, the question of the public interest, its nature, dimension, and definition becomes exponentially more important if the planning policy impacts on a national rather than local constituency. As we have said previously, the real concerns surrounding the predictions of what "planning" will be like in the political sphere constitute the greatest anxiety about the spread of this orientation toward public policy. To those concerned about the vitality of democratic institutions, this is as it should be.

American National Planners' Study (Survey of Planners) Questionnaire

Institute for Research in Social Science

Survey of Planners

Dear AIP Member:

As you are no doubt aware, the planning profession has been in the vortex of the controversy engendered by the critical issues of societal growth and change in America during the sixties and early seventies. The profession itself has undergone changes in response to the new demands and challenges that have and will confront planning in the United States. However, information regarding the individual planner's attitudes about factors inherent in the planning process is highly insufficient. Only you, as a professional planner, can provide this essential information, which is the reason we ask you to respond to the enclosed questionnaire.

This questionnaire is also being sent to a selected number of your colleagues in the AIP throughout the nation. We believe that you will find the substance of the questions both interesting and relevant. In consideration of the important demands placed upon your time, we have constructed the questions so that they can be answered with check marks, numbers, or other simple designations.

For your convenience we have enclosed a self-addressed, stamped envelope on which your name appears, exclusively for the purpose of reducing the costs of a second mailing to those who have not returned the original questionnaire. All information, however, is strictly confidential and will be used for academic research purposes only.

Will you please take the time to fill out the questionnaire? Your cooperation is greatly appreciated and your response is eagerly awaited.

Sincerely yours,

Michael L. Vasu
Associate AIP

National Problems and Priorities

1. We are faced with a great many problems in this country, none of which can be solved easily or inexpensively. Below are listed some of these problems. For each one please indicate whether you think we're spending too much money on it, too little, or about the right amount.

	too much	about right	too little
a. Improving and protecting the environment.			
b. Solving the problems of the big cities.			
c. Halting the rising crime rate.			
d. Improving the condition of Blacks.			
e. The military, armaments, and defense.			
f. Welfare.			

Issues in Planning

1. A number of planners have expressed different opinions about the question of whether planning possesses the ethical and intellectual requirements to be considered a profession: in the same sense as the more traditional professions, Law, Medicine, etc. Do you agree or disagree that planning is a profession?
   __ strongly agree   __ agree   __ undecided   __ disagree
   __ strongly disagree
2. What do you think should be the legitimate subject of concern of public planning agencies?
   __ the physical development of a community *exclusively*.
   __ *both* the physical and economic development of a community.
   __ the physical, economic, and social development of a community.
3. Do you think there exists today a body of knowledge and techniques sufficient to constitute a theory of planning?   __ yes   __ no
4. Do you think the United States should establish a federal agency responsible for comprehensive planning on a national basis?   __ yes   __ no

Your Position and Your Agency

1. By what type of agency are you presently employed?
   __ public   __ private

2. By which one of the following agencies are you employed?

   __ city   __ state   __ industry or business

   __ county   __ federal government __ college, university,

   __ metropolitan/   __ planning   or research

      regional   consultant   other _____

3. Please indicate which one of the following statements best describes your conception of what planning is:

   __ Ours is strictly a technical activity of applying the profession's engineering, statistical, and design tools to a given project or problem in order to determine a feasible solution and the blueprint for its accomplishment.

   __ Our recommendations are mostly technical but inherent in them are some unavoidable policy judgments on how the community's physical plan should be developed.

   __ We purposely integrate technical advice on the proposed use of community resources and recommend choices based on value judgments, as well as technical expertise.

Planners and the Planning Process

To what extent do you agree or disagree with the following statements? Mark the space above the abbreviated opinion category that best corresponds to your view. (SA = strongly agree; A = agree; U = undecided; D = disagree; SD = strongly disagree.)

1. Every government planner of integrity, no matter how specialized, must be guided by some conception of the public interest.

                                                  SA A U D SD

2. There is a solitary public interest in which all social and political groups hold a share.

                                                  SA A U D SD

3. Elections effectively serve the function of making local politicians accountable to the voters for their actions.

                                                  SA A U D SD

4. Citizen-participation groups involved in the public planning process are representative of the interests of their communities.

                                                  SA A U D SD

5. If communities are going to achieve truly comprehensive planning, the authority to control development must rest ultimately with the planning agency.

                                                  SA A U D SD

6. No plan produced by a public agency is neutral but benefits some interests and discriminates against others.

                                                  SA A U D SD

7. Comprehensive rational planning by the government is virtually impossible in a pluralistic society.

                                                  SA A U D SD

8. Politics can never be removed from planning because power in a community is distributed among
those who can best mobilize resources.

9. Urban planners, by virtue of their professional
training, are in the best position to be neutral
judges of the public interest.

SA A U D SD

10. The urban planner should *not* openly strive to sell
his plans by being an active participant in the
political process.

SA A U D SD

11. The urban planner in his capacity as an advisor
should ultimately accept the goals submitted by
the elected representatives of the voters.

SA A U D SD

12. The urban planner should base his recommendations on professional, rather than political, criteria.

SA A U D SD

SA A U D SD

Education

1. What was your major subject in undergraduate school? _____

2. Have you done graduate work in planning?
   __ No
   __ Yes, but work for a degree in
   planning not completed
   __ Yes, but toward a degree other
   than planning

   __ Yes, master's degree
   in planning granted
   __ Yes, doctoral degree
   in planning granted

3. If you have done graduate work toward a degree *other* than planning,
   please fill in the following:
   Major: _____
   Degree granted?   __ No   __ Yes—specify degree(s) _____

Planning Effectiveness and Structural Forms

1. In order for planning to function most effectively:
   a. Which *one* of the following forms of *local* government do you think is
      most desirable?
      __ *mayor council/manager* Administration of the community is integrated
      under the control of a professional administrator, a manager, hired by
      an elected council. Policy-making responsibility is shared by the
      council and the mayor. The mayor, who is either directly elected or
      chosen from within the council, has no formal veto power.
      __ *commission* The administration and policy-making functions of the
      community are both under the control of the mayor and elected
      commissioners, each of whom serves individually as the head of one

of the community's administrative agencies. The mayor is selected from within the council and has no formal veto power.

___ *weak mayor/council* The administration and policy-making functions of the community are both under the control of the mayor and council. The mayor, however, shares the administrative and policy-making responsibilities with the council and elected administrative agency heads. The mayor and council are directly elected.

___ *strong major/council* The administrative responsibility is concentrated in the hands of the mayor, who appoints and dismisses department heads. The mayor and council are directly elected and the mayor has very strong policy-making powers *vis-à-vis* the council.

b. Which *one* of the following *local* election schemes do you think is most desirable?

___ *non-partisan elections* Candidates have no political party designations.

___ *partisan elections.*

c. Which *one* of the following types of *local* representation do you think is most desirable?

___ *at-large elections* municipal officials elected by and representing the community as a whole.

___ *district or ward* municipal officials elected by and representing a single constituency.

Sources of Legitimacy

1. A number of planners have expressed different justifications or sources of legitimacy in order to defend to society at large their authority to "plan," (*i.e.*, impose restrictions on property rights, to intervene in various aspects of private enterprise, etc.). The following statements embody some of these sources of legitimacy. Please read all of them before answering the question *a* below.

___ A planner's source of legitimacy is his or her rational-technical knowledge and expertise.

___ A planner's source of legitimacy is his or her profession's more comprehensive view of the public interest.

___ A planner's source of legitimacy is his or her position as a public employee who serves the elected respresentatives of the community.

___ A planner's source of legitimacy is his or her position as an advocate for the goals of a client(s).

a. Please rank the above sources of legitimacy in order of importance to *you* as a planner (1 = most important; 2 = second most important; 3 = third most important; 4 = least important) by placing the appropriate number next to the corresponding statement.

Politics and Politicians

To what extent do you agree or disagree with the following statements? Check in the box below the opinion category that best corresponds to your view.

	strongly agree	agree somewhat	agree slightly	disagree slightly	disagree somewhat	disagree strongly
1. In order to get nominated, most candidates for political office have to make basic compromises and undesirable commitments.						
2. Politicians spend most of their time getting reelected or reappointed.						
3. Money is the most important factor influencing public policies.						
4. A large number of city and county politicians are political hacks.						
5. People are very frequently manipulated by politicians.						
6. Politicians represent the general interest *more* frequently than they represent special interests.						

Role of the Government

To what extent do you agree or disagree with the following statements? Mark the space above the abbreviated opinion category that best corresponds to your view. (SA = strongly agree; A = agree; U = undecided; D = disagree; SD = strongly disagree.)

1. If cities and towns around the country need help to build more schools, the government in Washington ought to give them the money they need.

       SA A U D SD

2. If minorities are not getting fair treatment in jobs and housing, the government in Washington should see to it that they do.

SA A U D SD

3. The government in Washington ought to see to it that everybody who wants to work can find a job.

SA A U D SD

4. The government should leave things like electric power and housing for private business to handle.

SA A U D SD

5. The government ought to help people get doctors and hospital care at low cost.

SA A U D SD

Background Characteristics

1. In what year were you born? 19___
2. In what year did you first begin work as a planner? 19___
3. What is your sex? ___ male ___ female
4. Generally speaking, do you consider yourself to be a ___ Democrat, ___ Republican, or ___ Independent?
4a. If Independent, are you closer to the ___ Democratic or ___ Republican party?
5. Generally how would you characterize your own political beliefs?
   ___ very liberal ___ moderate ___ very conservative
   ___ liberal ___ conservative
6. In the elections for president since you have been old enough to vote, would you say you have voted in ___ all of them, ___ most of them, ___ some of them, or ___ none of them?
7. The following are political activities in which some people participate. Please indicate those in which you have participated.
   a. During elections do you ever try to show people why they should vote for one of the parties or candidates? ___ yes ___ no
   b. In the past three or four elections have you attended any political meetings or rallies? ___ yes ___ no
   c. In the past three or four years have you contributed money to a political party or candidate or to any other political cause? ___ yes ___ no
   d. Have you ever done work for one of the parties or candidates? ___ yes ___ no
8. Please indicate your present AIP membership grade: ___ full ___ associate ___ intern

THANK YOU FOR YOUR ASSISTANCE

Scales and Indexes

Measures of Formal Education

The study employed two measures of formal planning education. The first is a measure which utilizes a criterion of presence or absence of formal planning degree (Formed 3). The second measures *exposure* to formal planning education (Formed 4). In all tables presented in the book except two, Formed 3 is utilized. However, the footnotes of the chapters—as well as the actual text in some cases—report the findings that resulted from using Formed 4. The results, in almost all cases, were identical. The specific construction of the variables proceeded as follows:

Formed 3 *(planning degree)* Select if undergraduate major or graduate major in planning, assign one, otherwise assign zero. The frequency distribution for the variable is presented in Table 1.

Formed 4 *(exposure to formal planning education)* Select if undergraduate major in planning or if planner had done *any* graduate work in planning, whether toward a formal degree in planning or not, assign one, otherwise zero. The frequency distribution for the variable is presented in Table 2. See Appendix A for the exact question.

The Planner's Role Index

The planner's role index consists of four questions arrayed in Likert fashion. The principal intensity structure relates to concerns developed in chapters two and three; namely, a role definition essentially technical/advisory, versus policy advocate. Questions utilized are 9, 10, 11, 12, under "Planners and the Planning Process" of the questionnaire in Appendix A.

Table 1

Frequency for Formal Planning Degree

Formed 3	Code	Absolute Frequency	Adjusted Frequency (%)
No Formal Degree	0	325	43.0
Formal Degree	1	431	57.0
Missing Data	9	19	Missing
Total		775	100.0

The construction of the instrument proceeded as follows: the original value of the index was initialized to zero, and subsequent values were added on the basis of strong support for the variable; i.e., IF (URPLNACT GE 4) ROLEA = ROLEA + 1, etc. This produced a set of five values (0, 1, 2, 3, 4) arrayed along a continuum expressing strong support for a technical role at the lower values (0, 1) of the continuum and strong support for a more policy oriented role at the upper range of values (3, 4). The frequency distribution is presented in Table 3. Analysis of the values utilized criteria developed in Allen L. Edwards, *Techniques of Attitude Scale Construction*. Evaluation was made of the normal deviate weighting of response categories. The result was a decision to collapse the distribution into three categories in the following fashion: 0 and 1, technician; 2, moderate; 3 and 4, advocate. (Note, advocates represent those planners expressing opposition to at least three of the four questions employed in the scale.)

Table 2

Frequency for Exposure to Formal Planning Education

Formed 4	Code	Absolute Frequency	Adjusted Frequency (%)
No Formal Education	0	113	14.9
Exposure to Formal Planning Education	1	643	85.1
Missing Data	9	19	Missing
Total		775	100.0

Table 3

Frequency for Planner's Role Index

Role	Value	N	(%)
Technician	0	105	13.5
	1	261	33.7
Moderate	2	242	31.2
	3	120	15.5
Advocate	4	29	3.7
	Missing	18	2.4
Total			100.0

Upper Socioeconomic Index: U.S. Public

The upper socioeconomic index reported in chapter four was constructed in the following fashion. The sample population of the 1974 General Social Survey who possessed a bachelor's degree or greater, made over $10,000 for the year, and who identified themselves as middle or upper class were assigned upper status, all others *not* upper status. (See also Table 4.18A.)

Planners and U.S. Public Participation Index

The Planners and U.S. Public Participation Index was constructed (for planners) on the basis of items 6 and 7 a, b, c, and d under "Background Characteristics" of the questionnaire in Appendix A (see chapter four for additional discussion). The index is a simple aggregate of the number of acts performed. The U.S. public data set for this variable is the Center for Political Studies, 1974 Population, American National Election Study (ICPR). The socioeconomic index for the U.S. public was constructed by assigning all those possessing a college degree or greater, middle or upper-class status, and making over $10,000 a year to upper status, all others *not* upper status.

Political Cynicism Scale

The political cynicism scale employed was (Agger, Goldstein, Pearl), in John P. Robinson, et al., *Measures of Political Attitudes* (Ann Arbor: Institute for Social Research, 1968). The *Statistical Package for the Social Sciences* (SPSS), Version 7, subroutine Guttman was the generating program. The construction of the scale proceeded as follows. The original values ran from Strongly Agree to Strongly Disagree. For all questions except question 6, the cynical response categories preceded the noncynical. Each item was dichotomized in the following manner: item 1 between b and c, item 2 between b and c, item 3 between c and d, item 4 between e and f, item 5 between d and e, item 6 (reversed) between e and f. Guttman-scaling procedures were employed and a composite cynicism scale ranging from zero through six was assigned to each individual. An evaluation of the items for their scalability indicated that they meet the requirement established for a valid Guttman Scale. The coefficient of scalability was .6419. The coefficient of reproducibility for the scale was .9354. The political cynicism scale itself was constructed utilizing the pattern of sample responses. Each respondent was assigned a scale score value based on the number of items passed. Those scoring zero and one were identified as politically cynical; those scoring two or three as politically neutral; and those scoring four, five, and six as politically trusting. The exact questions comprising the scale appear under "Politics and Politicians" in Appendix A. The frequency distribution for uncollapsed scale scores is presented in Table 4.

Table 4

Scores and Item Correlation Matrix for Political Cynicism Scale

Category Label	Code	Absolute Frequency	Relative Frequency (%)	Adjusted Frequency (%)	Cumulative Frequency (%)
Cynical	0.	39	5.0	5.1	5.1
	1.	113	14.6	14.9	20.1
	2.	246	31.7	32.5	52.5
	3.	257	33.2	33.9	86.4
	4.	77	9.9	10.2	96.6
	5.	23	3.0	3.0	99.6
Trusting	6.	3	0.4	0.4	100.0
	9.	17	2.2	Missing	100.0
Total		775	100.0	100.0	

Mean	2.397	Std Err	0.041	Median	2.423
Mode	3.000	Std Dev	1.132	Variance	1.281
Kurtosis	0.096	Skewness	0.054	Range	6.000
Minimum	0.0	Maximum	6.000		
Valid Cases	758	Missing Cases	17		

Interitem Correlation Matrix

	Reflect	Money	Hacks	Manplate	Nominate	Geninst
Reflect	1.0000	0.7030	0.3324	0.4520	0.6755	0.5845
Money	0.7030	1.0000	0.3867	0.5158	0.5191	0.3727
Hacks	0.3324	0.3867	1.0000	0.8702	0.4856	0.7451
Manplate	0.4520	0.5158	0.8702	1.0000	0.7020	0.4674
Nominate	0.6755	0.5191	0.4856	0.7020	1.0000	0.1234
Geninst	0.5845	0.3727	0.7451	0.4674	0.1234	1.0000
Scale Item	0.4554	0.3903	0.4877	0.4761	0.4151	0.2896

The Domestic Social Welfare Scale

The Domestic Social Welfare Scale in John P. Robinson, et al., *Measures of Political Attitudes* (Ann Arbor: Institute for Social Research, 1968), was employed. The SPSS, Version 7, subroutine Guttman was the generating program. The construction of the scale proceeded as follows. The original values were coded from Strongly Agree through Strongly Disagree. The strong support for positive government categories preceded the opposition to government involvement for all questions except question 4, for which the reverse is the case. Each item was dichotomized in the following manner: item 1 between d and e, item 2 between d and e, item 3 between c and d, item 4 between b and c, item 5 (reversed) between b and c. Guttman-scaling procedures were employed and a composite government-management scale score ranging from zero (low support) through five (high support) was assigned to each individual. An evaluation of the items for their scalability indicated that they meet the requirement established for a valid Guttman Scale. The coefficient of reproducibility was .9240 and the coefficient of scalability was .6398. Each respondent was assigned a scale score value based on the number of items passed. Those scoring zero or one were identified as low support; those scoring two or three as medium support; those scoring four or five as high support. The exact questions appear under "Role of Government" in Appendix A. The frequency distribution for the uncollapsed scale scores is presented in Table 5.

Table 5
Scores and Item Correlation Matrix for Domestic Social Welfare Scale

Category Label	Code	Absolute Frequency	Relative Frequency (%)	Adjusted Frequency (%)	Cumulative Frequency (%)
Low Support	0.	21	2.7	2.8	2.8
	1.	103	13.3	13.7	16.5
	2.	222	28.6	29.5	45.9
	3.	270	34.8	35.9	81.8
	4.	89	11.5	11.8	93.6
High Support	5.	48	6.2	6.4	100.0
	9.	22	2.8	Missing	100.0
Total		775	100.0	100.0	

Mean	2.594	Std Err	0.042		Median	2.613
Mode	3.000	Std Dev	1.141		Variance	1.303
Kurtosis	−0.163	Skewness	0.094		Range	5.000
Minimum	0.0	Maximum	5.000			
Valid Cases	753	Missing Cases	22			

Interitem Correlation Matrix

	Govcity	Jobhouse	Workwas	Private	Health
Govcity	1.0000	0.7916	0.6763	0.1548	1.0000
Jobhouse	0.7916	1.0000	0.7019	0.4255	0.6182
Workwas	0.6763	0.7019	1.0000	0.4610	0.5833
Private	0.1548	0.4255	0.4610	1.0000	0.6341
Health	1.0000	0.6182	0.5833	0.6341	1.0000
Scale-item	0.4835	0.5190	0.4606	0.3193	0.4367

Overview of
Selected Sample Characteristics

The purpose of this appendix is to provide a general overview of specific characteristics of the sample in a more extended format than was possible in the methodology section. The comparisons made in chapter three between our sample and the *Roster* were employed because the population of inference for our sample is the American Institute of Planners. However, it should be noted that Robert A. Beauregard's article "The Occupation of Planning: A View from the Census," also provides a description of U.S. planners focusing on their demographic characteristics. We choose not to make formal comparison with his data, because (in spite of the term *census*) the data he reports also come from samples and like our own are subject to sampling error. Moreover, his data by definition include AIP and ASPO members. While indeed there is substantial overlap between the two organizations (the AIP 1974 Survey reports 67.8 percent of its membership belong to ASPO) our sample is of the AIP exclusively.

The following section provides an age breakdown for the sample in five-year intervals. However, the statistics reported at the bottom are from the codebook and are computed on age in its continuous-variable format. Table 1 presents the frequency distribution for age. The exact question appears under "Background Characteristics" in Appendix A.

There is an experience breakdown for the sample in five-year intervals. However, the statistics reported at the bottom are from the codebook and are computed on experience in its continuous-variable format. Table 2 presents the frequency distribution for experience. The exact question appears under "Background Characteristics" in Appendix A.

There is an educational breakdown for the sample of planners. The responses found in Table 3, Table 4, Table 5, and Table 6 are responses to three questions that appear under "Education" in Appendix A.

Table 1

AIP Age Breakdown

Category Label	Code	Absolute Frequency	Relative Frequency (%)	Adjusted Frequency (%)	Cum Frequency (%)
25 and under	1.	27	3.5	3.6	3.6
26 to 30	2.	190	24.5	25.0	28.6
31 to 35	3.	152	19.6	20.0	48.6
36 to 40	4.	110	14.2	14.5	63.0
41 to 45	5.	91	11.7	12.0	75.0
46 to 50	6.	73	9.4	9.6	84.6
51 to 60	7.	79	10.2	10.4	95.0
61 and over	8.	38	4.9	5.0	100.0
	99.	15	1.9	Missing	100.0
Total		775	100.0	100.0	

Mean	38.711	Std Err	0.399	Median	35.940
Mode	29.000	Std Dev	11.011	Variance	121.241
Kurtosis	0.802	Skewness	1.001	Range	67.000
Minimum	21.000	Maximum	88.000		
Valid Cases	760	Missing Cases	15		

Table 2
AIP Experience Breakdown

Category Label	Code	Absolute Frequency	Relative Frequency (%)	Adjusted Frequency (%)	Cumulative Frequency (%)
5 and under	1.	244	28.9	29.8	29.8
6 to 10	2.	185	23.9	24.6	54.4
11 to 15	3.	116	15.0	15.4	69.8
16 to 20	4.	96	12.4	12.8	82.6
21 to 25	5.	68	8.8	9.0	91.6
26 and over	6.	63	8.1	8.4	100.0
	99.	23	3.0	Missing	100.0
Total		775	100.0	100.0	

Mean	12.194	Std Err	0.342	Median	9.557
Mode	5.000	Std Dev	9.370	Variance	87.802
Kurtosis	2.308	Skewness	1.349	Range	59.000
Minimum	0.0	Maximum	59.000		
Valid Cases	752	Missing Cases	23		

Table 3

AIP Undergraduate Majors

Category Label	Code*	Absolute Freq	Relative Freq (%)	Adjusted Freq (%)	Cum Freq (%)
Arch & Design	1.	188	24.3	24.7	24.7
Landscape Arch	2.	2	0.3	0.3	25.0
Geography	3.	51	6.6	6.7	31.7
Engineering	4.	78	10.1	10.2	41.9
Planning	5.	73	9.4	9.6	51.5
Economics	6.	51	6.6	6.7	58.2
Political Science	7.	86	11.1	11.3	69.5
Sociology	8.	30	3.9	3.9	73.5
Public Admin	10.	14	1.8	1.8	75.3
Urban Studies	11.	12	1.5	1.6	76.9
Business Admin	12.	23	3.0	3.0	79.9
History	13.	25	3.2	3.3	83.2
Mathematics	14.	6	0.8	0.8	84.0
Natural Science	15.	10	1.3	1.3	85.3
Other	16.	111	14.3	14.6	99.9
NA	17.	1	0.1	0.1	100.0
	99.	14	1.8	Missing	100.0
Total		775	100.0	100.0	

*Note: Coding scheme was designed to reflect traditional undergraduate majors found in standard university catalogs.

Table 4
AIP Graduate Work in Planning Breakdown

Category Label*	Code	Absolute Freq	Relative Freq (%)	Adjusted Freq (%)	Cum Freq (%)
No	1.	145	18.7	18.9	18.9
Yes but not complete	2.	120	15.5	15.6	34.6
Yes but not for MCP	3.	121	15.6	15.8	50.3
Yes masters in planning	4.	368	47.5	48.0	98.3
Yes Ph.D.	5.	13	1.7	1.7	100.0
	9.	8	1.0	Missing	
Total		775	100.0	100.0	

*Note: See Appendix A for question format.

Table 5
AIP Graduate Degree Breakdown

Category Label*	Code	Absolute Freq	Relative Freq (%)	Adjusted Freq (%)	Cum Freq (%)
Masters	1.	159	20.5	85.9	85.9
Ph.D.	2.	14	1.8	7.6	93.5
Grad certificate	4.	6	0.8	3.2	96.8
Ed.D.	5.	1	0.1	0.5	97.3
Law degree	6.	5	0.6	2.7	100.0
NA	3.	577	74.5	Missing	100.0
	9.	13	1.7	Missing	100.0
Total		775	100.0	100.0	

*Note: See Appendix A for question format.

Table 6
AIP Major of Graduate Degree Other Than Planning

Category Label*	Code	Absolute Freq	Relative Freq (%)	Adjusted Freq (%)	Cum Freq (%)
Arch & Design	1.	49	6.3	17.0	17.0
Landscape Arch	2.	2	0.3	0.7	17.6
Geography	3.	29	3.7	10.0	27.7
Engineering	4.	11	1.4	3.8	31.5
Economics	6.	16	2.1	5.5	37.0
Political Science	7.	20	2.6	6.9	43.9
Sociology	8.	8	1.0	2.8	46.7
Public Admin	10.	63	8.1	21.8	68.5
Urban Studies	11.	13	1.7	4.5	73.0
Business Admin	12.	14	1.8	4.8	77.9
History	13.	3	0.4	1.0	78.9
Mathematics	14.	1	0.1	0.3	79.2
Natural Science	15.	2	0.3	0.7	79.9
Other	16.	58	7.5	20.1	100.0
Total		289		100.0	

*Note: The total N for this table (289) reflects the fact that some planners reported two graduate degrees.

Data Sources

Data employed in the work were supplied by the Inter-University Consortium for Political Research (University of Michigan). The studies are as follows:

CPS 1974 American Election Study (ICPR)

J. Davis, *National Data Program for the Social Sciences: Spring, 1974 General Social Survey* (ICPR)

The ICPR is not responsible for either the analysis or interpretation of these data; however, their assistance in making them available is appreciated. The data were provided through the Louis Harris Political Data Center at The University of North Carolina at Chapel Hill. The data on planners were collected as a part of the 1974 American National Planners' Study (Survey of Planners), conducted through the Institute for Research in Social Science, The University of North Carolina at Chapel Hill.

Notes

Chapter 1

1. Thomas J. Watson, "Speech to the Bond Club of New York," pp. 1–4.
2. Walter F. Mondale, "Social Accounting, Evaluation, and the Future of Human Services."
3. Gar Alperovitz, "Notes towards a Pluralist Commonwealth," pp. 22–48.
4. G. David Garson and Michael L. Vasu, "Notes on the Political Issues of Decentralized Social Planning," pp. 2–20.
5. Marshall E. Dimock and Gladys O. Dimock, *Public Administration*, p. 312.
6. Alan Altshuler, *The City Planning Process*, p. 409.
7. Theodore J. Lowi, *The End of Liberalism*, pp. 101–186.
8. David C. Ranney, *Planning and Politics in the Metropolis*, p. 2.
9. Donald T. Allensworth, *The U.S. Government in Action*, p. 61.
10. Village of Euclid v. Ambler Realty Co., 297 Fed. 307, 316 (N.D. Ohio, 1924); rev'd 272 U.S. 365 (1926).
11. Mel Scott, *American City Planning Since 1890*, p. 301.
12. Ibid., p. 409.
13. Ibid., p. 323.
14. Ibid., p. 324.
15. Lawrence M. Friedman, *Government and Slum Housing*, p. 148.
16. Allensworth, *The U.S. Government in Action*, p. 61. The following section relies heavily on Allensworth.
17. Ibid., p. 62.
18. Ibid., p. 63.
19. For a comprehensive analysis of the status of state planning see Thad L. Beyle, Sureva Seligson, and Deil S. Wright, "New Directions in State Planning."
20. Ranney, *Planning and Politics in the Metropolis*, p. 13.
21. Ibid., p. 49.
22. Charles Abrams, *The Language of Cities*, p. 48.
23. Ranney, *Planning and Politics in the Metropolis*, p. 8.
24. Altshuler, *The City Planning Process*, pp. 5–6.
25. Deil S. Wright, "Governmental Forms and Planning Functions," p. 81.
26. Harold D. Lasswell, *Politics: Who Gets What, When, How*.
27. David Easton, *The Political System*, especially chapter five.
28. It should be noted that both definitions of politics utilized are different in emphasis rather than essence. The common conceptual variance shared by both definitions must be acknowledged. They are presented separately for analytical purposes, in order to facilitate comparison to salient features of the planning process.
29. Norman Beckman, "The New PPBS: Planning, Politics, Bureaucracy, and Salvation," p. 114.
30. David C. Ranney, *Planning and Politics in the Metropolis*, p. 111.
31. Francine Rabinovitz, *City Politics and Planning*, p. 126.
32. Charles R. Adrian, "Leadership and Decision-Making in Manager Cities," p. 210.
33. Ranney, *Planning and Politics in the Metropolis*, p. 111.
34. Ibid., p. 111.
35. Thomas R. Dye, *Politics in States and Communities*, p. 302.
36. Altshuler, *The City Planning Process*, pp. 354–55.
37. Ibid., p. 339.

38. Peter Bachrach and Morton Baratz, "Two Faces of Power," in *Cities and Suburbs,* ed. Bryan Downs.

39. Ibid., p. 239.

40. Guy Benveniste, *The Politics of Expertise,* p. 13.

41. Altshuler, *The City Planning Process,* pp. 4–5.

42. T. J. Kent, Jr., *The Urban General Plan,* p. 18.

43. Charles Abrams, *The Language of Cities,* p. 186.

44. For a survey research approach to community goals emphasizing mass and elite preferences, see John S. Jackson and William L. Shade, "Citizen Participation, Democratic Representation, and Survey Research."

45. Herbert A. Simon, *Administrative Behavior,* pp. 45–46.

46. Ibid., p. 5.

47. Ibid., p. 5.

48. Ibid., p. 7.

49. Dennis R. Judd and Robert E. Mendelson, *The Politics of Urban Planning,* p. 184.

50. Altshuler, *The City Planning Process,* p. 2.

51. Judd and Mendelson, *The Politics of Urban Planning,* p. 202.

52. Ranney, *Planning and Politics in the Metropolis,* p. 110.

53. Norton E. Long, "Planning and Politics in Urban Development," p. 168.

54. Altshuler, *The City Planning Process,* p. 348.

55. Ranney, *Planning and Politics in the Metropolis,* p. 19.

56. Judd and Mendelson, *The Politics of Urban Planning,* p. 179.

57. Ranney, *Planning and Politics in the Metropolis,* p. 14.

58. Ibid., p. 15.

59. Benveniste, *The Politics of Expertise,* p. 9.

60. Rabinovitz, *City Politics and Planning,* p. 139.

61. For studies that do deal with planners' attitudes, see Francine F. Rabinovitz and Stanley Pottinger, "Organization for Local Planning: The Attitudes of Directors."

62. Ranney, *Planning and Politics in the Metropolis,* p. 112.

Chapter 2

1. The term *planner* is operationally defined by membership in the American Institute of Planners, for reasons discussed in the next chapter.

2. David C. Ranney, *Planning and Politics in the Metropolis,* p. 42.

3. Ibid., pp. 19–38.

4. Ibid., p. 19.

5. Lawrence M. Friedman, *Government and Slum Housing,* p. 28.

6. Ibid., p. 27.

7. Mel Scott, *American City Planning Since 1890,* p. 10.

8. Friedman, *Government and Slum Housing,* p. 35.

9. Ranney, *Planning and Politics in the Metropolis,* p. 23.

10. Lawrence Veiller, quoted in Friedman, *Government and Slum Housing,* p. 35.

11. Ranney, *Politics and Planning in the Metropolis,* pp. 20–35.

12. William L. C. Wheaton and Margaret F. Wheaton, "Identifying the Public Interest," in *Urban Planning in Transition,* ed. Ernest Erber, p. 155.

13. Dennis R. Judd and Robert E. Mendelson, *The Politics of Urban Planning,* p. 180.

14. Ranney, *Planning and Politics in the Metropolis,* p. 24.

15. Melvin M. Webber, "Comprehensive Planning and Social Responsibility," in *Urban Planning and Social Policy,* ed. Bernard J. Frieden and Robert Morris, p. 11.

16. Jane Jacobs, *The Death and Life of Great American Cities.*

17. Bernard J. Frieden, "New Roles in Social Policy Planning," in *Urban Planning in Transition,* ed. Erber.

18. Henry Fagin, "Advancing the 'State of the Art'," in *Urban Planning in Transition,* ed. Erber.

19. Gans, "The Need for Planners Trained in Policy Formation," in *Urban Planning in Transition*, ed. Erber.

20. Bernard J. Frieden, "The Changing Prospects for Social Planning," p. 312.

21. Ranney, *Planning and Politics in the Metropolis*, p. 29.

22. Ibid.

23. Jacobs, *The Death and Life of Great American Cities*, p. 19.

24. Scott, *American City Planning Since 1890*, p. 89.

25. Ibid., p. 97.

26. Ranney, *Planning and Politics in the Metropolis*, p. 35.

27. Ibid.

28. John L. Handcock, "Planners in the Changing American City, 1900–1940."

29. Ranney, *Planning and Politics in the Metropolis*, p. 35.

30. Ibid. Also see Alan S. Kravitz, "Mandarinism: Planning as Handmaiden to Conservative Politics," in *Planning and Politics: Uneasy Partnership*, ed. Thad L. Beyle and George T. Lathrop.

31. Judd and Mendelson, *The Politics of Urban Planning*, especially chapter five.

32. Richard Hofstadter, *The Age of Reform*; Thomas R. Dye, *Politics in States and Communities*.

33. Edward C. Banfield and James Q. Wilson, *City Politics*, p. 115.

34. Hofstadter, *The Age of Reform*, pp. 175–85.

35. William L. Riordon, *Plunkitt of Tammany Hall*, p. 38.

36. Ranney, *Planning and Politics in the Metropolis*, p. 36.

37. Fred I. Greenstein, "The Changing Pattern of Urban Party Politics," in *Cities and Suburbs*, ed. Downs.

38. Riordan, *Plunkitt of Tammany Hall*, p. 28.

39. Robert K. Merton, "The Latent Functions of the Machine," in *Urban Government*, ed. Edward C. Banfield.

40. Banfield and Wilson, *City Politics*, pp. 38–46.

41. Merton, "The Latent Functions of the Machine," pp. 223–31.

42. Theodore J. Lowi, "Machine Politics Old and New."

43. Ibid.

44. Hofstadter, *The Age of Reform*, especially chapters four and five.

45. Ibid.

46. Ibid., pp. 185–96.

47. Ibid.

48. For a discussion of reformist philosophy see John Porter East, *Council Manager Government*.

49. Hofstadter, *The Age of Reform*, p. 8.

50. Banfield and Wilson, *City Politics*, p. 18.

51. Hofstadter, *The Age of Reform*, pp. 8–9.

52. Banfield and Wilson, *City Politics*, pp. 33–48.

53. Ibid., p. 41.

54. Andrew D. White, "Municipal Affairs Are Not Political," in *Urban Government*, ed. Banfield.

55. Samuel P. Hays, "The Politics of Reform in Municipal Government in the Progressive Era," pp. 157–69.

56. Banfield and Wilson, *City Politics*, pp. 140–41.

57. Ibid., p. 138.

58. Ibid., p. 171.

59. East, *Council Manager Government*, especially chapter two.

60. Ibid., pp. 74–90.

61. Ibid., p. 61.

62. Banfield and Wilson, *City Politics*, p. 170.

63. Donald K. Price, "The Promotion of the City Manager Plan," in *Urban Government*, ed. Banfield, p. 289.

64. East, *Council Manager Government*, p. 36.

65. Edward Banfield, "Good Government," in *Urban Government*, ed. Banfield, pp. 267–70.

66. East, *Council Manager Government*, p. 35.

67. Brand Witlock, "The Absurdity of Partisanship," in *Urban Government*, ed. Banfield, pp. 275–78.

68. Eugene C. Lee, *The Politics of Nonpartisanship*, pp. 28–35.

69. Hays, "The Politics of Reform in Municipal Government," pp. 162–65.

70. See, for example, Robert L. Lineberry and Edmund P. Fowler, "Reformism and Public Policies."

71. The analytical dichotomy of planning doctrine into traditional ideology versus advocacy is to facilitate comparison of both to features generic in the municipal-reform movement. The process of debate over ideology and doctrine in planning is, perhaps, more dynamic than this simple typology expresses. Nonetheless, many of the areas of controversy within planning relate essentially to the questions raised in the debate between proponents of the classical model of planning and those of advocacy planning. For a discussion of traditional ideology see Judd and Mendelson, *The Politics of Urban Planning*, chapter five. For a discussion of the classic model see Richard S. Bolan, "Emerging Views of Planning."

72. Bolan, "Emerging Views of Planning," p. 234.

73. Kravitz, "Mandarinism: Planning as Handmaiden to Conservative Politics," in *Planning and Politics*, ed. Beyle and Lathrop, pp. 243–57.

74. Judd and Mendelson, *The Politics of Urban Planning*, p. 193.

75. Kravitz, "Mandarinism: Planning as Handmaiden to Conservative Politics," pp. 243–57.

76. Ranney, *Planning and Politics in the Metropolis*, p. 40.

77. Bolan, "Emerging Views of Planning," p. 236.

78. Altshuler, *The City Planning Process*, p. 299.

79. Wheaton and Wheaton, "Identifying the Public Interest," p. 153.

80. Ernest Erber, *Urban Planning in Transition*, p. xxv.

81. Altshuler, *The City Planning Process*, p. 303.

82. Deil S. Wright, "Governmental Forms and Planning Functions: The Relation of Organization and Structures to Planning Practice," p. 69.

83. Ranney, *Planning and Politics in the Metropolis*, pp. 35–42.

84. Francine F. Rabinovitz, *City Politics and Planning*, pp. 135–39.

85. T. J. Kent, Jr., *The Urban General Plan*; Robert A. Walker, *The Planning Function in Urban Government*.

86. Ranney, *Planning and Politics in the Metropolis*, p. 35.

87. Ibid., pp. 49–60.

88. Francine F. Rabinovitz and J. Stanley Pottinger, "Organization for Planning: The Attitudes of Directors," pp. 27–32.

89. Robert Goodman, *After the Planners*, pp. 155–57.

90. John Friedmann, "The Future of Comprehensive Urban Planning: A Critique"; Altshuler, *The City Planning Process*; Melville Branch, *Planning: Aspects and Applications*.

91. Branch, *Planning: Aspects and Applications*, pp. 297–308.

92. Ibid., p. 300.

93. Ibid., pp. 298–302.

94. Altshuler, *The City Planning Process*, p. 302.

95. Anthony James Catanese, *Systematic Planning: Theory and Application*, p. 38.

96. Altshuler, *The City Planning Process*, p. 303.

97. Branch, *Planning: Aspects and Applications*, p. 301.

98. Friedmann, "The Future of Comprehensive Urban Planning: A Critique," p. 315.

99. Goodman, *After the Planners*, p. 157.

100. Frances Fox Piven, "Planning and Class Interests," p. 308.

101. Judd and Mendelson, *The Politics of Urban Planning*, p. 188; Altshuler, *The City Planning Process*, p. 396.

102. Altshuler, *The City Planning Process*, p. 2.

103. Francine F. Rabinovitz, "Politics, Personality, and Planning," p. 20.

104. Hays, "The Politics of Reform in Municipal Government." While Hays expresses the belief in centralization of executive authority as a goal of municipal reform, he clearly does not accept "rationality" or "municipal efficiency" as the explanation.

105. Altshuler, *The City Planning Process*, p. 313.

106. Judd and Mendelson, *The Politics of Urban Planning*, p. 178.

107. Robert Mayer, Robert Moroney, and Robert H. Morris, *Centrally Planned Change*, p. 112.

108. Ibid., p. 219.

109. Goodman, *After the Planners*, p. 158.

110. Ibid., quotation found on p. 159.

111. Donald N. Michael, "Urban Policy in the Rationalized Society," p. 287.

112. Martin H. Krieger, "Some New Directions for Planning Theories"; Martin Meyerson, "Building the Middle Range Bridge for Comprehensive Planning"; Paul Davidoff, "Advocacy and Pluralism in Planning"; Lisa Peattie, "Reflections on Advocacy Planning."

113. Walker, *The Planning Function in Urban Government*; Kent, *The Urban General Plan*.

114. Meyerson, "Building the Middle Range Bridge for Comprehensive Planning."

115. Altshuler, *The City Planning Process*, p. 324.

116. Kravitz, "Mandarinism: Planning as Handmaiden to Conservative Politics," pp. 243–57.

117. Edward C. Banfield, "The Uses and Limitations of Comprehensive Planning in Massachusetts," in *Taming Megalopolis*, ed. H. Wentworth Eldridge, p. 713.

118. Altshuler, *The City Planning Process*; Lowi, *The End of Liberalism*.

119. Charles Lindblom, "The Science of 'Muddling Through,'" in *A Reader in Planning Theory*, ed. Faludi, pp. 151–61.

120. Davidoff, "Advocacy and Pluralism in Planning," p. 332.

121. Altshuler, *The City Planning Process*, p. 325.

122. Peattie, "Reflections on Advocacy Planning," p. 81.

123. Ibid., p. 87.

124. Altshuler, *The City Planning Process*, p. 333.

125. Davidoff, "Advocacy and Pluralism in Planning," p. 332.

126. Piven, "Planning and Class Interests," p. 310.

127. Peattie, "Reflections on Advocacy Planning," pp. 80–84.

Chapter 3

1. See chapter two.

2. Ibid.

3. John Friedman, "The Future of Comprehensive Urban Planning: A Critique," p. 315.

4. Goodman, *After the Planners*, p. 157.

5. Alan S. Kravitz, "Mandarinism: Planning as Handmaiden to Conservative Politics," in *Planning and Politics*, ed. Thad L. Beyle and George Lathrop, pp. 252–54.

6. For a comprehensive reader on the status of planning theory, see Andreas Faludi, ed., *A Reader in Planning Theory*.

7. The analytical dichotomy of planning doctrine into traditional ideology versus advocacy is to facilitate comparison of both to features generic in the municipal reform movement. The process of debate over ideology and doctrine in planning is perhaps more dynamic than this simple typology expresses. Nonetheless, many of the areas of

controversy within planning relate essentially to the questions raised in the debate between proponents of the classical model of planning and those of advocacy planning. For a discussion of traditional ideology, see Judd and Mendelson, *The Politics of Urban Planning*, chapter five.

8. See note 26.

9. James A. Davis, *National Data Program for the Social Sciences: Spring 1974 General Survey*. See Appendix A for the questionnaire. Appendix B contains information relating to the Guttman Scales and scaling techniques employed. Appendix C contains more extensive documentation relating to item selection, scale development, and sampling design.

10. See Appendix A for the questionnaire.

11. Delbert C. Miller, *Handbook of Research Design and Social Measurement*, p. 77.

12. Arnold S. Linsky, "Stimulating Responses to Mailed Questionnaires: A Review," pp. 82–101.

13. The author is also grateful to Dr. Frank Munger, Institute for Research in Social Science, University of North Carolina, Chapel Hill. See also Appendix D.

14. Linsky, "Stimulating Responses to Mailed Questionnaires," p. 85.

15. Davis, *National Data Program for the Social Sciences: Spring 1974 General Survey*.

16. Francine Rabinovitz, *City Politics and Planning*. See also Appendix D.

17. John P. Robinson, Jerrold G. Rusk, and Kendra B. Head, *Measures of Political Attitudes*.

18. Allen L. Edwards, *Techniques of Attitude Scale Construction*.

19. Miller, *Handbook of Research Design and Social Measurement*, p. 55.

20. Ibid., p. 56.

21. Charles H. Backstrom and Gerald D. Hursh, *Survey Research*, p. 33.

22. American Institute of Planners, *AIP Newsletter*, 9 (June 1974).

23. Deil S. Wright, "Governmental Forms and Planning Functions: The Relation of Organization and Structures to Planning Practice," p. 77.

24. John Neter and William Wasserman, *Applied Linear Statistical Models*.

25. According to AIP code of professional responsibility, all planners serve the public interest. American Institute of Planners, *Roster*, Article 9.

26. Rabinovitz, *City Politics and Planning*, p. 22.

27. Judd and Mendelson, *The Politics of Urban Planning*, p. 191.

28. Edward C. Banfield and James Q. Wilson, *City Politics*, p. 191.

29. Ibid., p. 189.

30. Alan Altshuler, *The City Planning Process*, p. 302. Altshuler indicates that such a conception reflects the ideal type of comprehensive planning.

31. Ibid., p. 334.

32. Quoted in Banfield and Wilson, *City Politics*, pp. 188–93.

33. Paul Davidoff, "Advocacy and Pluralism in Planning," p. 331.

34. Paul Davidoff and Thomas A. Reiner, "A Choice Theory of Planning," p. 108.

35. The relationship between formal education and attitudes toward master planning was also run using an operational definition of formal planning education that included simple exposure to planning course work. The conclusions presented remained unchanged. Moreover, years of experience was introduced both as a control variable and to assess its independent effect. The independent effect of experience was also significant ($p < .04$). However, the theoretical significance of this difference is far less relevant; that is, over 85% of both experience groups agree that no plan is indeed neutral—the difference is at the Disagree level, where those with 10 years or more experience are slightly more likely to disagree: 10.0% versus 5.7%, respectively.

36. Altshuler, *The City Planning Process*, p. 409.

37. Faludi, ed., *A Reader in Planning Theory*, p. 1.

38. Quoted in Yehezkel Dror, "The Planning Process: A Facet Design," in *A Reader in Planning Theory*, ed. Faludi, pp. 327–30.

39. Ibid.

40. Altshuler, *The City Planning Process*, p. 344.

41. The relationship between formal planning education and conceptions of the planning process was also run using an operational definition of formal planning education that included exposure to planning coursework. The conclusions presented here remain unchanged. Also, the independent effect of experience on the planner's conception of the planning process was nonsignificant.

42. Altshuler, *The City Planning Process*, pp. 392–400.

43. Ibid.

44. American Institute of Planners, *Roster*, Article 9.

45. Peter Marcuse, "Professional Ethics and Beyond: Values in Planning," p. 264–73.

46. Altshuler, *The City Planning Process*, pp. 392–400.

47. Ibid.

48. In addition, the relationship between formal planning education and attitudes toward planning as a profession was also run using an operational definition of formal planning education that included simple exposure to planning coursework. The conclusions presented here remain unchanged. Also, the independent effect of experience was nonsignificant.

49. Altshuler, *The City Planning Process*, p. 396.

50. Ibid., p. 397.

51. Ibid.

52. Quoted in ibid.

53. Ibid.

54. The relationship between formal planning education and the existence of a theory of planning was also run using an operational definition of formal planning education that included simple exposure to planning coursework. The conclusions presented here remain unchanged. While controlling for experience did not alter the nature of the relationship, the independent effect of experience was significant ($p < .01$); however, that relationship as indicated above vanished when we controlled for formal education and agency type. The direction of the difference for experience was such that 69.4% of planners with over ten years agreed there was a theory of planning versus 60.5% of those with less than ten years.

55. Rabinovitz, *City Politics and Planning*, p. 11.

56. Beckman, "The Planner as a Bureaucrat," in *A Reader in Planning Theory*, ed. Faludi, p. 251.

57. Ibid.

58. Francine F. Rabinovitz, "Politics, Personality and Planning," in *A Reader in Planning Theory*, ed. Faludi, p. 265.

59. Ibid., p. 267.

60. Ibid.

61. Ibid., p. 268.

62. Ibid., p. 269. See also Ranney, *Planning and Politics in the Metropolis*, pp. 139–59. For a general discussion of roles and professional norms in planning, see John W. Dyckman, "What Makes Planners Plan?", pp. 164–67.

63. Ibid.

64. Davidoff, "Advocacy and Pluralism in Planning," p. 333.

65. Ibid., p. 331.

66. See Appendix B for a complete discussion of the index.

67. The relationship between formal planning education and type of role was also run using an operational definition that included simple exposure to planning coursework. The relationship was also significant ($p < .01$) and in the same direction.

68. Altshuler, *The City Planning Process*, p. 303.

69. Ibid. Also see Richard Bolan, "Emerging Views of Planning"; Melville Branch, *Planning: Aspects and Applications*; Melville Branch, *Urban Planning Theory*.

70. Edward Banfield, "Ends and Means in Planning," in Faludi, ed., *A Reader in Planning Theory*, p. 141.

71. Ibid., p. 140.

72. Bolan, "Emerging Views of Planning," p. 234.

73. Ibid.

74. Quoted in Banfield, "Ends and Means in Planning," p. 145.

75. Ibid.

76. Ibid., p. 144.

77. Charles E. Lindblom, "The Science of 'Muddling Through,'" in *A Reader in Planning Theory*, ed. Faludi, pp. 151–69.

78. Ibid., p. 156.

79. Ibid., p. 157.

80. Ibid.

81. Altshuler, *The City Planning Process*, p. 299.

82. Ibid., p. 299.

83. Ibid., p. 300.

84. Ibid., see chapter five.

85. Ibid., p. 324.

86. Faludi, *A Reader in Planning Theory*, p. 117.

87. Ibid.

88. Amitai Etzioni, "Mixed-scanning: A Third Approach to Decision-Making," *A Reader in Planning Theory*, ed. Faludi, pp. 217–29. Quotation is on p. 200.

89. Ibid.

90. Ibid., pp. 223–24.

91. Many issues related to this debate are at the center of concerns addressed by the traditional model of planning and advocacy. Clearly, the divisions between poles also include points in between, a not-mixed scanning would be an example.

92. Ernest Erber, *Urban Planning in Transition*.

93. See Robert Mayer, Robert Moroney, and Robert Morris, *Centrally Planned Change* for an excellent discussion of issues inherent in centralism.

94. Ibid.

95. Melvin M. Webber, "Comprehensive Planning and Social Responsibility," in *A Reader in Planning Theory*, ed. Faludi, p. 97.

96. The relationship between formal planning education and the legitimate subject of concern of public planning was also run using an operational definition of formal planning education that included simple exposure to planning coursework. The conclusions presented here remain unchanged. The independent effect of experience was statistically significant ($p < .002$); the direction of that relationship was such that while 92.6% of planners with under ten years of experience thought the legitimate subject of concern of public-planning agencies was the physical, social, and economic development of the community, 82.9% of those with over ten years thought so.

97. The relationship between formal planning education and the possibility of comprehensive rational planning was also run using an operational definition of formal planning education that included simple exposure to planning coursework. The relationship was significant ($p < .01$). Planners with exposure to formal planning coursework were both more likely to agree and to disagree, i.e., they constituted a much smaller proportion of the undecided category. The independent effect of experience was nonsignificant.

98. Altshuler, *The City Planning Process*, p. 309.

99. Erber, *Urban Planning in Transition*, p. xvi.

100. Quoted in Robert Goodman, *After the Planners*, p. 159.

101. Martin Meyerson, "The Next Challenge for the Urban Planner: Linking Local and National Economic Planning," p. 375.

102. The relationship between formal planning education and the desirability of a

federal agency for comprehensive planning was also run using an operational definition of formal planning education that included simple exposure to planning coursework. The conclusions presented here remain unchanged. The independent effect of
experience was nonsignificant.

Chapter 4

1. Studies on which this contention is based include the following: Alan A. Altshuler, *The City Planning Process*, p. 401; Anthony James Catanese, *Planners and Local
Politics*, p. 18; Dennis R. Judd and Robert E. Mendelson, *The Politics of Urban Planning*,
pp. 176–202. For a critical analysis of the liberal ideology in planning see, Alan S.
Kravitz, "Mandarinism: Planning as Handmaiden to Conservative Politics," in *Planning
and Politics: Uneasy Partnership*, ed. Beyle and Lathrop, pp. 132–37.

2. David C. Ranney, *Planning and Politics in the Metropolis*, p. 35; Deil S. Wright,
"Governmental Forms and Planning Functions: The Relation of Organization and
Structures to Planning Practice," in *Planning and Politics: Uneasy Partnership*, pp. 68–69;
Rabinovitz, *City Politics and Planning*, pp. 132–37.

3. Philip E. Converse, "The Nature of Belief Systems in Mass Publics," in *Ideology and
Discontent*, ed. David E. Apter, p. 206.

4. Ibid., p. 207.

5. Ibid.

6. Ibid., pp. 212–16.

7. Ibid.

8. Lloyd A. Free and Hadley Cantril, *The Political Beliefs of Americans*.

9. James W. Prothro and C. M. Griggs, "Fundamental Principles of Democracy: Bases
of Agreement and Disagreement."

10. Herbert McClosky, "Consensus and Ideology in American Politics," pp. 361–82.

11. Ibid., pp. 370–82.

12. Treatises on ideology, liberalism, and conservatism include Louis Hartz, *The Liberal Tradition in America*; Henry Steele Commager, *The American Mind*; Clinton Rossiter,
Conservatism in America; and Robert B. Lane, *Political Ideology*.

13. For an analysis of planning during the New Deal see Mel Scott, *American City
Planning Since 1890*, especially chapter five.

14. Converse, "The Nature of Belief Systems in Mass Publics," pp. 232–56.

15. Ibid.

16. For a review of the literature with some new findings in this regard, see Norman
H. Nie, Sidney Verba, and John R. Petrocik, *The Changing American Voter*.

17. Seymour Martin Lipset, *Political Man*.

18. Converse, "The Nature of Belief Systems in Mass Publics," p. 214.

19. Aage R. Clausen, *How Congressmen Decide*.

20. See Hartz, *The Liberal Tradition in America*; Clinton Rossiter, *Conservatism in
America*.

21. Clausen, *How Congressmen Decide*, pp. 100–101.

22. Ibid.

23. Lloyd A. Free and Hadley Cantril, *The Political Beliefs of Americans*, p. 5.

24. Clausen, *How Congressmen Decide*, p. 101.

25. Catanese, *Planners and Local Politics*; Ranney, *Planning and Politics in the Metropolis*,
especially chapter two.

26. Melvin M. Webber, "Comprehensive Planning and Social Responsibility," in
Urban Planning and Social Policy, ed. Bernard J. Frieden and Robert Morris, p. 22.

27. Ranney, *Planning and Politics in the Metropolis*, p. 19.

28. Kravitz, "Mandarinism: Planning as Handmaiden to Conservative Politics," in
Planning and Politics, ed. Beyle and Lathrop, pp. 224–48.

29. Catanese, *Planners and Local Politics*, p. 18.

30. Ernest Erber, ed., *Urban Planning in Transition*, p. xvi.

31. Ibid.

32. Altshuler, *The City Planning Process*, p. 313.

33. H. Wentworth Eldredge, "Toward a National Policy for Planning the Environment," in *Urban Planning in Transition*, ed. Ernest Erber.

34. See, Angus Campbell, et al., *The American Voter*.

35. The elite/mass literature is too extensive to review entirely. In addition to the references already presented, for one of particular importance to planning see Kenneth Prewitt, *The Recruitment of Political Leaders*.

36. Planners are self-defined "middle-income professionals." For additional aspects in the way of a statistical profile, see *American Institute of Planners Newsletter* (June 1974).

37. The American Institute of Planners reports that approximately 90% of planners made $10,000 or more for the sample year. See *American Institute of Planners Newsletter* (June 1974).

38. Campbell, et al., *The American Voter*, pp. 184–209.

39. On subject social class, planners, because of income and education were assumed to be middle class for the purpose of comparing the two cumulative distribution functions. However, the measures employ the frequencies of both middle and upper class for comparison purposes and the relationship remains statistically significant.

40. Francine Rabinovitz, *City Politics and Planning*, pp. 136–40; Catanese, *Planners and Local Politics*, pp. 10–28.

41. The relationship between formal planning education and political ideology, controlling for agency type, was also run using an operational definition of formal education restricted to those with and without planning degrees. The relationship discussed here remained the same; namely, for public planners the relationship was statistically significant ($p < .03$) with those having formal degrees more liberal and less conservative. Also, the difference was *not* statistically significant ($x^2 = .04910, df = 2$) for private planners. Moreover, the independent effect of experience was nonsignificant.

42. Campbell, et al., *The American Voter* p. 543.

43. McClosky, "Consensus and Ideology in American Politics," pp. 377–82.

44. Clausen, *How Congressmen Decide*, pp. 46–47.

45. Ibid.

46. For the most current analysis, including a summary of existing literature, see Nie, et al., *The Changing American Voter*, pp. 23–42.

47. Converse, "The Nature of Belief Systems in Mass Publics," p. 211.

48. Anthony Downs, *An Economic Theory of Democracy*.

49. H. T. Reynolds, *Politics and the Common Man*, p. 160.

50. Campbell, et al., *The American Voter*.

51. Ibid., pp. 143–45.

52. Sidney Verba and Norman Nie, *Participation in America*.

53. Ibid.

54. Ibid., p. 127.

55. Ibid., p. 130.

56. Ibid., especially chapter eleven.

57. Deil S. Wright, "Governmental Forms and Planning Functions: The Relation of Organization and Structures to Planning Practice," p. 69.

58. David C. Ranney, *Planning and Politics in the Metropolis*, pp. 35–45.

59. Rabinovitz, *City Politics and Planning*, pp. 135–39.

60. Ibid.

61. R. E. Agger, N. M. Goldstein, S. A. Pearl, "Political Cynicism: Measurement and Meaning," pp. 477–85; John P. Robinson, Jerrold G. Rusk, Kendra B. Head, *Measures of Political Attitudes*, pp. 433–34.

62. Jeffrey C. Rinehart and E. Lee Bernick, "Political Attitudes and Behavior Patterns of Federal Civil Servants"; Robinson, Rusk, Head, *Measures of Political Attitudes*, pp. 433–34. While the Hatch Act covers federal employees specifically, many states have

adopted similar measures. In addition, the entire question of Dillon's Rule and the relationship of municipalities to the state dictated that questions be included that involved types of political participation not in violation to the Federal Hatch Act.

63. Deil S. Wright, "Governmental Forms and Planning Functions: The Relation of Organization and Structures to Planning Practice," pp. 65–82.

Chapter 5

1. Deil S. Wright, "Governmental Forms and Planning Functions: The Relation of Organization and Structures to Planning Practice," p. 69.

2. Francine Rabinovitz, *City Politics and Planning*, pp. 130–40.

3. Ibid.

4. R. E. Agger, N. M. Goldstein, S. A. Pearl, "Political Cynicism: Measurement and Meaning," pp. 477–85.

5. Appendix B contains a complete discussion of scaling techniques.

6. Maureen McConaghy, "Maximum Possible Error in Guttman Scales," pp. 343–58.

7. Fred N. Kerlinger, *Foundations of Behavioral Research*, pp. 659–93.

8. The particular factor analysis utlized was the PA2 program (principal factoring with iteration) in the Statistical Package for the Social Sciences. A minimum eigen value parameter of 1.0 was employed as the criterion for determining the number of factors extracted. Factor rotation employed was orthogonal. In order to address the concern that planners' attitudes would be interrelated, we also employed an oblique factor analysis. This transformation also rendered a factor matrix in which the political cynicism variables loaded on the first factor extracted (data not displayed).

9. See Appendix A for questionnaire.

10. As in chapter three there are two measures of formal planning education employed. One is based upon a degree in the field versus no degree. The second measures a domain more appropriately called exposure to formal planning education. Moreover, in our initial regression approach we employed a measure of formal education that possessed the ordinal measurement level (zero for no exposure, to five for high exposure); our analysis of both regression output as well as contingency tables indicated a dichotomized variable would suffice as an appropriate measure of the concept.

11. John Neter and William Wasserman, *Applied Linear Statistical Models*, pp. 424–26.

12. In other words the introduction of experience as a control variable produced a statistically significant difference in the levels of cynicism among the various subgroups, over and above education and agency type.

13. Bolan, "Emerging Views of Planning," pp. 233–45.

14. Ibid., p. 234.

15. Altshuler, *The City Planning Process*, p. 303.

16. Alan S. Kravtiz, "Mandarinism: Planning as Handmaiden to Conservative Politics," in *Planning and Politics: Uneasy Partnership*, Beyle and Lathrop, eds., pp. 243–57. David C. Ranney, *Planning and Politics in the Metropolis*, pp. 40–42.

17. Judd and Mendelson, *The Politics of Urban Planning*, p. 193.

18. Ibid., pp. 178–79.

19. Frances Fox Piven, "Planning and Class Interests," p. 308.

20. Kravitz, "Mandarinism: Planning as Handmaiden to Conservative Politics," pp. 252–54.

21. Altshuler, *The City Planning Process*, p. 325.

22. Eugene C. Lee, *The Politics of Nonpartisanship*, pp. 28–35.

23. Edward C. Banfield and James Q. Wilson, *City Politics*, pp. 138–45.

24. Ernest Erber, ed., *Urban Planning in Transition*, p. xxv.

25. Rabinovitz, *City Politics and Planning*, pp. 136–40.

26. Moreover, experience looked at independently exerted no effect on attitudes toward the public interest.

27. Altshuler, *The City Planning Process,* pp. 299–315.

28. Judd and Mendelson, *The Politics of Urban Planning,* p. 192–93.

29. Exposure to formal education was operationally defined to include planners having undergraduate degree, graduate coursework, or a graduate degree in planning. No formal planning education included all others. The second definition was employed to address the very valid concern that under certain circumstances, simple exposure to planning education would act as a mechanism for the transfer of professional norms. See Appendix B for the construction of the two measures.

30. Both groups were equally likely to agree (26.6% for planners with under ten years versus 27.9% for planners over ten years). Moreover, planners having over ten years of experience were less undecided and as stated in the text more likely to disagree that the planner possessed the capacity to be a neutral judge of the public interest.

31. Sherry R. Arnstein, "A Ladder of Citizen Participation," p. 216.

32. In addition, the independent effect of experience on attitudes toward citizen participation was nonsignificant.

33. John Porter East, *Council Manager Government.*

34. Ibid., especially chapter 2.

35. Banfield and Wilson, *City Politics,* p. 170.

36. East, *Council Manager Government,* pp. 35–40.

37. Banfield and Wilson, *City Politics,* pp. 170–86.

38. Lee, *The Politics of Nonpartisanship,* pp. 20–35.

39. Banfield and Wilson, *City Politics,* pp. 151–87.

40. Samuel P. Hays, "The Politics of Reform in Municipal Government in the Progressive Era," pp. 157–69.

41. Ibid.

42. Lee, *The Politics of Nonpartisanship,* pp. 138–40.

43. Robert L. Lineberry, and Edmund P. Fowler, "Reformism and Public Politics in American Cities."

44. Terry N. Clark, "Community Structure, Decision Making and Public Policy in Fifty-one American Communities," pp. 576–93.

45. Lee, *The Politics of Nonpartisanship,* pp. 138–40.

46. Kerneth Prewitt, *The Recruitment of Political Leaders,* pp. 147–49.

47. Ibid.

48. Prewitt, *The Recruitment of Political Leaders,* pp. 129–50.

49. The relationship between formal planning education and forms of local government was also run using an operational definition of formal planning education as exposure to planning coursework. The conclusions presented here remained unchanged. The independent effect of years of experience on form of government or type of election was nonsignificant. The effect of experience on representation (at large versus district) is discussed in the text.

50. Altshuler, *The City Planning Process,* p. 313.

51. William L. C. Wheaton and Margaret F. Wheaton, "Identifying the Public Interest," in *Urban Planning in Transition,* ed. Ernest Erber, p. 155.

52. Robert Mayer, Robert Moroney, and Robert Morris, *Centrally Planned Change,* p. 112.

53. John P. Robinson, Jerrold G. Rusk, and Kendra B. Head, *Measures of Political Attitudes,* p. 191.

54. Neter and Wasserman, *Applied Linear Statistical Models,* pp. 423–26.

Chapter 6

1. Alan Altshuler, *The City Planning Process,* p. 303.

2. Ibid., p. 301.

3. Ibid., p. 300.

4. Ernest Erber, ed., *Urban Planning in Transition*, p. xviii.

5. Dennis R. Judd and Robert E. Mendelson, *The Politics of Urban Planning*, p. 192.

6. Altshuler, *The City Planning Process*, p. 324.

7. E. David Stoloff, "Competence to Plan Social Strategies," in *Urban Planning in Transition*, ed. Erber, p. 296.

8. Erber, *Urban Planning in Transition*, p. xxv.

9. Altshuler, *The City Planning Process*, p. 325.

10. Ibid.

11. Ibid.

12. Erber, *Urban Planning in Transition*.

13. Altshuler, *The City Planning Process*, especially chapter five.

14. Ibid., p. 342.

15. Ibid., p. 348.

16. Francine F. Rabinovitz, "Politics, Personality and Planning," in *A Reader in Planning Theory*, ed. Faludi, p. 267.

17. Altshuler, *The City Planning Process*, p. 313.

18. Robert Mayer, Robert Moroney, and Robert Morris, *Centrally Planned Change*. This work provides an excellent perspective on the entire question of national planning.

19. Frances Fox Piven, "Social Planning or Politics," *Urban Planning in Transition*, ed. Erber, p. 46.

20. Erber, ed., *Urban Planning in Transition*, p. xv.

21. Lowi, *The End of Liberalism*, p. 29.

22. Ibid., p. 49.

23. Ibid., p. 101.

24. Ibid.

25. Marcuse, "Professional Ethics and Beyond: Values in Planning," p. 265.

26. Ibid., p. 266.

27. Melville Branch, "Critical Unresolved Problems of Urban Planning Analysis," p. 47.

28. Judd and Mendelson, *The Politics of Urban Planning*, see introduction.

29. Quoted in Lowi, *The End of Liberalism*, p. xiv.

30. Paul Davidoff and Thomas A. Reiner, "A Choice Theory of Planning," in *A Reader in Planning Theory*, ed. Faludi, p. 21.

31. Donald L. Foley, "British Town Planning: One Ideology or Three," in *Urban Planning in Transition*, ed. Erber, pp. 69–93.

32. Ibid., p. 77.

33. Ibid., p. 78.

34. Duncan MacRae, "Scientific Communication, Ethical Argument, and Public Policy," pp. 38–39.

35. Ibid., p. 40.

Bibliography

Abrams, Charles. *The Language of Cities*. New York: Viking Press, 1971.

Adrian, Charles R. "Leadership and Decision-Making in Manager Cities." *Public Administration Review* 18 (1958): 208–222.

Agger, Robert; Goldrich, Daniel; and Swanson, Bert S. *The Rulers and the Ruled*. New York: John Wiley & Sons, 1964.

Agger, Robert E.; Goldstein, N. M.; and Pearl, S. A. "Political Cynicism: Measurement and Meaning." *Journal of Politics* 23 (1961): 477–85.

Aleshire, Robert A. "Planning and Citizen Participation: Costs, Benefits and Approaches." *Urban Affairs Quarterly* 5 (1970): 369–92.

Allensworth, Donald. *The U.S. Government in Action: Public Policy and Change*. Pacific Palisades, California: Goodyear Publishing Co., 1972.

Almond, Gabriel A., and Coleman, James C., eds. *The Politics of the Developing Areas*. Princeton, New Jersey: Princeton University Press, 1960.

Alperovitz, Gar. "Notes towards a Pluralistic Commonwealth." *Review of Radical Political Economics* 4 (1972): 22–48.

Altshuler, Alan. *The City Planning Process: A Political Analysis*. Ithaca, New York: Cornell University Press, 1965.

————. "The Goals of Comprehensive Planning." *Journal of the American Institute of Planners* 31 (1965): 186–95.

American Institute of Planners, *Roster*. Washington, D.C.: AIP, 1974.

Apter, David E., ed. *Ideology and Discontent*. New York: Free Press, 1964.

Arnstein, Sherry R. "Ladder of Citizen Participation." *Journal of the American Institute of Planners* 35 (1969): 216–304.

Babcock, Richard F. *The Zoning Game*. Madison, Wisconsin: University of Wisconsin Press, 1966.

Bachrach, Peter, and Daratz, Morton S. *Power and Poverty: Theory and Practice*. New York: Oxford University Press, 1970.

Backstrom, Charles H., and Hursh, Gerald D. *Survey Research*. Chicago: Northwestern University Press, 1963.

Banfield, Edward C., and Wilson, James Q. *City Politics*. New York: Vintage Books, 1963.

Banfield Edward C., ed. *Urban Government*. New York: Free Press, 1969.

Beauregard, Robert A. "The Occupation of Planning: A View from the Census." *Journal of the American Institute of Planners* 42 (1976): 187–92.

Beckman, Norman. "The New PPBS: Planning, Politics, Bureaucracy and Salvation." In *Planning and Politics: Uneasy Partnership*. Edited by Thad L. Beyle and George Lathrop. New York: Odyssey Press, 1970.

Benveniste, Guy. *The Politics of Expertise*. San Francisco: Glendessary Publishing Co., 1972.

Berry, Brian J. L., ed. *City Classification Handbook: Methods and Applications*. New York: John Wiley & Sons, 1972.

Beyle, Thad L.; Seligson, Sureva; and Wright, Deil S. "New Directions in State Planning." *Journal of the American Institute of Planners* 35 (1969): 334–39.

Beyle, Thad L., and Lathrop, George T., eds. *Planning and Politics: Uneasy Partnership*. New York: Odyssey Press, 1970.

Blalock, Hubert M., Jr. *Causal Inferences in Non-experimental Research*. Chapel Hill, North Carolina: University of North Carolina Press, 1964.

――――. *Social Statistics*. 2nd ed. New York: McGraw-Hill, 1972.

Bolan, Richard S. "Emerging Views of Planning." *Journal of the American Institute of Planners* 33 (1967): 233–45.

Bolan, Richard S., and Nuttall, Ronald L. *Urban Planning and Politics*. Lexington, Massachusetts: Lexington Books, 1975.

Branch, Melville. *Planning: Aspects and Applications*. New York: John Wiley & Sons, 1966.

――――. "Critical Unresolved Problems of Urban Planning Analysis." *Journal of the American Institute of Planners* 44 (1978): 47–59.

――――, ed. *Urban Planning Theory*. Stroudsburg, Pennsylvania: Dowden, Hutchinson and Ross, Inc., 1975.

Brooks, Michael. *Social Planning and City Planning*. Chicago: American Society of Planning Officials, 1970.

Brooks, Michael, and Stegman, Michael. "Urban Social Policy, Race and the Education of Planners." *Journal of the American Institute of Planners* 34 (1968): 275–86.

Campbell, Angus, et al. *The American Voter*. New York: John Wiley & Sons, 1960.

Catanese, Anthony James. *Planners and Local Politics*. Beverly Hills, California: Sage Publications, 1974.

――――. *Systematic Planning: Theory and Application*. Lexington, Massachusetts: Lexington Books, 1970.

Chapin, F. Stuart. *Urban Land Use Planning*. Urbana, Illinois: University of Illinois Press, 1965.

Clark, Terry N. "Community Structure, Decision Making and Public Policy in Fifty-one American Communities." *American Sociological Review* 33 (1968): 576–93.

Clausen, Aage R. *How Congressmen Decide: A Policy Focus*. New York: St. Martin's Press, 1973.

Commager, Henry Steele. *The American Mind: An Interpretation of American Thought and Character since the 1880's*. New Haven, Connecticut: Yale University Press, 1950.

Converse, Philip. "The Nature of Belief Systems in Mass Publics." In *Ideology and Discontent*, edited by David E. Apter. New York: Free Press, 1964.

Crenson, Mathew A. *The Unpolitics of Air Pollution*. Baltimore: Johns Hopkins University Press, 1971.

Dahl, Robert A. *Who Governs: Democracy and Power in an American City.* New Haven, Connecticut: Yale University Press, 1961.

Daland, Robert T., and Parker, John A. *Urban Growth Dynamics.* New York: John Wiley & Sons, 1962.

Davidoff, Paul. "Advocacy and Pluralism in Planning." *Journal of the American Institute of Planners* 31 (1965): 331–37.

Davidoff, Paul, and Reiner, Thomas A. "A Choice Theory of Planning." *Journal of the American Institute of Planners* 28 (1962): 103–14.

Davis, James A. *National Data Program for the Social Sciences: Spring 1974 General Social Survey.* Ann Arbor, Michigan: Inter-University Consortium for Political Research, 1974.

Dimock, Marshall Edward, and Dimock, Gladys Ogden. *Public Administration.* 4th ed. New York: Holt, Rinehart, and Winston, 1969.

Downs, Anthony. *An Economic Theory of Democracy.* New York: Harper & Row, 1957.

Downs, Bryan, ed. *Cities and Suburbs.* Belmont, California: Wadsworth Publishing Co., 1971.

Dyckman, John W. "What Makes Planners Plan?" *Journal of the American Institute of Planners* 27 (1961): 164–67.

Dye, Thomas R. *Politics in States and Communities.* Englewood Cliffs, New Jersey: Prentice-Hall, 1973.

East, John Porter. *Council Manager Government: The Political Thought of Its Founder, Richard S. Childs.* Chapel Hill, North Carolina: University of North Carolina Press, 1965.

Easton, David. *The Political System: An Inquiry into the State of Political Science.* New York: Alfred A. Knopf, 1953.

Edwards, Allen L. *Techniques of Attitude Scale Construction.* New York: Appleton-Century-Crofts, 1957.

Eldredge, H. Wentworth, ed. *Taming Megalopolis.* New York: Doubleday, 1967.

Erber, Ernest, ed. *Urban Planning in Transition.* New York: Grossman Publishers, 1970.

Etzioni, Amitai. *Modern Organizations.* Englewood Cliffs, New Jersey: Prentice-Hall, 1964.

Eulau, Heinz, and Prewitt, Kenneth. *Labyrinths of Democracy: Adaptation, Linkages, Representation, and Policies in Urban Politics.* Indianapolis: Bobbs-Merrill Company, 1973.

Faludi, Andreas, ed. *A Reader in Planning Theory.* New York: Pergamon Press, 1973.

Flanigan, William H. *Political Behavior of the American Electorate.* Boston: Allyn and Bacon, Inc., 1972.

Free, Lloyd A., and Cantril, Hadley. *The Political Beliefs of Americans.* New Brunswick, New Jersey: Rutgers University Press, 1971.

Frieden, Bernard J. "The Changing Prospects for Social Planning." *Journal of the American Institute of Planners* 33 (1967): 311–23.

Frieden, Bernard J., and Morris, Robert, eds. *Urban Planning and Social Policy.* New York: Basic Books, 1968.

Friedman, Lawrence M. *Government and Slum Housing.* Chicago: Rand McNally Co., 1968.

Friedmann, John. "The Future of Comprehensive Urban Planning: A Critique." *Public Administration Review* 31 (1971): 325–25.

———. *Retracking America: A Theory of Transactive Planning.* New York: Anchor Press, 1973.

Friedmann, John, and Hudson, Barclay. "Knowledge and Action: A Guide to Planning Theory." *Journal of the American Institute of Planners* 40 (1974): 2–14.

Gans, Herbert J. *People and Plans.* New York: Basic Books, 1968.

Garson, G. David, and Vasu, Michael L. "Notes on the Political Issues of Decentralized Social Planning." Paper presented at the Northeastern Political Science Association Meeting, 1976.

Goodman, Robert. *After the Planners.* New York: Simon & Schuster, 1971.

Greer, Scott. *Urban Renewal and American Cities.* Indianapolis: Bobbs-Merrill, 1965.

Handcock, John L. "Planners in the Changing American City, 1900–1940." *Journal of the American Institute of Planners* 33 (1967): 290–303.

Hartz, Louis. *The Liberal Tradition in America.* New York: Harcourt Brace Jovanovich, 1955.

Hawley, Amos. "Community Power and Urban Renewal Success." *American Journal of Sociology* 68 (1963): 422–31.

Hays, Samuel P. "The Politics of Reform in Municipal Government in the Progressive Era." *Pacific Northwest Quarterly* 55 (1964): 157–69.

Hofstadter, Richard. *The Age of Reform: From Bryan to F.D.R.* New York: Alfred A. Knopf, 1955.

Hollander, Myles, and Wolfe, Douglas A. *Nonparametric Statistical Methods.* New York: John Wiley & Sons, 1973.

Hunter, Floyd. *Community Power Structures.* Chapel Hill, North Carolina: University of North Carolina Press, 1953.

Jackson, John S., and Shade, William L. "Citizen Participation, Democratic Representation, and Survey Research." *Urban Affairs Quarterly* 9 (1973): 57–89.

Jacobs, Jane J. *The Death and Life of Great American Cities.* New York: Vintage Books, 1961.

Judd, Dennis R., and Mendelson, Robert E. *The Politics of Urban Planning: The East St. Louis Experience.* Urbana, Illinois: University of Illinois Press, 1973.

Kaplan, Harold. *Urban Renewal Politics.* New York: Columbia University Press, 1963.

Kelly, Francis, et al. *Research Design in the Behavioral Sciences: Multiple Regression Approach.* Carbondale, Illinois: Southern Illinois University Press, 1969.

Kent, T. J., Jr. *The Urban General Plan.* San Francisco: Chandler Publishing Co., 1964.

Kerlinger, Fred N. *Foundations of Behavioral Research*. 2nd ed. New York: Holt, Rinehart, and Winston, 1973.

Kessel, John. "Governmental Structure and Political Environment." *The American Political Science Review* 56 (1962): 615–20.

Krieger, Martin H. "Some New Directions for Planning Theories." *Journal of the American Institute of Planners* 40 (1974): 156–63.

Lane, Robert B. *Political Ideology*. New York: Free Press, 1962.

Lasswell, Harold D. *Politics: Who Gets What, When, How*. New York: Meridian Books, 1958.

Lee, Eugene C. *The Politics of Nonpartisanship*. Berkeley and Los Angeles, California: University of California Press, 1960.

Lindblom, Charles. "The Science of 'Muddling Through.'" *Public Administration Review* 19 (1959): 79–88.

Lineberry, Robert L., and Fowler, Edmund P. "Reformism and Public Policies in American Cities." *The American Political Science Review* 61 (1967): 701–16.

Lineberry, Robert L., and Sharkansky, Ira. *Urban Politics and Public Policy*. New York: Harper & Row, 1971.

Linsky, Arnold S. "Stimulating Responses to Mailed Questionnaires: A Review." *Public Opinion Quarterly* 39 (1975): 82–101.

Lipset, Seymour Martin. *Political Man*. Garden City: Doubleday & Co., 1963.

Long, Norton E. "Planning and Politics in Urban Development." *Journal of the American Institute of Planners* 25 (1959): 167–69.

_____. *The Unwalled City: Reconstituting the Urban Community*. New York: Basic Books, 1972.

Lowi, Theodore J. *The End of Liberalism: Ideology, Policy, and the Crisis of Public Authority*. New York: W. W. Norton and Co., 1969.

_____. "Machine Politics Old and New." *The Public Interest* 9 (1967): 83–92.

McClosky, Herbert. "Consensus and Ideology in American Politics." *American Political Science Review* 58 (1964): 361–82.

McConaghy, Maureen. "Maximum Possible Error in Guttman Scales." *Public Opinion Quarterly* 39 (1975): 343–57.

MacRae, Duncan, Jr. "Scientific Communication, Ethical Argument, and Public Policy." *American Political Science Review* 65 (1971): 38–50.

Marcuse, Peter. "Professional Ethics and Beyond: Values in Planning." *Journal of the American Institute of Planners* 42 (1976): 264–74.

Martin, Roscoe C., et al. *Decisions in Syracuse*. Bloomington, Indiana: Indiana University Press, 1961.

Mayer, Robert; Moroney, Robert; and Morris, Robert H. *Centrally Planned Change: A Reexamination of Theory and Experience*. Urbana, Illinois: University of Illinois Press, 1974.

Mazziotti, Donald F. "The Underlying Assumptions of Advocacy Planning: Pluralism and Reform." *Journal of the American Institute of Planners* 40 (1975): 38–46.

Meyerson, Martin. "Building the Middle Range Bridge for Comprehensive

Planning." *Journal of the American Institute of Planners* 22 (1956): 58–64.

———. "The Next Challenge for the Urban Planner: Linking Local and National Economic Planning." *Journal of the American Institute of Planners* 42 (1976): 374–84.

Meyerson, Martin, and Banfield, Edward C. *Politics, Planning, and the Public Interest.* New York: Free Press, 1964.

Michael, Donald. *The Unprepared Society.* New York: Basic Books, 1968.

———. "Urban Policy in the Rationalized Society." *Journal of the American Institute of Planners* 31 (1965): 283–88.

Miller, Delbert C. *Handbook of Research Design and Social Measurement.* New York: David McKay Co., 1970.

Mondale, Walter F. "Social Accounting, Evaluation, and the Future of Human Services." *Evaluation* 1 (1972): 29–34.

Morgan, David R., and Kirkpatrick, Samuel A., eds. *Urban Political Analysis: A Systems Approach.* New York: Free Press, 1972.

Neter, John, and Wasserman, William. *Applied Linear Statistical Models.* Homewood, Illinois: Richard D. Irwin, Inc., 1974.

Nie, Norman H.; Verba, Sidney; and Petrocik, John R. *The Changing American Voter.* Cambridge, Massachusetts: Harvard University Press, 1976.

Peattie, Lisa. "Reflections on Advocacy Planning." *Journal of the American Institute of Planners* 34 (1968): 80–88.

Piven, Francis Fox. "Planning and Class Interests." *Journal of the American Institute of Planners* 41 (1975): 308–10.

Prewitt, Kenneth. *The Recruitment of Political Leaders: A Study of Citizen-Politicians.* Indianapolis: Bobbs-Merrill, 1970.

Protho, James W., and Griggs, C. M. "Fundamental Principles of Democracy: Bases of Agreement and Disagreement." *Journal of Politics* 22 (1960): 276–94.

Rabinovitz, Francine. *City Politics and Planning.* New York: Atherton Press, 1969.

———. "Politics, Personality and Planning." *Public Administration Review* 27 (1967): 18–24.

Rabinovitz, Francine, and Pottinger, Stanley J. "Organization for Local Planning: The Attitudes of Directors." *Journal of the American Institute of Planners* 33 (1967): 27–32.

Ranney, David C. *Planning and Politics in the Metropolis.* Columbus, Ohio: Charles E. Merrill Publishing Co., 1969.

Reynolds, H. T. *Politics and the Common Man.* Homewood, Illinois: Dorsey Press, 1974.

Rinehart, Jeffrey C., and Bernick, E. Lee. "Political Attitudes and Behavior Patterns of Federal Civil Servants." *Public Administration Review* 35 (1975): 603–11.

Riordan, William L. *Plunkitt of Tammany Hall.* New York: E. P. Dutton & Co., 1963.

Robinson, Ira M., ed. *Decision Making in Urban Planning: An Introduction to Methodologies.* Beverly Hills, California: Sage Publications, 1972.

Robinson, John P.; Rusk, Jerrold G.; and Head, Kendra B. *Measures of Political Attitudes*. Ann Arbor, Michigan: Institute for Social Research, 1968.

Rodwin, Lloyd. *Nations and Cities*. Boston: Houghton-Mifflin, Co., 1970.

Rossi, Peter, and Dentler, Robert A. *The Politics of Urban Renewal*. New York: Free Press, 1961.

Rossiter, Clinton. *Conservatism in America*. 2nd ed. New York: Vintage Books, 1962.

Schnore, Leo, and Alford, Robert. "Forms of Government and Socio-Economic Characteristics of Suburbs." *Administrative Science Quarterly* 8 (1963): 1–17.

Schon, Donald A., et al. "Planners in Transition: Report on a Survey of Alumni of M.I.T.'s Department of Urban Studies." *Journal of the American Institute of Planners* 42 (1976): 193–202.

Scott, Mel. *American City Planning Since 1890*. Berkeley and Los Angeles, California: University of California Press, 1969.

Sharkansky, Ira. *Public Administration: Policy-Making in Governmental Agencies*. 2nd ed. Chicago: Markham, 1970.

Siegel, Sidney. *Nonparametric Statistics for the Behavioral Sciences*. New York: McGraw-Hill, 1956.

Simon, Herbert A. *Administrative Behavior*. 2nd ed. New York: Macmillan, 1957.

Stouffer, Samuel A. *Communism, Conformity, and Civil Liberties*. Gloucester, Massachusetts: P. Smith, 1955.

Tugwell, Rexford Guy. *Model for a New Constitution*. Palo Alto, California: James E. Freel, 1971.

Verba, Sidney, and Nie, Norman H. *Participation in America: Political Democracy and Social Equality*. New York: Harper & Row, 1972.

Walker, Robert A. *The Planning Function in Urban Government*. Chicago: University of Chicago Press, 1950.

Watson, Thomas J. "Speech to the Bond Club of New York." *I.F. Stone's Biweekly* 18 (1970): 1–4.

Webber, Melvin M. "The Roles of Intelligence Systems in Urban Systems Planning." *Journal of the American Institute of Planners* 21 (1965): 289–95.

Williams, Oliver P., and Adrian, Charles R. *Four Cities*. Philadelphia: University of Pennsylvania Press, 1963.

Wright, Deil S. "Governmental Forms and Planning Functions: The Relation of Organization and Structures to Planning Practice." In *Planning and Politics: Uneasy Partnership*. Edited by Thad L. Beyle and George Lathrop. New York: Odyssey Press, 1970.

United States Commission on Civil Rights. *Above Property Rights*. Washington, D.C.: Government Printing Office, 1972.

Index

The Author

Michael Lee Vasu is assistant professor of political science
at North Carolina State University at Raleigh.

The Book

Typeface: Mergenthaler V-I-P Palatino

Design and composition: The University of North Carolina Press

Paper: Sixty pound Olde Style by S. D. Warren Company

Binding cloth: Roxite B 51544 by Holliston Mills, Incorporated

Printer and binder: Edwards Brothers Incorporated

Published by The University of North Carolina Press

DATE DUE